Human Resource Management

Evolving Roles & Responsibilities

Human Resource Management

Evolving Roles & Responsibilities

Lee Dyer
Editor

Gerald W. Holder
Consulting Editor

The Bureau of National Affairs, Inc., Washington, D.C.

Library of Congress Cataloging-in-Publication Data

Human resource management—evolving roles &
responsibilities.

(ASPA/BNA series ; 1)
Includes indexes.
1. Personnel management. I. Dyer, Lee, 1939—
II. Holder, Gerald W. III. Bureau of National Affairs
(Washington, D.C.) IV. Series.
HF5549.A9574 Vol. 1 658.3 s [658.3]   88-21252
ISBN 0-87179-601-5

Printed in the United States of America
International Standard Book Number: 0-87179-601-5

Preface

It has been 15 years since the first volume of the original ASPA Handbook of Personnel and Industrial Relations was published. A great deal has changed in our profession since then. No longer is PAIR (personnel and industrial relations) the accepted acronym for the management of human resources, primarily because our roles and our accountabilities are so different.

Human resource executives have been broadening their horizons and learning new ways to make a bigger contribution to their organizations. So, too, does the focus of this new HRM (human resource management) series indicate the extent to which the field has changed and how pace-setting human resource executives have been reshaping management practice. We have tried to reflect those changes in this new series.

The original series was eight volumes with a heavy emphasis on "how-to-do-it." This new series, comprised of six volumes, focuses more heavily on the why than the how, on strategy and integration rather than the specifics of execution.

The very process we used to develop this series indicates the shift in orientation. Each of the six volumes had a different well-known academician as its editor. These individuals were supported by at least one consulting editor, a senior practitioner in the HRM field whose role was to provide the "real world" perspective so necessary to this kind of project. And the overall series was guided by an editorial advisory board made up of practitioners, academicians, and representatives of BNA and ASPA. Members of the editorial advisory board are listed opposite the title page of this Volume.

Collectively, we struggled through the development of each volume and its chapters, striving to achieve the proper balance between a macro perspective of the profession and an evolutionary approach to the material presented. Our target audience—middle to upper level practitioners and those who aspire to such positions—was a constant presence during all of our discussions.

The six volumes in this series and their key players are:

1. *Human Resource Management: Evolving Roles and Responsibilities* edited by Lee Dyer, professor at Cornell University with

Jerry Holder, retired vice president of human resources for Marion Laboratories, as consulting editor. Additional consulting editors included Robert Berra of Monsanto, Leo Contois of Consolidated Foods (retired) and Garth Dimon of Bristol-Meyers.

2. *Human Resource Planning, Employment and Placement* edited by Wayne Cascio, professor at the University of Colorado with Donald Sweet of Hawkins Associates, Inc. as consulting editor.

3. *Compensation and Benefits* edited by Luis R. Gomez-Mejia, professor at the University of Colorado with consulting editors Ray Olsen of TRW and Wes Leibtag of the University of Illinois.

4. *Employee and Labor Relations* edited by John Fossum, professor, University of Minnesota, with Jerauld Mattson of International Multifoods as consulting editor.

5. *Developing Human Resources* edited by Kenneth N. Wexley, professor, Michigan State University with John Hinrichs of Management Decision Systems as consulting editor.

6. *Managing Human Resources in the Information Age* with Randall S. Schuler of New York University as editor and James Walker of Walker and Associates as consulting editor.

This new management series reflects the coming of age of human resource management. ASPA is grateful to the individuals whose work is reflected in its pages and proud to mark this professional transition with such an outstanding series.

Ronald C. Pilenzo
Alexandria, VA
June 1988

Introduction

This first volume of the new ASPA/BNA Series on *Human Resource Management* serves as a backdrop for the more functionally oriented volumes to follow. It takes an expansive and integrative look at existing and emerging trends and issues relevant to the practice and study of HRM, broadly defined.

The volume is a paean to change. Many of the issues it addresses have only recently come to the fore. Likewise, many of the concepts and technologies it explores have just now reached a point permitting systematic and coherent examination. In this respect, the volume captures the dynamic nature of the HRM field.

Strategy for handling these changes provides the overarching theme. Each chapter deals with different aspects of the field's struggle to become significantly more business-driven, policy-oriented, proactive, and rational. Equally important are the resulting issues regarding the proper roles of line and staff in managing human resources and effective ways to demonstrate the "value added" of HR functions and professionals.

Interestingly, this emphasis on change was not a predetermined theme. Nonetheless, each author cites compelling evidence of significant change—the temptation is to call it progress— and sees a need for even greater change in the years to come. Each chapter reflects a tone of, at best, slightly muted impatience. The message is clear: While we have come far, there is still so far to go. Fortunately, none of the authors shrinks from the task of mapping out these remaining trails.

An overview for the volume is provided in Chapter 1, "A Strategic Perspective of HRM." In this chapter Lee Dyer and Jerry Holder document the current preoccupation with strategy among HR practitioners and scholars and briefly analyze its historical evolution. The authors then turn their attention to the key components of HR strategy and three basic HR strategies: inducement, investment, and involvement.

Chapter 1 also addresses the implications of a strategic focus for today's HR managers and professionals. In particular, it examines the changing role of the HR function and the knowledge and skill bases required of those who would play this new role. The chapter closes with a look at factors favoring and retarding the strategic evolution and speculates as to where the chips eventually will fall.

Chapters 2 and 3, which cover, respectively, HR planning and environmental scanning, are best considered in tandem. In Chapter 2, Jim Craft takes a fresh look at the formal and informal processes through which HR strategies are made. The chapter is organized around a comprehensive model which provides a unique slant on this somewhat familiar topic. Craft's input-output model incorporates both processes and products; it thus reflects, in a rare way, the symbiotic relationships among these critical components. Like Dyer and Holder, Craft explores the various internal and external factors influencing the choice of HR strategy, but he also analyzes the mechanisms that can bring these factors into strategic deliberations. Readers familiar with Craft's writings find this chapter to be a vintage example: thoroughly analytical and carefully balanced, with just a touch of iconoclasm.

The external environment and its role as a significant shaper of HR strategy is discussed in both Chapters 1 and 2, but Chapter 3 is where the topic of environmental scanning receives its just due. Here, Larry Schrenk, a pioneer of the art, examines the rationale underlying the scanning process, the nature of the process, its products, and its place in a broader planning framework. To highlight the discussion, Schrenk provides a specific example of the development and implementation of an environmental scanning system at Honeywell.

The chapter serves as a step-by-step guide to the scanning process, from the planning stages through data collection and analysis. Schrenk places particular emphasis on the pragmatic uses of the data, such as identifying strategic issues and framing them so as to demand and suggest action. Thus, the chapter focuses less on inputs and more on the quality of outputs from the scanning process and the resulting decisions.

Chapters 4 and 5 catch the reader coming and going on the issue of assuring HR effectiveness. In Chapter 4, John Boudreau shows how the use of utility analysis in decision-making stages promotes effective allocation of resources to various activities and programs. In the following chapter, Anne Tsui and Luis Gomez-Mejia explore ways to systematically analyze and evaluate the cumulative results of these decisions — that is, HRM effectiveness.

Boudreau's thesis is that it is insufficient to propose significant expenditures on HRM activities and programs simply because they are "good for morale," "done down the street," or "popular in Japan." Today's competitive conditions demand that decision makers justify proposed investments in HRM, at least in part, on the basis of their anticipated financial returns. Enter utility (that is, cost-benefit) analysis, an approach that not only facilitates the financial quantification of HRM, but also helps to clarify possible tradeoffs between financial and less tangible outcomes and to do so even under conditions of uncertainty.

Using a running case study, Boudreau demonstrates the application of utility analysis to a series of increasingly complex HR decisions. At each juncture, he carefully delineates the relevant issues, shows how to calculate the significant costs and benefits, and indicates ways to deal with uncertainties. A unique feature is his use of break-even analysis, which facilitates informed decision making even when calculating precise dollar returns is impossible, as it usually is. Bedtime reading it isn't. Persistent readers, however, will reap invaluable insights into this exciting new area of HRM.

While more informed decisions should produce more favorable results, Chapter 5 examines this assumption more closely. In this chapter, Tsui and Gomez-Mejia address two distinct types of HR effectiveness; organizational HR effectiveness or how well the organization is utilizing its pool of human resources, and functional HR effectiveness, or the extent to which HR department is contributing to organizational HR effectiveness. After first exploring various proposed approaches to evaluation, the authors document actual practices reported in their survey of 70 ASPA-member firms. The wide gap between prescription and practice revealed in this survey is as striking as it is disappointing.

However, Tsui and Gomez-Mejia find that many, if not all, of the possible reasons for this gap could be overcome by a clearer notion of what evaluation is all about. Chapter 5 provides this clarification through a carefully drawn conceptual framework of the evaluation process. One particularly helpful feature is a full enumeration of plausible effectiveness criteria catalogued as to type of effectiveness (overall or functional), type of measure (quantitative or qualitative), and focus (process or content). Another useful aspect is the painstaking application of these criteria across the three main levels of organizational analysis: strategic, managerial, and operational. The chapter concludes with a carefully conceived set of prescriptions to guide nascent evaluators.

Going global: Increasingly, this is the watchword among big and not-always-so-big business, which in turn has opened up a whole new dimension of HRM. In Chapter 6, Peter Dowling, a noted scholar of international HRM explores this emerging area of the field. Unlike earlier chapters, Chapter 6 concerns an area in which research has clearly been outpaced by practice and by a fairly wide margin. Nonetheless, by drawing on disparate sources, Dowling is able to document a number of essential distinctions between domestic and international HRM across two basic types of international organizations: multi-domestic and global.

To supplement this source material, Dowling also conducted his own survey of 34 members of the International Chapter of ASPA (ASPA/I). The results of this survey provide up-to-date analyses of preferred organizational arrangements for international HRM, major activities pursued, major problems encountered, and issues of particular currency. Whereas pleas for improved practices characterize the earlier chapters of this volume, Dowling concludes with an urgent appeal for more and better research and, in particular, for organizational access to and financial support for academics who would do such research.

As may now be clear, this volume is aimed at three primary audiences: Upper-level managers, whether outside or inside the HR function; HR professionals at all levels and of all stripes; and academics teaching and researching in the field. For the first group, and particularly those managers at — or striving to be at — the leading edge, the intent was to produce a volume which faithfully reflects their efforts and desires, and which thus will prove indispensable to their work and that of their staffs. For the second group, the goal was to provide a relevant and compelling source of professional development and a useful recurring reference source. And for the third group, we aimed to produce a volume suitable for classroom use that would also stimulate fruitful research ideas. It is by and for these individuals and purposes, then, that the volume should be evaluated.

Lee Dyer
Ithaca, NY
June 1988

About the Authors

Chapter 1.1

A Strategic Perspective of Human Resource Management

Lee Dyer (Ph.D., University of Wisconsin-Madison) is a professor of Human Resource Studies and Director of the Center for Advanced Human Resource Studies at the New York State School of Industrial and Labor Relations, Cornell University. Dyer has served as a consultant in the development of HR strategies, policies, and planning processes for several major corporations. He serves on the editorial boards of *Human Resource Planning, Human Resource Management,* and *Human Resource Management Australia.* He has published over 40 articles and book chapters, in addition to ten books and monographs, and has lectured widely on a variety of HRM topics in the U.S., Europe, and Australia.

His teaching and research interests focus on HR strategy, HR planning and decision-making, and comprehensive employee relations.

Gerald W. Holder is president of GWH & Associates and a professor at the Barney School of Business, the University of Hartford. Prior to these affiliations, Holder was a senior vice president of administration for Marion Laboratories, from which he retired in 1986. He also served as director of corporate personnel administration at Abbott Laboratories. Holder has been an active member in ASPA, serving on various committees and most recently serving as the chairman of ASPA's advisory council.

The authors thank James A. Craft and George T. Milkovich for their helpful comments on an earlier draft of this chapter.

The research for this chapter was carried out with the support from the U.S. Army Research Institute, contract SFRC 3 MDA 903-87-K-0001. The views, opinions, and/or findings contained in this chapter are those of the authors and should not be construed as an official Department of the Army policy or decision.

Chapter 1.2

Human Resource Planning and Strategy

James A. Craft (Ph.D., University of California-Berkeley) is a professor of Business Administration and coordinator of the Human Resources

Interest Group in the Graduate School of Business Administration at the University of Pittsburgh. He is currently on the board of directors and chairman of the research committee for the Pittsburgh Personnel Association, an ASPA affiliate chapter and president of the Western Pennsylvania Industrial Relations Research Association. He has served as an associate editor for the journal *Human Resource Planning*, and remains a member of its editorial board. His research, teaching, and consulting interests are in the areas of HR planning and strategy, labor relations, and management theory.

The author wishes to thank the following HR executives and scholars for their comments and ideas on this chapter: Donald E. Crean, Lee Dyer, Charles R. Greer, Stella Nkomo, J.R. Phelp, Mary C. Rothenberger, Edward Sussna, and William Thomas.

Chapter 1.3

Environmental Scanning

Lorenz P. Schrenk (Ph.D., Ohio State University) is director of human resource planning and talent at Honeywell, Inc. His background includes assignments as Honeywell's first corporate manager of human resource planning and first corporate manager of health care management. His previous experience includes work as a research scientist, as manager of a research and development group in life sciences, and as a manager of multidisciplinary applied research and product development programs.

Schrenk holds a BA in History from George Washington University and masters and doctoral degrees in experimental psychology from Ohio State University.

Chapter 1.4

Utility Analysis

John W. Boudreau (Ph.D., Purdue University) is an associate professor of Personnel and Human Resource Studies at the New York State School of Industrial and Labor Relations, Cornell University. Professor Boudreau has consulted with several Fortune 500 companies in developing decision-making frameworks, staffing programs, and career management programs. He has published articles in such journals as *Journal of Applied Psychology, Organizational Behavior and Human Performance, Personnel*

Psychology, and *Industrial Relations,* as well as authored numerous book chapters and presented papers in the United States and Europe. Boudreau's research interests include HRM decision making; applications of economic, accounting, and financial theories to HR decisions; organizational staffing, and HR strategic planning.

The research for this chapter was carried out with the support from the U.S. Army Research Institute, contract SFRC 3 MDA 903-87-K-0001. The views, opinions, and/or findings contained in this chapter are those of the author and should not be construed as an official Department of the Army policy or decision.

Chapter 1.5

Evaluating Human Resource Effectiveness

Anne S. Tsui (Ph.D., University of California-Los Angeles) is an assistant professor of organizational behavior and human resource management at the Graduate School of Management, University of California-Irvine. Prior to that she was at the Fuqua School of Business, Duke University. Her experience in HRM includes stints with the University of Minnesota hospitals and Control Data Corporation. She has published widely in a variety of academic and professional journals on such topics as managerial effectiveness and HRM effectiveness. Her current research activities focus on the design and implications of multiple assessments of managerial effectiveness and the role of the HR function in organizations.

Luis R. Gomez-Mejia (Ph.D., University of Minnesota) is an Associate Professor in the Department of Strategy and Organization Management at the University of Colorado at Boulder. He has had over eight years of field experience in human resource management at Control Data Corporation and the City of Minneapolis and has also been a consultant to numerous private and public sector organizations. Dr. Gomez-Mejia has authored over 50 publications in the areas of compensation and evaluation of personnel programs which have appeared in such journals as *Personnel Psychology, Industrial Relations, Industrial and Labor Relations, Academy of Management Journal, Strategic Management Journal* and *Journal of Psychology.* He is the editor of *Compensation and Benefits,* the third volume in the ASPA/BNA Series on HRM, scheduled for publication in 1989.

Chapter 1.6

International HRM

Peter J. Dowling (Ph.D., Flinders University of South Australia) is international associate director of the Graduate School of Management, Monash University, Melbourne, Australia. Before taking this position, he served as senior lecturer in the Graduate School of Management, University of Melbourne. From 1985-1986 he was a visiting professor at the New York State School of Industrial and Labor Relations, Cornell University. His current research concerns the similarities and differences between domestic and international HRM and the crossnational transferability of HR practices.

The author wishes to thank the board of directors of ASPA/International for their support and assistance with the survey detailed in this chapter. In particular, the assistance of Daniel W. Kendall, Patrick V. Morgan, and Roy Richardson of ASPA/I is gratefully acknowledged. The author is also grateful for the research assistance provided by Helen De Cieri.

Contents

1.1

A Strategic Perspective of Human Resource Management

Lee Dyer

Gerald W. Holder

The decade of the 1980s has brought another transformation in the practice and study of human resource management (HRM): The field has discovered, and indeed begun to embrace, a strategic perspective. The intellectual energy invested in discussing the nature, extent, and desirability of this development clearly indicates that something significant is afoot. Understand it or not, believe in it or not, like it or not, strategy is well on its way to becoming the cutting edge, guiding much of what HR professionals do and think.

The Strategic Focus

Just how thoroughly the strategic perspective will permeate HRM is impossible to predict, but the available evidence suggests a major movement in the making. The topic has certainly made deep inroads into the professional journals, particularly those oriented to practitioners and even more particularly those aimed at HR planners.[1] Several recent books on HRM have a strategic focus,[2] some research has been published,[3] and more is underway.[4] Strategy has become an obligatory topic at major meetings where HR professionals gather to talk shop. Furthermore, an increasing number of HR consultants are hawking their recently acquired strategic expertise.

A few companies — IBM, General Electric (GE), Hewlett Packard, Eli Lilly, Marion Laboratories, Lincoln Electric, and

United Parcel Service (UPS), for example — have gained considerable status as a result of their strategic approaches to HRM. Still others — Chaparral Steel, New United Motors Manufacturing, Inc. (NUMMI), Motorola, and Federal Express — have more recently generated considerable publicity for their efforts along these lines. Many others are no doubt making more quiet forays into the strategic waters, as indicated by available surveys.[5]

Influences Leading to Strategic HRM

What lies behind this flurry of activity? Much of it can be attributed to business necessity. The past ten years have been particularly challenging for American business. In the rush to competitiveness, many firms have been forced to rethink and recast their basic business strategies. As a consequence, all organizational resources, including human resources, have come under close scrutiny. In many cases, this approach led initially to piecemeal, and sometimes draconian, responses. However, over the longer run, it has also encouraged at least a few firms to engage in a deeper level of thought and action. For some organizations, the natural outcome of this introspection has been a more strategic approach to the management of people.

On its own, business necessity may not have turned the tide completely, but it has been aided and abetted by several important trends. First, the 1980s witnessed a steady erosion in the influence of factors which traditionally gave HR professionals much of their *raison d'etre*. In particular, the labor movement continued to lose some of its punch, and both the promulgation and enforcement of employment laws and regulations withered, most notably at the federal level. For some HR professionals, then, strategy provided a means, and indeed a particularly convenient and salient means, of using time and resources previously devoted to dealing with outside demands.

A second facilitating force, never to be underestimated, is the pervasive bandwagon effect. All the activity noted earlier is certain to generate yet more activity. If strategy represents the cutting-edge, what company, what HR professional wants, or can afford, to be left behind? Thus primed by a fortunate confluence of events and fueled by a steady stream of exhortations, success stories, and insecurities, the strategic perspective has rapidly worked its way into the consciousness of the HR community, and by extension into the role prescriptions of many line managers.

Traditional vs. Strategic HRM

Before describing how strategic HRM works, it may be helpful to look at ways this approach differs from earlier ones that have driven the development of the field. Observers have reported a variety of details, but there is a fair amount of agreement on the critical distinctions between traditional and strategic approaches to HRM.[6]

Organizational Level

Strategic — Because strategies involve decisions about key goals, major policies, and the allocation of resources, they tend to be formulated at the top.

Traditional — The design and implementation of personnel programs or activities (such as training sessions or job evaluation plans) usually is handled by middle-level personnel specialists, and the day-to-day administration of policies and programs usually is carried out by line managers at various levels assisted by middle- to lower-level personnel generalists.[7]

Focus

Strategic — Strategies are business-driven and focus on organizational effectiveness; thus, in this perspective, people are viewed primarily as resources to be managed toward the achievement of strategic business goals.

Traditional — This perspective emphasizes individual HR outcomes (for example, performance, turnover, job satisfaction) or, more often, programs or activities, and tends to view people, or at least their behaviors and attitudes, as ends in and of themselves.[8]

Framework

Strategic — Strategies by their very nature provide unifying frameworks which are at once broad, contingency-based, and integrative. They incorporate a full complement of HR goals and activities designed specifically to fit extant environments and to be mutually reinforcing or synergistic.

Traditional — This approach treats personnel programs or activities in relative isolation, separated from both their environments and one another.

Roles

Strategic — As the foregoing suggests, strategy-making generally is the responsibility of line managers, with personnel playing a supportive role.

Traditional — The role of line managers is downplayed in deference to the personnel function and the professionals who staff it.[9]

Steps in Strategic HRM

In general, strategies outline the goals that key organizational decision makers intend to accomplish and, at least to some extent, how they intend to accomplish them. Large companies develop strategies at three levels: at the corporate level, within divisions or strategic business units, and within various functions.[10] At the first, or corporate, level, strategy indicates the businesses an enterprise intends to pursue; the second level shows how the company intends to compete in each of the targeted businesses (for example, by becoming a low-cost producer or a highly innovative product developer). The third level specifies the expected contribution of each major function such as marketing, manufacturing, or research and development to each business' competitive strategy. All three types of strategies, collectively referred to in this chapter as business strategies, often contain HR issues and implications.

Strategic HRM consists of three major tasks. The first task, which arises during the formulation of business strategies, is to assure that the HR issues and implications of various alternatives or proposals are fully considered. The next task involves establishing HR goals and action plans — that is, HR strategies — to support the business strategies.[11] And the final task requires working with line managers as principal clients to ensure that established action plans are indeed implemented.

Assessing Feasibility

The first task is accomplished by assessing each serious strategic proposal in terms of its feasibility and desirability from an HR perspective. Feasibility depends, first, on whether the numbers and types of key people required to make the proposal succeed can be obtained on a timely basis and at a reasonable cost[12] and second, whether the behavioral expectations assumed by the strategy (for example, retention rates and productivity levels) have some reasonable chance of being met. [13]

As Figure 1 suggests, making these HR-related judgments requires an extensive knowledge of not only the proposed business strategies, including any implied or stated changes in the organizational environment, such as structures or technologies, but also any constraining factors in the organization's internal or external environments. For example, judging a proposal to grow a business significantly through ongoing new product development requires first identifying the key personnel (for example, researchers and process engineers) and then estimating how many new persons the strategy would require. Next, attention would turn to the internal supply of relevant talent and, allowing for likely turnover, an estimate of its probable availability when needed. If internal shortfalls seem likely, feasibility depends on whether hiring from external labor markets can fill the anticipated deficiencies in a timely and affordable manner. (This process of HR planning is described in greater detail in Chapter 1.2 of this volume.)

Determining Desirability

Desirability is addressed by examining the implications of strategic proposals in terms of sacrosanct HR policies or conditions. A strategy of rapid retrenchment, for example, would be called into question at a company with a full employment policy, unless the required employee dislocations could be accomplished without layoffs. In many companies, a proposal that called for rapid increases in productivity would be flagged if the heightened pressure on employees might lead to morale problems and a propensity to unionize. In other companies, a strategy dependent on a new technology which uses new, untried chemicals would be contraindicated if the possibility of serious health risks to employees existed.

Desirability, even more than feasibility, is a judgment call. The same basic information is required: a thorough knowledge of the business proposal, including its organizational and technological implications, and a data base of existing and expected conditions in the organization's internal and external environments. (For details on environmental scanning, see Chapter 1.3 of this volume.)

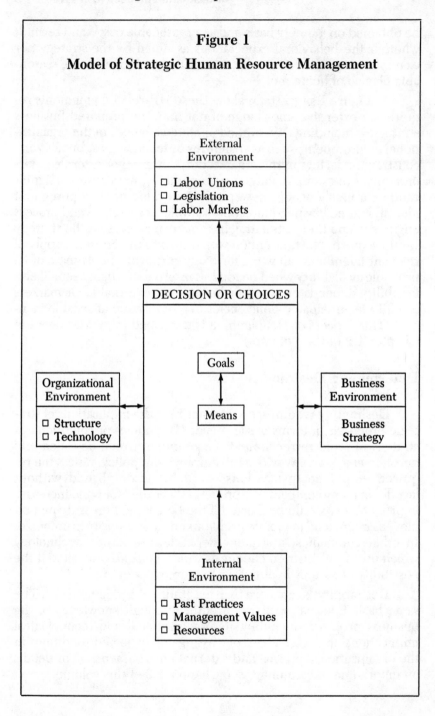

Figure 1

Model of Strategic Human Resource Management

When the investigation suggests that a particular proposal could be infeasible or undesirable from an HR perspective, it is reconsidered. This does not necessarily mean that the idea must be scrapped or even altered. Other more compelling, and thus overriding, considerations may outweigh HR concerns; adverse business conditions, for example, have led to layoffs in companies, such as Kodak, Control Data, and Data General, which previously had prided themselves on being full employment companies. Even in situations where HR concerns do not prevail, the HR analyses that were conducted may prove useful during the next major strategic HRM task, the formulation of a supporting HR strategy.

Defining Goals

As previously suggested, HR strategy consists of decisions concerning major HR goals and the primary means to use in pursuit of these goals. While HR goals and means are necessarily situation-specific, a generic set of areas that might be considered is defined in Figure 2.

HR goals define the main issues to be worked on and they derive primarily from the content of the business strategy, although they may be tempered by information about other relevant environments (see Figure 1). To cite an example, many businesses today are striving to become lower-cost producers. This strategy typically requires, among other things, reducing labor costs. This, in turn, often translates into at least two types of HR goals: higher performance standards (contribution) and reduced headcounts (composition). In some firms it may also translate into a third and fourth type of HR goal: maintaining employee quality (competence) and morale (commitment), especially as the organization begins to reduce the work force. The relevance of the latter two issues might be influenced by outside factors, such as the availability of replacement talent in the labor market in case of a subsequent upturn, or the threat of unionization.

Means of Achieving Goals

With HR goals in place, HR strategists are left with the task of deciding on means. Two matters are at issue: One involves priorities, which ultimately determine resource allocations, and the other

Figure 2

Human Resource Strategy

Goals

CONTRIBUTION—The organization's individual or group behavior and performance goals.

> Some organizations seek little more than reliable role behavior (coming to work on time and doing what is assigned), while others attempt to attain a modicum of initiative, creativity and flexibility, and still others expect a high degree of innovative, creative and even spontaneous behavior and flexibility. In any of these situations, performance expectations may rank from relatively modest to very high.

COMPOSITION—The organization's headcount, staffing ratio, and skill mix goals.

> At any point in time, some organizations choose to run fat, others lean; some attempt to staff up, others down; some try to enhance staff groups, others to pare them; some seek to increase the ratio, for example, of engineers to technicians, others to decrease it.

COMPETENCE—The general level of ability an organization wishes to attain among various groups of employees.

> Some employers try to attain only the barest minimum of ability required by the jobs at hand, others look for a close match between ability and job requirements, and still others strive for a work force that is generally overqualified.

COMMITMENT—The general level of employee attachment sought and the degree of identification with organization goals desired.

> Some organizations seek only a casual attachment of a strictly instrumental, work for outcomes nature; others desire a moderate degree of attachment based on both instrumental and emotional ties; and still others try to develop a high degree of attachment and a nearly total identification with the organization and/or its goals.

Means

STAFFING—The process of matching people with jobs.

> Involves the use of both external and internal staffing mechanisms. Typical policy issues involve the relative amount of emphasis on external and internal staffing, the stringency of selection standards, the amount of effort for career management, and whether or not layoffs are to be used when cutbacks are called for.

Figure 2 continued

DEVELOPMENT—The process of enhancing the knowledge, skills, and abilities of employees.

Typical policy issues involve the degree of emphasis on development and the choice of means to achieve the development, whether on or off the job.

REWARDS—The process of compensating employees and providing them with special forms of recognition.

Typical policy issues involve the general level of pay to be offered, the steepness of pay structure(s), the bases for determining individual rates of pay (for example, seniority or merit), and the types and levels of benefits to be provided.

WORK SYSTEM—The process of designing jobs and workplaces.

Typical policy issues involve whether employees are to work primarily individually or in teams, whether jobs or team assignments are to be narrow or broad (enriched), and the degree of control employees are to exercise over the work.

SUPERVISION AND PERFORMANCE MANAGEMENT—The process of directing and evaluating the work of others.

Some policy issues involve the amount of emphasis to be placed on supervision (vs. self-management), the closeness of the supervision to be provided, and the role of supervisors (e.g., director, supporter, facilitator).

EMPLOYEE RELATIONS—The process of providing support to employees.

Four areas are involved: communication, voice (avenues for upward communication), due process (means of redressing grievances), and employee assistance (for such things as alcohol and drug abuse, family problems, etc.). Since these are optional (in nonunion settings), a major policy issue involves whether to do them at all. If the decision is affirmative, other issues involve extent and types of activities.

LABOR RELATIONS—The process of dealing with unions or the threat of unionization where present.

In unionized companies some policy issues involve the nature of the relationship to seek with the union (for example, adversarial or cooperative) and how much cooperative behavior to engage in outside the formal bargaining relationship. In nonunionized firms, the major policy issue involves the amount of effort to put into staying nonunion.

GOVERNMENT RELATIONS—The process of dealing with governmental regulators and, where necessary, the courts.

Some policy issues involve the amount of effort to put into complying with existing legislation and regulations (such as non-compliance, basic compliance, or over-compliance (model citizen), and how much to put into lobbying to affect existing or proposed legislation and regulations.

involves major policies. Priorities are necessary since few organizations can, or would desire to, put equal emphasis on all the program areas listed in Figure 1. Major policies provide guidance to those who design the specific programs or activities that underly the HR strategy.

To a large extent, HR goals determine priorities and policies, although the decision-making process certainly allows for some latitude. A company seeking high levels of routine performance, for example, might emphasize rewards by offering generous levels of contingency-based pay (such as incentives, bonuses, or gainsharing plans). A company more interested in inducing initiative, creativity, and flexibility, however, might put its money toward designing work systems that emphasize employee participation (for example, job enrichment or self-managing work teams).

The general rule is: The tighter the external and internal fit, the better the strategy. External fit refers to the degree of consistency between HR goals on the one hand and the exigencies of the underlying business strategy and relevant environmental conditions on the other. Internal fit measures the extent to which HR means follow from HR goals and other relevant environmental conditions, as well as the degree of coherency or synergy among the various HR means.

Chaparral Steel—A Working Example

One company which clearly meets the conditions noted above is Chaparral Steel.[14] A so-called mini-mill, the company's business strategy is to outdo the major manufacturers and importers through niche marketing, product innovation, and low prices. This strategy is made possible by a very flat and flexible organizational structure, continuous introduction of state-of-the-art production technologies, and tight cost controls.

Chaparral's HR strategy, which has evolved over time, features the following goals:

- High performance standards (a constant drive to do "better") and expectations of initiative and creativity from all employees (contribution)

- Minimal management (four layers), minimal staffs, some slack at lower management levels (for flexibility), lean headcounts on the production floor (composition)

- High skill levels and considerable personal flexibility (competence)

- High identification with the company and its business goals (commitment)

To achieve these goals, Chaparral has put in place a tightly integrated set of HR activities. Greatest emphasis is placed on the work system and a policy of participative management which is, according to one manager, "not consensus management, but [rather] driving decisions down to the lowest possible level." For example, all research and development and quality control work is done by line supervisors and production employees, not by specialized departments; supervisors are responsible for their own hiring, training, and safety programs; and production employees regularly serve on special project teams to look after customer concerns and evaluate new technologies.

The work system is supported by very high hiring standards (the company looks for "home-grown entrepreneurs") and extensive training efforts, including sabbaticals. Financial rewards include profit sharing (six percent of pre-tax profits goes into the plan) and special bonuses for extraordinary achievements. The company also has an active employee relations effort, which features constant communication about company goals and performance; an egalitarian atmosphere — no time clocks, all salaried employees, no reserved parking, no fancy offices; and no union.

Chaparral is a highly productive company: Labor costs run 9 to 10 percent of sales, about one-fourth the industry standard; output per person is a little over three times the industry average. Gordon Forward, the chief executive officer, attributes about 60 percent of the company's productivity advantage to its advanced automation, and about 40 percent to its HR strategy.

Evolution of Strategic HRM

As is now clear, an organization's HR strategy results from a series of managerial decisions about priorities and policies designed either to influence or to adapt to dominant environmental forces. By extension, broader developments in HRM — which are, after all, simply the sum of prevailing organizational patterns — emerge in much the same way. Once again, Figure 1 can serve as a useful framework for examining first, the evolution of the forces acting on managerial decision makers and then, the dominant patterns in their responses. For brevity, the analysis is collapsed into two broad time periods: the 30 to 35 years following World War II and the 1980s.

1945 through the 1970s

In retrospect, the period from the mid-1940s to about 1970 was a golden age for American business. The demand for goods and services, especially early on, was practically insatiable and the United States entered the period possessing more than one-half the world's usable industrial capacity.[15] The name of the game was to produce and market.

Business Operations

Business strategies — perhaps too grandiose a term for the reality of the 50s and 60s — focused on maintaining uninterrupted production and, to a lesser extent, on distribution and advertising. Costs, quality, and other aspects of product differentiation, while not matters of total indifference, were often secondary concerns.

In terms of organizational structure, the drift was toward immense size, centralization, and bureaucratization.[16] A number of important technological breakthroughs took place but they pertained more to products than to processes. Perceived threats of widespread technological obsolescence and displacement among blue-collar workers proved to be seriously overdrawn.[17]

This comfortable pattern of operation changed very little even well into the 1970s. Unfortunately, however, the business environment did. Oil shocks and recessions took their toll, but the longer-term challenge came from foreign competition. In 1970, about 20 percent of the goods produced in the United States were competing with foreign-made products either here or abroad; by 1980, the figure was closer to 70 percent.[18] American share of world markets fell by 23 percent during the 1970s, in part because of managements' failure to adjust their business strategies to meet these changing circumstances.[19]

Labor Relations

Just as business had prospered immediately after World War II, so had the American labor movement. In 1945, union membership reached 35 percent of the nonagricultural labor force, and it stayed at that level for over a decade. Labor militance also was high; lost time due to strikes reached unprecedented levels in the mid-1940s and, at the time, this situation seemed likely to continue. This clearly was a vexing prospect for employers, given the large rewards they stood to reap from uninterrupted production. The corresponding HR challenge was to find paths of accommodation and stabilization in ongoing labor-management relations and to stave off the unions where they had yet to make inroads.

By all accounts, this challenge was admirably met. Labor relations specialists were assigned responsibility for negotiating and administering contracts in a manner satisfactory to both their bosses and the unions; that is, without strikes or other disruptions. The specialists learned to do this successfully, particularly during the 1950s. With a few major exceptions, a general pattern of managed adversarialism held sway in union-management relations well into the 1970s.[20]

At the same time, personnel managers and specialists in newly-formed personnel departments were developing and expanding programs and procedures that had gained acceptance during the war. These innovations included job analysis, psychological testing, technical training, job evaluation, and other techniques of wage and salary administration.[21] While much of this effort was aimed at forestalling the spread of unions,[22] it was also particularly well-suited to the large, centralized bureaucracies of the time.

The 1960s and, particularly, the 1970s brought a diminution of labor's power. By 1970, union membership had dwindled to 27.3 percent of the nonagricultural labor force; by 1980, it had dropped to 21.9 percent. Organizing attempts declined and became increasingly less successful, partly because of managements' enhanced willingness and new-found capability to resist unions in nonviolent ways.

Legislative Developments

As the influence of unions dwindled, the action picked up on the legislative front. The litany of federal laws, executive orders, and regulations during the socially tumultuous 60s and early 70s is legion: Title VII, the Age Discrimination in Employment Act, the Equal Pay Act, Executive Orders 11246 and 11375 — the list goes on and on. Between 1960 and 1975, according to one estimate, the number of regulations administered by the U.S. Department of Labor tripled from 43 to 134.[23]

Enforcement of these statutes and directives peaked during the 1970s. Several sizable and highly publicized consent decrees and judgments came down, many of which supported women, who were entering the labor force in unprecedented numbers.[24] In a survey taken in the mid-1970s, personnel professionals singled out government regulation as a major instigator of change in their organizations during the previous decade.[25] Unfortunately, no similar survey was taken among top and other line managers. However, it appears that except for the most socially conscious and legally vulnerable employers, most managers saw these legal developments as somewhat less central and significant.

Once again, much of this regulatory activity wound up on the shoulders of the ever-expanding personnel departments. By the mid-1970s, virtually all medium-sized and large companies had established equal employment opportunity units within their personnel functions.[26] In addition, a cadre of capable professionals had developed to carry out and champion the often sophisticated analyses and actions required to meet or exceed the basic legal requirements.

HR Activities

Despite a general preference for the status quo among labor relations specialists and their union counterparts,[27] a few unionized and, many more nonunionized firms found themselves experimenting with a host of activities — quality circles, quality of worklife programs, and the like — to bolster productivity, enhance product quality, and improve employee morale.[28] Greater attention also was paid to the burgeoning number of so-called knowledge workers in the expanding high-tech and service sectors. Many of these activities arose from an emerging sense of professionalism in the personnel community and a concomitant desire to be on the cutting edge of the field. However, the general emphasis was on relatively disassociated programs and practices rather than a broader concept of HR strategy.[29]

1980 to Present

During the past decade, globalization continued unabated. Deregulation brought competition to the airlines, railroads, truckers, bankers, telephone companies, oil and gas producers, and broadcasters. Evolving technologies blurred traditional industry lines, generating competing products and services from unexpected sources. Institutional investors and corporate raiders became bolder and more assertive, thereby increasing the pressure on management to produce immediate financial returns and constant increases in shareholder value. And a worldwide recession occurred.

Business Operations

In the face of these developments, some managements sought refuge in asset shuffling, protectionism, and even reregulation.[30] But many companies belatedly began the process of corporate revitalization. Business strategies, structures, technologies, and processes underwent significant changes. Strategies were reformulated to assure that every product and service offered a clear competitive advantage (such as low cost, high quality, a unique feature, or an innovative application).[31] Firms of all sizes, but particularly the huge bureaucracies of the post-war era, were restructured and often downsized: Between 1980 and 1987, about one-half of the *Fortune* 1,000 firms experienced at least one significant reorganization.[32] Decentralization — driving business decisions out to operating units and down to the lowest feasible level, or "getting back to the basics" and "close to the customer" in the vernacular — came into vogue once again.

Huge investments were made in process technologies — computer-aided design and manufacturing, robotics, computer-integrated manufacturing, point-of-sale ordering and inventory systems, fault-tolerant transaction processing systems, and multifunctional work stations, to name just a few — in attempts to increase efficiency, improve quality, and enhance flexibility in manufacturing and, to a lesser extent, the service sector.[33] In recent years, these new technologies have altered the jobs of an estimated 40 to 50 million Americans, or about 40 percent of the civilian labor force.[34]

Labor and Legislative Trends

Commensurate with these events, the labor movement continued its downward slide; by the late 1980s union membership was less than 18 percent of the nonagricultural labor force. Competitive realities forced several large and visible unions to make significant concessions in wages, benefits, and work rules. In 1986, negotiated wage settlements reached record low levels for the fifth consecutive year according to the Bureau of Labor Statistics.[35] Strikes reached their lowest point in forty years, and until very recently, organizing came to a virtual standstill.

Consistent with the spirit of deregulation and rugged individualism, the Reagan administration neither instigated nor supported any major legal initiatives in the HR arena. Enforcement lapsed. To some extent, state governments and the courts filled this vacuum,[36] but on balance the legal heat felt by employers in the 80s has been well below the level of the preceding decade.

HR Activities

The big HR challenge, then, was to keep up with the changes on the business front. One apparent effect of this challenge was an increasing involvement by top and other line managers in HR matters. The impetus for managements' involvement came when the initial moves toward competitiveness — especially massive layoffs, dislocations, and wage and salary freezes or cuts — resulted in HR implications too far-reaching and serious to ignore or delegate. This impetus was sustained where enhanced levels of contribution and commitment on the part of all employees became recognized as necessary conditions for business success.

One, perhaps surprising, result of this metamorphosis was an enlarged role for the personnel function. Personnel managers and specialists were increasingly called upon to understand the businesses in which they operate, to be familiar with extant or evolving business strategies, to propose strategic HR solutions to strategic business issues, and to work closely with line management to implement these solutions. This relationship differed greatly from that of having continually to press line managers for action simply because of contractual or legal requirements or because the action seemed professionally appropriate. Not surprisingly, the change proved somewhat discomforting to some personnel professionals.

These new-found partnerships between line managers and HR staff resulted in a wealth of organizational experimentation. Some experiments were relatively limited in scope and aimed at fairly specific goals. Federal Express, for example, implemented a systematic program of information, incentives, and controls to keep headcounts in line.[37] Several companies — Digital Equipment, Hallmark, Pacific Bell, Worthington Industries — successfully redeployed and retrained significant portions of their work forces to enhance performance without layoffs.[38] Pay for performance, such as merit pay, bonuses, gainsharing, and profit sharing, enjoyed a resurgence in companies where employee motivation was a concern.[39] Earlier experiments with employee participation through quality circles, quality of worklife programs, semiautonomous work groups, and self-managed work teams — in the auto and steel industries, for example — were expanded and adopted by a wide variety of firms and industries.[40]

More extensive efforts are now underway. Virtually every manufacturer committed to maintaining production in this country has been forced to undertake productivity and quality improvement programs of one type or another. Some — for example, Outboard Marine — built new modular plants in low-wage areas in the south. Other companies, such as Allen-Bradley, made substantial investments both in new technologies and in the people who install and operate them, while still others concentrated mainly on human resources.[41] A typical example of the HR approach is NUMMI, the joint venture between General Motors and Toyota in California. Here, in partnership with the United Auto Workers, the emphasis is on participative management — semiautonomous work groups, open communications, extensive training — in combination with Japanese production techniques. The plant, which General Motors had closed down because of labor and production problems, now regularly outperforms more technologically advanced facilities in terms of both productivity and quality.[42]

State of Strategy in Practice

As these various forms of experimentation have taken hold, the resulting internal anomalies have required still more changes in HR priorities and policies to preserve internal consistency.[43] And as these adjustments have been made, organizations have at some point become embroiled in the evolution of an HR strategy. This, then, constitutes one group in the strategy fold.

Along with this group, a smaller number of companies have been, and in some cases still are, involved in even more ambitious efforts. For example, several well-known corporations — Bank of America, Corning Glass Works, GE, Kodak, Motorola, Polaroid, and Xerox, among others — have found their paternalistic HR strategies (some would say cultures) to be unsustainable in the face of continuing competitive pressures and depressed earnings. All these companies are engaged in the struggle to specify and implement more performance-oriented HR strategies corporate-wide.

To these two groups of companies, a third can be added: the firms that have maintained their basic HR strategies through the turmoil. This group includes long-timers such as IBM, Hewlett Packard, Eli Lilly, Marion Laboratories, and Lincoln Electric, as well as such newcomers as Chaparral Steel and Federal Express.

Collectively, these three groups seem to represent the current action with respect to HR strategy. Regrettably, little is known about many of these efforts at this time. Nonetheless, the essence of what they are trying to do can be captured through a more extensive look at a few specific examples.

Illustrative HR Strategies

Given the current level of activity in HR strategy, any discussion must resort to some sort of typology or taxonomy to identify and define generic patterns. Although a generally accepted typology or taxonomy has yet to emerge,[44] the framework presented in Figure 1, when applied to available information on various HR strategies, helps to identify a few prevailing patterns.

Three strategic types — labelled inducement, investment, and involvement — can be discussed in detail, with reference to Tables 1, 2, and 3 for comparisons of the relevant environmental conditions, goals, and means associated with each strategy. These particular HR strategies are not necessarily the most prevalent or promising ones; no such claims are possible given the present state of knowledge. The purpose is to demonstrate a few of the methods that various organizations are using to achieve external and internal consistency in their HR priorities and policies, at least among selected employee groups.[45]

Inducement Strategy

The origins of the inducement strategy date back to 1911 and the work of the much-maligned Frederick Winslow Taylor, the father of scientific management. Its evolution, however, probably owes more to the philosophies expounded by James B. Lincoln in the late 1930s, and particularly to the highly successful and well-

Table 1

HR Strategies Relating to Environment

ENVIRONMENTAL CONDITION	HR STRATEGY		
	INDUCEMENT	INVESTMENT	INVOLVEMENT
□ Business Strategy	□ Based on Price and/or Quality	□ Based on Differentiation: Quality, Features, Service, etc.	□ Based on Innovation, Flexibility
□ Organizational Structure	□ Flat, Centralized	□ Tall, Centralized	□ Flat, Decentralized, Many Task Forces, Small Units
□ Technology	□ Traditional, Evolutionary Change	□ Modern, Somewhat Rapid Change	□ Varies
□ Labor Supply	□ Adequate	□ Somewhat Tight	□ Somewhat Tight
□ Legislation			
□ Labor Unions	□ Sometimes	□ Hardly Ever	□ Sometimes
□ Management Philosophy	□ Much Attention to HR (Cost)	□ Much Attention to HR, Paternalistic	□ Much Attention to HR, Theory Y
□ Resources for HR	□ Low	□ High	□ Intermediate

Table 2

HR Strategies Relating to Goals

GOALS	HR STRATEGY		
	INDUCEMENT	INVESTMENT	INVOLVEMENT
□ Contribution	□ Some Initiative and Creativity, Very High Performance Standards, Modest Flexibility	□ High Initiative and Creativity, High Performance Standards, Some Flexibility	□ Very High Initiative and Creativity, High Performance Expectations, High Flexibility
□ Composition	□ Lean Headcount (Core and Buffer), Low Skill Mix, Minimal Staffs	□ Comfortable Headcount (Core and Buffer), High Skill Mix, Moderate Staffs	□ Comfortable Headcounts (Core and Buffer), High Skill Mix, Minimal Staffs
□ Competence	□ Adequate	□ High	□ Very High
□ Commitment	□ High, Instrumental	□ High, Identification with Company	□ High, Identification with Work and Company

Table 3
HR Strategies Relating to Means

MEANS	HR STRATEGY		
	INDUCEMENT	INVESTMENT	INVOLVEMENT
□ Staffing	□ Careful Selection, Few Career Options, Use of Temps, (Minimal Layoffs)	* Careful Selection, Extensive Career Development, Some Flex, Minimal (or no) Layoffs	□ Careful Selection, Some Career Development, Much Flex, Minimal (or no) Layoffs
□ Development	□ Minimal	* Extensive, Continuous Learning	* Extensive, Continuous Learning
□ Rewards	* Flat Structure, High-Variable, Piece-Rate, Profit Sharing, Minimal Benefits	□ Tall Structure, Competitive-Fixed, Job Based, Merit, Many Benefits	□ Flat Structure, High-Partially Variable, Skill-Based, Gain-sharing, Flex Benefits
□ Work System	□ Narrow Jobs, Employee Paced, Individualized	□ Broad Jobs, Employee Initiative, Some Groups	* Enriched Jobs, Self-Managed Work Teams
□ Supervision	□ Minimal, Directive	□ Extensive, Supportive	* Minimal, Facilitative
□ Employee Relations	□ Some Communication, Some Voice, Egalitarian	* Much Communication, High Voice, High Due Process, High Employee Assistance	□ Much Communication, High Voice, Some Due Process, Some Employee Assistance, Egalitarian
□ Labor Relations	□ Union Avoidance, or Conflict	□ Non-Issue	□ Union Avoidance, and or Cooperative
□ Government Relations	□ Compliance	* Over-Compliance	□ Compliance

*Indicates priority program areas.

publicized application of his ideas at the Lincoln Electric Company.[46]

Business Environment

The environmental conditions giving rise to the inducement strategy are outlined in the first column of Table 1. The business environment tends to be very competitive, with firms competing largely on the basis of low prices and/or the quality of their products or services. Decision-making power is highly centralized, although organizational structures tend to be relatively flat with few layers and wide spans of control. The technology is traditional, simple, and evolves slowly. External environmental conditions are largely benign, although militant unions are not unheard of. Top management pays a good deal of attention to human resources, particularly HR costs. At Lincoln Electric, for example, management considers employees to be the second most important stakeholder group in the organization, just behind customers and well ahead of stockholders. At UPS, another well-known inducer, the ". . . ability to manage labor and hold it accountable is the key to [the company's] success."[47]

HR Goals

With respect to contribution (as shown in Table 2), the inducement strategy is aimed first and foremost at encouraging very high levels of reliable role behavior. Employee initiative or flexibility is at most a modest concern, while encouraging innovation, creativity, or spontaneity plays no part in this strategy.

Since cost is a major consideration, inducers seek to run lean, particularly with respect to overhead and staff jobs. Another major HR goal is to hold down the ratio of comparatively skilled to unskilled employees. Competence, in contrast, is a secondary goal. Despite a low tolerance for incompetence, no attempt is made to develop employee skills beyond levels required by current tasks.

Commitment is encouraged, although it usually is not a preoccupation. At any rate, commitment is instrumentally based — i.e., we pay, you stay — although some inducers, such as Lincoln Electric, reinforce it with a touch of paternalism and a strict no-layoff policy.[48]

Means to Achieve HR Goals

Advocates of the inducement strategy are seldom cited as cutting-edge practitioners of HRM. They are largely unmoved by the successive waves of fads that wash over the field. Instead, their forte lies in getting the best out of the basics.

As Table 3 shows, the focal activity of inducers' incentive plans is pay. Despite a preoccupation with cost control, inducers offer opportunities for very high earnings. But the emphasis is on opportunities. Inducers are among the most avid users of performance-based pay schemes, such as incentive pay, performance bonuses, gainsharing, and profit sharing. In every way possible, high pay is made contingent on high levels of contribution.

Lincoln Electric, for example, applies piece-rate plans to every possible job in the shop, even some classified as indirect labor, and among the sales force. All other employees are on merit pay. The profit-sharing plan, which encompasses all employees, distributes bonuses on the basis of performance appraisal ratings — inducement style, rather than on the traditional basis of earnings. In good years, which is most years at Lincoln, the bonuses often match or exceed regular earnings; semi-skilled shop workers can and do earn $40,000 a year or more. Many of Lincoln's employees at all levels are also stockholders as a result of a long-standing and relatively generous stock purchase plan. Even at UPS where the Teamsters union has resisted incentive pay, hourly rates exceed those of most comparable firms and, with overtime pay, many drivers earn $35,000 to $40,000 a year. UPS also offers a profit-sharing plan and, for management, a stock ownership plan.

But, even inducers do not rely on pay alone. Work systems are carefully designed and managed; jobs tend to be narrowly defined and work standards are tightly controlled. Despite the general loathing of staff jobs among inducers, UPS employs over 1,000 industrial engineers — the company has 152,000 employees — and uses state-of-the-art electronic stopwatches and computer programs to time and retime tasks and jobs and to project appropriate performance standards.

Those inducers that use incentive pay plans deemphasize supervision and rely on employees to manage themselves; the others give supervision a good deal of attention. In either case, supervision tends to be directive: "A sorter is expected to handle

1,124 packages an hour and is allowed no more than one mistake per 2,500 packages. UPS counts on strict supervision to overcome the occasional human lapses."[49]

Selection, while not central, is used to identify qualified candidates who also will respond positively to and be comfortable with the inducement strategy. Noncontributors are weeded out early. Career management and employee development receive little emphasis, and what training is done tends to be task-oriented and carried out on the job.

Employee relations activities — communication, voice, due process, and employee assistance — are not major concerns, although most inducers tend to be egalitarian with respect to amenities and perks. Unionized inducers often have strained relations with their unions, particularly with respect to work systems and supervision — witness, for example, the running war between UPS and the Teamsters. Government relations tend to focus on compliance, nothing more.

Investment Strategy

The investment strategy has its origins in the welfare capitalism of the 1920s, but also borrows ideas from the human relations movement of the 40s and 50s and the more recent human capital theorists. The greatest success of this strategy has occurred in start-up companies with intensely paternalistic founders of long-standing influence. IBM, Hewlett Packard, and Eli Lilly are classic examples; Polaroid was.

Business Environment

As noted in the middle column of Table 1, the business strategies in investment oriented firms center around product or service differentiation (for example, unique features, brand identification, or superior service) rather than price, which in turn allows for relatively generous cost structures. Most — although certainly not all — are highly centralized and, until recently, were relatively tall organizations having many layers of management. State-of-the-art, and thus rapidly changing, technology is a common feature.

Investors worry more than inducers about evolving trends in external environments. This information helps to fashion personnel policies and programs attractive to the highly trained talent their business strategies and technologies demand, to maintain postures as good corporate citizens, and to remain nonunion. Top management also pays a good deal of attention to internal HR matters and provides generous funding to back up this concern.

HR Goals

When it comes to contribution, excellence is a common theme among investors. Performance standards are high, although not excessively so, and employees are expected routinely to exercise a fair amount of initiative and creativity in carrying out their tasks (see the middle column in Table 2). Continual technological change also requires a certain amount of employee flexibility, especially since most investors eschew layoffs.

Competence is clearly the preferred path to achieve the desired levels of employee contribution. Investors exhibit an unrelenting and uncompromising preoccupation with employee quality. Attract and develop the best, they seem to say, and contribution will naturally follow. Since this approach works only if employees remain for a long time, attaining a high level of employee commitment is also an important goal for investors.

Because of their full employment policies, composition of the work force also matters greatly to investors. The primary aim is flexibility. In the past, some investors deliberately overstaffed, both in terms of numbers and in skill mixes, and maintained relatively large staff groups to enhance organizational adaptability. Recently, faced with unprecedented levels of competition, some investors find that their biggest current HR challenge is to figure out how to downsize without laying off employees or undermining traditional levels of employee contribution, competence, and commitment. If the competition continues, the trend ultimately may call into question the long-term viability of the investment strategy.

Means to Achieve HR Goals

Investors are not, as is frequently assumed, the premiere practitioners of McGregor's Theory Y style of people management.[50] Briefly, advocates of Theory Y believe that most employees naturally desire to use their capabilities fully and do a good job and therefore are most likely to thrive and produce in a nurturing environment characterized by challenging jobs, participative decision making, and non-directive leadership. In contrast, investors rely on a kid glove version of Theory X. Management establishes performance and related standards, fashions the accompanying amenities, and maintains close control. Employees are expected to exercise judgment and initiative in their work, but investors do not advocate or encourage high levels of employee participation in a wide range of firm affairs. The prevailing organizational values are personal growth, respect, equity, justice, and security, not autonomy and involvement.[51]

The emphasis on employee competence naturally leads investors to be big spenders on employee development (as indicated in Table 3). Much of the money goes toward employee socialization, but a good deal is devoted to various types of skill-based training. Employees at virtually all levels are trained not only for their current jobs, but also for future moves and even, when the time comes, for retirement. Much of the managerial and supervisory training involves the essentials of effective people management, especially employee relations.

Employee relations incorporates four subactivities (see Exhibit 1) and investors like to be on the cutting edge of all four.[52] They employ a wide variety of communication media to provide employees with both factual and symbolic information. They also encourage an ongoing flow of information up the organization through a range of mechanisms: opinion surveys, skip-level meetings, sensing sessions, and the like.

Investors also make every effort to assure that employees receive fair treatment in all aspects of the employment relationship. This concern is solidly backed by due process mechanisms, such as open doors, "speak out" programs, and grievance procedures. Investors are prominent providers of employee assistance programs, child care programs, family leaves, alternative work schedules, wellness programs, nonsmoking policies, and company-sponsored social events. The message: investors care.

Along with employee development and employee relations, investors emphasize staffing. Selection policies are designed to attract highly qualified employees who also hold the proper values. Career management and counseling programs emphasize long-term development within the company. Extensive HR planning and ongoing coordination among external and internal staffing and development activities are employed in the interest of employment stabilization.[53] Government relations receives extra resources, and investors commonly go well beyond the basic requirements in such areas as equal employment opportunity, affirmative action, and safety and health. Again, investors care.

In contrast, investors tend to downplay rewards. Most pay competitively and, in keeping with their paternalistic tendencies, offer attractive benefit packages. Merit pay may be used but more hard-core incentive schemes, such as bonuses and profit-sharing plans are rare.

Work systems, as suggested earlier, receive relatively little attention and are usually traditional: Jobs and performance standards are fairly well-defined; bosses boss and workers work. Supervision is ever-present and supportive; it basically is viewed as a delivery system for employee development and employee relations activities. Labor relations tends to be a nonissue since most investors are nonunion and rely on the other elements of their HR strategies to stay that way.

Involvement Strategy

The involvement strategy contains vestiges of the human relations movement, particularly its organizational offshoots,[54] but gains most of its theoretical justification from subsequent job enrichment research,[55] quality of worklife programs,[56] and industrial democracy. Because of its democratic underpinnings, involvement is the most highly touted HR strategy in the current literature.[57] Applications include the HR strategies at Chaparral Steel, NUMMI, and Marion Laboratories discussed earlier in this chapter. Another example, which represents a conversion rather than a start-up, is Motorola's well-known "participative management program."[58]

Business Environment

The involvement strategy has been tried, at least in part, by many different types of organizations pursuing a number of different business strategies. Its greatest success, however, seems to have been achieved by organizations operating under two rather diverse sets of circumstances. The first set is companies doing business in markets that are highly competitive on the basis of low prices and/or high quality — markets similar to those of inducers. The second group is firms pursuing business strategies that rely either on innovation to provide continually differentiated products or services, or on agility to move from niche to niche as markets change or competitors begin to catch up. Both sets, but especially the latter, tend to be relatively small, decentralized companies or business units within larger companies that have either flat or unconventional (for example, matrix) organizational structures, and state-of-the-art flexible systems technology.

The external environment also plays a role. Proponents say that the involvement strategy is particularly well-suited to today's highly educated and narcissistic labor force, which presumably has a great need to experience high levels of autonomy, challenge, and influence at work. Top managers tend to adopt a Theory Y philosophy concerning the internal management of people and to back their beliefs with at least moderate funding levels for HR experimentation. Despite the open hostility of many unions to the involvement strategy, a number of applications have occurred in unionized environments.[59]

HR Goals

The major goal of the involvement strategy is to achieve a very high level of employee commitment.[60] Involvers seek a deep psychological commitment from employees based on a close identification with the organization, its mission, and its work (see Table 2). This differs radically from the more instrumental commitment associated with the inducement strategy.

Of course, high levels of employee commitment should result in equally high levels of employee contribution. Contribution in this context involves a good deal more than a high level of output on a particular job. The goal is for employees at all levels to exercise considerable initiative, creativity, and spontaneity in solving a wide range of organizational problems, as well as to display a high degree of flexibility in adapting to ongoing organizational change.

This, in turn, requires very competent employees. As might be expected, the definition of competence encompasses not only specific job skills, but also a full range of knowledge and skills, including problem-solving and social skills, even at the lowest organizational levels.

Composition goals are generally downplayed in the involvement strategy, although its supporters suggest, and such cases as Chaparral Steel, prove that companies adopting this strategy can operate with fewer levels of management and smaller staff groups than would be possible under other HR strategies. However, offsetting differentials in headcounts may occur at lower organizational levels and in skill upgrades at these levels. Some overstaffing also may be necessary to provide the needed training and to achieve desired levels of organizational adaptability.

Means to Achieve HR Goals

The whole idea behind the involvement strategy is to enhance the power and contribution of employees at all organizational levels by redistributing authority, increasing both the downward and upward flow of work-related information, and enhancing the knowledge base and skills of employees.[61]

Not surprisingly, the work system is the main means used to achieve this goal (see Table 3). The basic policy is to drive all decisions involving work goals and means down to the lowest feasible level. In practice, this policy translates, in limited cases, into job enrichment and, in more extensive applications, into the formation of semiautonomous work groups and self-managed work teams.[62] It may also involve the liberal use of task forces and other temporary groups. These units function not only to accomplish work — often work that would otherwise be done by staff functions — but also to foster maximum participation and involvement. Accompanying features include such policies as flex-work and flex-time, which also enhance employee control over the work situation.

Supervision plays a key role in the involvement strategy, particularly in the early stages. The central concept is facilitation. Supervisors at all levels assist subordinates in creating and communicating units' missions and goals and in allocating and making decisions properly, by providing information, encouraging openness and trust, and lending support.[63] Social control is provided primarily through peer pressure rather than supervisory direction.

Since participation and facilitation are beyond the experience of many employees and supervisors, involvers usually find it necessary to do considerable training and development, particularly when such a strategy is first adopted. Much of the emphasis is on developing problem-solving, interpersonal, and group facilitation skills, and economic and financial knowledge, rather than more traditional job skills and knowledge.

While work design, supervision, and development are central to the success of the involvement strategy, other HR activities provide support. Careful selection, for example, assures that those hired possess the skills, or at least the aptitudes and attitudes, demanded by the involvement strategy. Careers are redefined in terms of skill growth and cross-functional movement so as to overcome reduced opportunities for upward mobility, and career counseling communicates and facilitates this concept. Layoffs are minimized for philosophical reasons, but also in an attempt to protect investments in employees and enhance organizational adaptability.

With the heavy emphasis on so-called intrinsic rewards, involvers have tended to deemphasize the role of pay and benefits. However, experience increasingly suggests that this policy eventually bumps up against the philosophical, and actual, inconsistency of spreading responsibility without enhancing payoffs. For this reason, many involvers have implemented more sophisticated compensation programs, such as skill-based pay, which rewards employees for learning new skills and jobs; gainsharing, and payoff schemes that are tied to long-term corporate earnings through profit-sharing and stock ownership plans.[64] Bonuses, for example, are an integral part of Motorola's "participative management system."[65]

Involvers downplay employee relations. The underlying assumption is that forums for discussing and deciding work-related issues obviate the need for employee relations oriented communication or special voice programs (such as speak out programs, opinion surveys, and open doors). Involvers also seem to believe that employee involvement somehow lessens the likelihood of personal grievances or problems; thus due process and employee assistance programs are less central in the involvement strategy than in, for example, the investment strategy. Nevertheless, since participation and involvement are recognized as inconsistent with status differentials, egalitarianism governs the provision of amenities and perks. Indeed, participation often starts around these issues.

While most involvers would no doubt prefer to be nonunion, the involvement strategy is not inconsistent with unionization. Its implementation in a unionized environment, however, requires a level of union-management cooperation and trust that typically takes much effort to achieve.[66]

Involvers do not stress government relations. Indeed, maintaining compliance with equal employment opportunity and affirmative action legislation can prove difficult if and when employees are allowed to participate in decisions about hiring, promotions, and the allocation of training opportunities and rewards.

As these brief descriptions show, the inducement, investment, and involvement strategies share very few common priorities or policies other than high performance standards and careful selection. Yet, each of the three, and probably many others, clearly can be made to work if it fits the prevailing business strategy, organizational structure, technology, and external and internal environmental conditions and is molded into a coherent and synergistic whole. Notwithstanding current rhetoric,[67] no one best HR strategy stands out. Although HRM practitioners and students might wish otherwise, the inescapable conclusion is that what is best, depends.

The Changing Role of the Personnel/HRM Function

The complexities of strategic HRM are not easy to conquer. Among other things, implementing a strategy usually involves significant changes in the prevailing priorities and practices of traditional personnel departments and the professionals who staff them. The obvious, but often stated, prescription is that both HR professionals and practices must become more strategic in thought and action. But, what does this mean? What are the specific implications for the HRM function? For HRM professionals? And how prepared are they to meet these challenges? Some preliminary answers to these questions lie in the experiences of the companies that have adopted or are in the process of adopting the strategic perspective.

Strategic Partnerships

The recommended role for the personnel function is that of a "strategic partner."[68] This role typically has four aspects. First, top corporate and divisional personnel executives cooperate with their line counterparts in formulating and, from time to time, reviewing broad HR strategies (inducement, investment, involvement, or whatever) appropriate to their organizations. Second, top corporate HR executives fully participate in all top-level business strategy sessions as equals to chief financial officers, general counsels, and subsidiary operating heads,[69] while lower-level HR managers operate in a similar fashion with divisional and functional managements.

This permits early evaluation of proposals in terms of their feasibility and desirability from an HR perspective, as well as early warning of upcoming HR issues. But, participation occurs routinely and is not limited to situations known to involve HR issues.[70]

A third aspect is that HR executives, managers, and specialists work closely with line managers on an ongoing basis to assure that all components of the business strategies are adequately implemented. Lastly, the HR function itself is managed strategically and has its own departmental strategy which lays out priorities, directs the allocation of resources, and guides the work of various subfunctional specialists.

This concept of strategic partnership no doubt has been fully implemented in only a handful of firms. Other companies, in which the strategic perspective is just now taking hold, however, are pursuing it in a number of ways. For example, some HR executives and managers have taken it upon themselves to formulate broad HR strategies suitable for their organizations. They then use these visions at every opportunity to guide and influence the decision making of top line executives on HR policy matters. Other HR managers have worked to heighten line managements' awareness of HR issues and to assure that these executives seek professional expertise whenever such issues arise in their strategic deliberations. Still other HR executives have gained the right of review and concurrence during the formal strategic planning process on any and all strategic moves and plans prior to implementation.[71]

The basic goal of these personnel executives and managers is to exercise leadership in all matters concerning HR strategy and policy. They constantly search for ways in which their organizations might achieve or enhance a competitive advantage through better people management.[72] They question the wisdom of business strategies that appear risky because of potential HR problems. When strategic business directions change, they take the lead in evaluating the continued relevance of broad HR strategies and in making any necessary changes.

In addition, HR executives exercise leadership within their own functions in developing more strategic orientations. Strategic teams analyze the content of business and HR strategies, evaluate the relevant strengths and weaknesses of the function, and, ultimately, formulate an appropriate functional, or departmental, strategy. While a wide variety of issues are addressed in such strategies,[73] at a minimum they include four components: (1) a mission statement, or a set of prioritized goals for the function and the major subfunctions (e.g., employment, training, compensation); (2) a proposed organizational structure — decentralization is common these days; (3) a program portfolio to outline priorities and policies; and, (4) ultimately, a budget to address the issue of resource allocation. This broad framework is then used by the various subfunctions, or by cross-subfunctional teams, to guide program development and improvement.

Bringing strategy within the HR function also alters how success is defined and measured. Form — that is, program elegance or process counts, such as number of managers trained — gives way to substance, in particular, the nature of the contribution toward the achievement of HR goals and, in the longer run, to the success of the organization's business strategies (see Chapter 1.5 of this volume).

In brief, HR executives and managers that have adopted the strategic perspective are attempting to demonstrate "value added";[74] that is, to show through word and deed that they are capable of thinking about and operating their functions strategically, and that this capability can and does make a difference to the organization's bottom line.

Implications for HR Professionals

As strategic thinking begins to permeate a personnel function, its members come to view their work quite differently. They begin to evolve into "Type A" HR professionals.[75] They become more business-oriented: They apply their professionalism to key business issues and work with line managers as business partners, helping to find solutions that contribute (or do the least harm) to the well-being of all organizational stakeholders, including employees. They also become more future-oriented, proactive, broad in focus, and willing to take risks.

These changes obviously can be traumatic for personnel executives, managers, and specialists whose training and experience are more traditional. Some individuals have found, and others are finding, it necessary to acquire a whole new set of knowledge and skills.[76] Priority areas in which this new knowledge is needed include the following:

- An understanding of business and organizational environments — markets, customers, products, services, finances, structures, and technologies

- An appreciation of the contributions expected of various organizational units toward broader business strategies and the major problems and obstacles facing those individuals who manage and operate these units

- A fairly firm grasp of major trends in various components of the external environment — labor unions, legislation, and labor markets — so as to ascertain their significance for proposed business or HR strategies

- A sufficiently thorough understanding of various elements of the internal environment — ongoing personnel problems, dominant management values concerning human resources, and resource restrictions — to gain their fair share in the formulation of HR and functional strategies

- A broader view of the activities they perform and a fuller appreciation of the ways in which these fit into the bigger picture

Managers at or near the top should have visionary abilities or, more realistically, planning and analytical skills that can help bring business and HR components together in meaningful ways.[77] Diagnostic skills are important since quick fixes, gimmicks, and a follow-the-leader mentality can no longer be relied upon.[78] Other consulting skills come in handy during both the formulation of strategies and their implementation. Another key attribute, although not exactly a skill, is flexibility, since compromises are inevitable. Like other department heads, HR people can easily forget what is best for the business in their desire to obtain what is optimal from an HR point of view.[79] Finally, as the stakes become higher, HR managers need a concomitant ability to assess and face up to risks.

State of the Practice

Unfortunately, no one knows how many HR functions or professionals are accomplished, aspiring, or abstaining strategists. All three categories quite clearly have some practitioners. A few companies, as earlier noted, have completed the transition and some have been operating strategically for years.[80] The current commotion over strategy, would suggest that many other firms are struggling with the transition and learning as they go.[81] Many more are undoubtedly nonstarters.

The nonstarters probably fall into two categories. The first group includes companies in situations where implementing strategy would be an irrational course of action. This group incorporates, for example, the HR functions and professionals in organizations dominated by "paper entrepreneurs" whose preoccupation with buying and selling "properties" precludes any interest in operations. Other organizations unlikely to adopt strategy include those so engrossed with the here and now that any type of strategic thinking is at best tomorrow's dream. The rest of the nonstarters fall in this group largely of their own volition. Some holdouts no doubt are hampered by uncertainty over what to do or doubts about their ability to do it. So far these nonstarters have been fortunate enough not to have their managements demand a more strategic role from them. Many are no doubt persuaded that such a demand will never come and that the strategy kick, as so many fads before, will soon lose its luster.

Which way will events go? Will the strategy approach continue to gain momentum and eventually come to dominate the practice and study of HRM? Or is it, after all, just another passing fancy?

A Look Ahead

A look ahead shows that some forces will continue to push HRM toward the strategic perspective, while others will have the opposite effect. The outcome is far from certain, but, on balance, the first set of forces seems to have the upper hand. Cautious forays into strategic HRM seem likely to continue, which, when combined with the current activity, may eventually give strategy a dominant position within the HRM field.

Forces Favoring the Strategic Perspective

On the business side, virtually everyone expects the competitive pressures that built up during the late 1970s and through the 1980s to continue. Protectionist legislation and re-regulation may offer temporary respite for a few firms in selected industries — the larger steel companies, for example, and the airlines — but most organizations will continue to face stiff competition from a variety of both domestic and foreign companies.[82] This is true not only in the manufacturing sector where considerable progress toward global competitiveness has already been made,[83] but also in the service sector where the process is only now beginning.[84]

Restructurings and downsizings are expected to continue, although they will, by necessity, be fewer in number and, usually, less massive in proportions than those of the 1970s.[85] Freezes and cuts in pay and benefits will continue to tempt hard-pressed employers. But, management will find these measures increasingly difficult to attain and sustain as the continuing erosion of living standards intensifies and as serious labor shortages emerge in certain occupations and areas of the country.[86] Many firms, therefore, will need slightly more creative ways to attain essential increases in productivity, product and service quality, and organizational innovation and adaptability. Based on the experience of those few companies which have already worked through this process, it is easy to see that the search for these new policies will inevitably concentrate mainly on some mixture of technology and HRM.[87]

Technologists will continue to discover, however slowly and painfully, the necessity of dealing with the human side of their systems, in terms of both the design and the subsequent installation and operation of hardware and software.[88] But, they and their managements will need help. Furthermore, some situations simply will not yield to technological solutions, at least in the foreseeable future, and the only answer will lie in better organization and management so as to use the full capacity of every type of employee at every level. Help will be needed here, also.

Thus, developments in the business and organizational environments will continue to create critical HR issues that will be difficult to ignore and unlikely to yield to traditional piecemeal solutions. In some cases, these developments will be further complicated by some already noticeable trends in the external environment.

One trend, previously alluded to, comes in the form of impending shortages in certain sectors of the labor market.[89] Over the next few years, labor force growth will slow significantly. In particular, the number of 16 to 24 year olds will decline each year between now and 1995.[90] The resulting shortage of high school and college graduates will exacerbate already existing shortages in fields such as science and engineering. It also means that the deficiencies in many of our public school systems will become harder to ignore.

As a result, an increasing number of employers, particularly in potentially high-growth areas such as high tech and some parts of the service sector (e.g., restaurants, hotels, retail stores, hospitals, nursing homes, banks, and insurance companies) will face some difficult decisions. In essence, these employers will have to either alter significantly or even abandon otherwise sound business strategies or take on previously unacceptable employees, including some portion of the million or so youngsters who drop out of school or graduate ill-prepared to do even the simplest tasks.[91] A good many executives and managers are no doubt ill-prepared to make this decision or to deal with the consequences of pushing ahead. They will need, and perhaps even want, help in coming to grips with the issues involved.

The second complication emanating from the external environment, more limited in its effect, emerges from a significant shift in strategy among some labor unions. A few, most notably the trend-setting United Auto Workers, have used and will continue to use their clout to gain a voice in the strategy and policy-making nexus of the companies with which they deal.[92] This has two effects. First, it forces a more systematic approach to strategy making than otherwise would occur. Second, it necessarily complicates the process, making it more difficult to forge workable business and, in particular, supporting HR strategies.[93] Witness, for example, the well-publicized events within General Motors' Saturn project. This area represents the "frontier" of labor-management relations[94] and it will not yield to traditional solutions.

The accumulation of these business, organizational, and environmental pressures, of course, does not assure the emergence of carefully considered HR strategies. After all, some powerful forces are pushing in other directions.

Forces Against the Strategic Perspective

The most powerful of the countervailing forces probably is top management. The easy cases presumably have seen the light; the remaining holdouts undoubtedly either do not know of or have no reason to think they need HR strategy. Some of these managers (the "paper entrepreneurs") have little or no interest in operations; others have what they perceive to be more pressing problems; and still others feel that management's only obligation to employees is to provide today's job today. All these organizations will be hard sells. Even when HR issues are unavoidable, many managers will simply activate their well-fed addictions to the quick fix.

Few of these managers are likely to encounter a groundswell of countermanding forces from within their organizations. In most cases, such protests would have to come from personnel functions, and, as previously noted, many personnel executives and managers now lack, and seem reluctant to develop, the necessary knowledge, skills, and risk-taking propensity.

This hesitancy does have some basis. Despite the virtues of the strategic approach found in the advocacy literature, the supportive empirical evidence, with only a few exceptions,[95] consists almost entirely of the small number of anecdotal case studies cited in this chapter. Theorists and researchers are a long way from demonstrating convincingly that the potential rewards of this approach to HRM are worth the considerable costs involved.

Another inhibiting factor concerns anticipated developments in the legal arena. A backlash is building as a result of the human costs of the present economic restructuring and the relative inaction during the Reagan administration. Congress, backed by organized labor, has generated a spate of new legislation and even some interest in enforcement.[96] This federal activity matches continuing initiatives from the states and the courts. While much of the impending action is unlikely to have strategic consequences (except for perhaps plant closing legislation), it will probably provide a convenient and comfortable diversion for HR practitioners who are otherwise disinclined to move further into business issues or all the way into HR strategy.

The Likely Outcome

What is the likely outcome of all this pulling and tugging? The pioneers and their early followers will continue to forge ahead, and those that learn to turn HRM to a competitive advantage will find themselves far ahead. The pressure will continue to build on many of the others, particularly in the service sector, as intensifying competitive pressures continue to expose the high costs of HR mismanagement and the successes of the leading-edge companies receive even greater publicity. Under this pressure, or in anticipation of it, a larger number of HR professionals will become familiar with the precepts of strategic HRM and the result will be an ongoing wave of cautious experimentation with strategy that conceivably might reach half the medium-sized and larger organizations in the country.

Because of the continuing need to become cost competitive (and the drying up of the downsizing and pay-cut options), much of this experimentation will focus on traditional concepts of productivity. But, since the United States can hardly aspire to being the low cost producer of much of anything, most businesses will be forced, as many already have been, into business strategies focusing on product or service differentiation (in extreme cases, for example, there may even be some service forthcoming from the service sector) and/or niche marketing. Thus, productivity will have to mean much more than efficiency.

As a result, management will need to demand more of employees in terms of innovativeness, creativity, spontaneity, and flexibility. Organizational structures and even technologies will become increasingly malleable and flexible, as will the utilization of employees.[97] Management will make much greater use of "disposable employees."[98] Traditional organizational expectations of employee commitment and loyalty will continue to be rethought, as will traditional employee expectations of organizational commitment and loyalty — a process which some observers say began when massive cutbacks and layoffs first occurred.

All of these changes hold great potential for creating a monumental backlash among employees and, ultimately, in society. Modest signs of this backlash are already evident in the current legislative and legal developments previously noted and in some of the recent successes of the labor movement.[99] How far all this goes will depend on two things. The first factor is whether businesses can successfully generate competitiveness and profitability — no one wants to annoy, let alone slaughter, a golden goose. The second mitigating factor concerns the quality of management actions to offset negative aspects of restructuring and recalibrating. In brief, much depends on the ability of HR professionals to help generate and implement high quality HR strategies.

Consultants and academics, attracted by the glitter if not the gold, can be expected to follow — and attempt to act on — these developments with great interest and, indeed, gusto. As a result, professional journals and magazines will take on even more of a strategic hue, thus feeding the budding applications. As consensus begins to emerge, textbooks will come to be organized around one or another of a small number of strategic perspectives. Useful research results will begin to emerge. For a while, maybe even a long while, strategy may provide the dominant and integrative model that has thus far eluded the practice and study of HRM.

◆

Notes

1. See, for example, any recent issue of *Personnel Administrator, Personnel Journal, Human Resource Management,* or *Human Resource Planning.*
2. Beer et al.; Fombrun, Tichy, and Devanna; Foulkes, 1986; and Lawler, 1986.
3. For reviews, see Dyer, 1984 and 1985.
4. DeBejar and Milkovich; Schuler and Jackson, 1987(b).
5. Heidrick and Struggles.
6. Mahoney and Deckop.
7. Tichy, Fombrun, and Devanna.
8. Mahoney and Deckop.
9. Beer et al.
10. Schendel and Hofer.
11. Dyer, 1983.
12. Or alternatively, whether in the case of a strategy that calls for cutting back in a particular business, those no longer needed can be reallocated or released quickly or cheaply enough.
13. Schuler, 1987.
14. Forward.
15. Bluestone and Harrison.
16. By the mid-1960s, it will be recalled, John Kenneth Galbraith (1967) was first moved to warn of the emerging "technostructure."
17. Hunt and Hunt.
18. Reich, p. 121.
19. Bluestone and Harrison, p. 140.
20. Kochan, Katz, and McKersie.
21. Jacoby.
22. Dunlop and Myers.
23. Dunlop.
24. Fullerton and Tschetter.
25. Janger.
26. Ibid.
27. Freedman; Kochan.
28. Kochan, Katz and McKersie, pp. 40–45.
29. Tichy, Fombrun and Devanna.
30. Reich termed this activity "paper entrepreneurialism" and "historic preservation."
31. Porter.
32. Russell.
33. Greenhouse; Pava; Walton, 1985(a); Zuboff, 1985.
34. Hoerr, Pollock, and Whiteside.
35. Work, Seamonds, and Black.
36. Hoerr et al.
37. Wagel.
38. Saporito.
39. Lawler.
40. Port; Port and Wilson.
41. Lawler; Walton, 1985(b).
42. Bernstein and Zellner; Levine.
43. Lawler.
44. Unfortunately, students of HR strategies, unlike those of business strategies, have only just begun to tackle the needed research (DeBejar and Milkovich; Dyer, 1984; Lawrence).
45. For a similar, although more normatively oriented, exercise, see Walton, 1985(b).
46. Zager; Volard.
47. Machalara, p. 1.
48. Zager.
49. Machalara, p. 1.
50. McGregor.
51. Foulkes, 1981.
52. Foulkes, 1981.
53. Dyer, Foltman, and Milkovich.
54. Likert.
55. Hackman and Oldham.
56. Morhman and Lawler.

57. See, for example, Lawler; Walton, 1985(b), 1986.
58. O'Toole; Weisz.
59. Kochan, Katz and McKersie; Lawler, 1986.
60. Walton, 1985(b).
61. Lawler.
62. For a working example, see Frohman.
63. Lawler.
64. Milkovich.
65. Weisz.
66. Kochan, Katz and McKersie; Lawler.
67. Lawler; Walton, 1985(b), 1986.
68. Holder.
69. Levine.
70. McLaughlin.
71. Dyer and Heyer.
72. Schuler and Jackson, 1987(a); Schuler and McMillan.
73. Kanter and Buck.
74. Mills, Chapter 15.
75. Holder.
76. Murphy.
77. Casual observation suggests that more than a few personnel executives and managers have seen their strategic aspirations founder because their planning and ana-lytical skills were inferior to those of their line counterparts.
78. McLaughlin.
79. Holder.
80. Burdick.
81. Hoerr.
82. Choate and Langer.
83. See, for example, Treece.
84. Quinn and Gagnon.
85. *New York Times*, August 23, 1987.
86. Bernstein, Anderson and Zellner; Fullerton and Tschetter.
87. *Business Week*, Feb. 13, 1984; Drucker.
88. Hoerr, Pollock, and Whiteside; Howard; Hunt and Hunt; Pava; Walton, 1985(a).
89. Bernstein, Anderson and Zellner.
90. Fullerton and Tschetter.
91. Choate and Lainger.
92. Kochan, Katz and McKersie, p. 17.
93. Bernstein and Zellner; Schlesinger.
94. Kochan, Katz and McKersie, p. 17.
95. See, for example, DeBejar and Milkovich.
96. Hughey.
97. Choate and Langer; Reich; Piore and Sabel.
98. Pollock and Bernstein.
99. Kotlowitz.

Editor's Note: In addition to the references shown below there are other significant sources of information and ideas on HRM strategy.

Books

Lincoln, J.F. 1951. *Incentive Management: A New Approach to Human Relationships in Industry and Business.* Cleveland: Lincoln Electric.

Manzini, A.D. and J.D. Gridley 1986. *Integrating Human Resources and Strategic Business Planning.* New York: American Management Association.

Taylor, F.W. 1911. *The Principles of Scientific Management.* New York: Harper & Row.

Walker, J. 1980. *Human Resource Planning.* New York: John Wiley & Sons.

Journals
Human Resource Management
Human Resource Planning

Periodicals
Business Week
Wall Street Journal

◆

References

Beer, M., B. Spector, P.R. Lawrence, D.Q. Mills, and R.E. Walton. 1984. *Managing Human Assets*. New York: The Free Press.

Bernstein, A. and W. Zellner. 1987. "Detroit vs. the UAW: At Odds Over Teamwork." *Business Week*, (August 24):54–55.

Bernstein, A., R.W. Anderson, and W. Zellner. 1987. "Help Wanted." *Business Week* (August 10):48–53.

Bluestone, B. and B. Harrison. 1982. *The Deindustrialization of America*. New York: Basic Books.

Burdick, W.E. 1986. "Impact/Influence: Defining and Charting a Course for Personnel Vitality." In *Strategic Human Resources Management: A Guide for Effective Practice*, ed. F.K. Foulkes. Englewood Cliffs, NJ: Prentice-Hall.

Choate, P. and J.K. Langer. 1986. *The High-Flex Society*. New York: Alfred A. Knopf.

DeBejar, G. and G. Milkovich. 1985. "Human Resource Strategy at the Business Level: Description and Correlates." Paper presented at the First Annual Research Symposium of the Human Resource Planning Society, Philadelphia, December 4–6.

Drucker, P.F. 1986. "Goodbye to the Old Personnel Department." *The Wall Street Journal* (May 22).

Dunlop, J.T. 1976. "The Limits of Legal Compulsion," *Labor Law Journal*, 27:67–74.

Dunlop, J.T. and C.A. Myers. 1955. "The Industrial Relations Function in Management: Some Views on its Organizational Status." *Personnel* 31:406–413.

Dyer, L. 1983. "Bringing Human Resources into the Strategy Formulation Process." *Human Resource Management* 22, 3:257–271.

_____. 1985. "Strategic Human Resource Management and Planning." In *Research in Personnel and Human Resource Management, Vol. 3*, ed. K.R. Rowland and G.R. Ferris. Greenwich, CT: JAI Press.

_____. 1984. "Studying Human Resource Strategy: An Approach and an Agenda." *Industrial Relations* 23, 2:156–169.

Dyer, L., F.F. Foltman, and G.M. Milkovich. 1985. "Contemporary Employment Stabilization Practices." In *Industrial Relations and Human Resource Management: Text, Readings, and Cases*, eds. T.A. Kochan and T.A. Barocci. Boston: Little, Brown.

Dyer, L. and N.O. Heyer. 1986. "Human Resource Planning at IBM." In *Human Resource Planning: Tested Practices of Five Major U.S. and Canadian Companies*, ed. L. Dyer. New York: Random House.

Fombrun, C., N.M. Tichy, and M.A. Devanna. 1984. *Strategic Human Resource Management*. New York: John Wiley & Sons.

Forward, G.E. 1986. "Wide-Open Management at Chaparral Steel." *Harvard Business Review* (May-June):96–102.

Foulkes, F.K. 1981. "How Top Non-Union Companies Manage Their Employees." *Harvard Business Review* (September-October):90–96.

————. ed. 1986. *Strategic Human Resources Management: A Guide for Effective Practice*. Englewood Cliffs, NJ: Prentice-Hall.

Freedman, A. 1979. *Managing Labor Relations*. New York: The Conference Board.

Frohman, M.A. 1984. "Human Resource Management and the Bottom Line: Evidence of the Connection." *Human Resource Management* 23:315–334.

Fullerton, H.N., Jr. and J. Tschetter. 1983. "The 1995 Labor Force: A Second Look." *Monthly Labor Review* (November):3–10.

Gailbraith, J.K. 1967. *The New Industrial State*. Boston: Houghton Mifflin.

Greenhouse, S. 1987. "Revving Up the American Factory." *New York Times* (January 11): Business Section, p. 1.

Hackman, J.R. and G.R. Oldham. 1980. *Work Redesign*. Reading, MA: Addison-Wesley.

Heidrick and Struggles. 1984. *Human Resources: Function in Transition*. New York: Heidrick and Struggles.

Hoerr, J. 1985. "Human Resource Managers Aren't Corporate Nobodies Anymore." *Business Week* (December 2):58–59.

Hoerr, J., W.G. Glaberson, D.B. Moskowitz, V. Cahah, M. Pollock, and J. Tasini. 1985. "Beyond Unions." *Business Week* (July 8):72–77.

Hoerr, J., M.A. Pollock, D.E. Whiteside. 1986. "Management Discovers the Human Side of Automation." *Business Week* (September 29):70–75.

Holder, G. 1986. "Human Resource Professionals: Adaptations to Changes in the Function." Paper presented at the 18th Annual Meeting of the PMA Personnel Section, Key Biscayne, FL, February 10.

Howard, R. 1985. *Brave New Workplace*, New York: Viking.

Hughey, A. 1987. "Congress Takes Up Labor's Cause." *New York Times* (August 23): Business Section, p. 1.

Hunt, H.A., and T.L. Hunt. 1983. *Human Resource Implications of Robotics*. Kalamazoo, MI: W.E. Upjohn Institute for Employment Research.

Jacoby, S.M. 1985. *Employing Bureaucracy: Managers, Unions, and the Transformation of Work in American Industry, 1900–1945*. New York: Columbia University Press.

Janger, A.R. 1977. *The Personnel Function: Changing Objectives and Functions.* New York: The Conference Board.

Kanter, R.M. and J.D. Buck. 1985. "Reorganizing Part of Honeywell: From Strategy to Structure." *Organizational Dynamics* 13, 3:5–25.

Kochan, T.A. 1980. *Collective Bargaining and Industrial Relations.* Homewood, Ill.: Richard D. Irwin.

Kochan, T.A., H.C. Katz, and R.B. McKersie. 1986. *The Transformation of American Industrial Relations.* New York: Basic Books.

Kotlowitz, A. 1987. "Labor's Turn?: Unions May Be Poised to End Long Decline, Recover Some Clout." *Wall Street Journal* (August 28):1.

Lawler, E.E. III. 1986. *High Involvement Management.* San Francisco: Jossey-Bass.

Lawrence, P.R. 1985. "The History of Human Resource Management in American Industry." In *Human Resource Management: Trends and Challenges*, ed. R.E. Walton and P.R. Lawrence, Boston: Harvard Business School Press.

Levine, H.Z. 1986. "Highlights of AMA's 57th Annual Human Resources Conferences, Part 2." *Personnel* (October):41–45.

Likert, R. 1961. *New Patterns of Management.* New York: McGraw-Hill.

McGregor, D. 1960. *The Human Side of Enterprise.* New York: McGraw-Hill.

McLaughlin, D.J. 1986. "The Turning Point in Human Resources Management." In *Strategic Human Resources Management: A Guide for Effective Practice*, ed. F.K. Foulkes. Englewood Cliffs, NJ: Prentice-Hall.

Machalara, D. 1986. "Up to Speed: United Parcel Service Gets Deliveries Done by Driving its Workers." *Wall Street Journal* (April 22):1.

Mahoney, T.A. and J.R. Deckop. 1986. "Evolution of Concept and Practice in Personnel Administration/Human Resource Management (PA/HRM)." *Journal of Management* 12, 2:223–242.

Milkovich, G.T. In press. "A Strategic Perspective on Compensation Management." In *Research in Human Resources Management, Vol. 6*, ed. K. Rowland and G. Ferris. Greenwich, CT: JAI Press.

Mills, D.Q. 1985. *The New Competitors.* New York: John Wiley & Sons.

Morhman, S.A. and E.E. Lawler III. 1984. "Quality of Work Life." In *Research in Personnel and Human Resource Management, Vol. 2*, ed. K.R. Rowland and G.R. Ferris. Greenwich, CT: JAI Press.

Murphy, R.H. 1986. "A Line Manager's View of the Human Resource Role." In *Strategic Human Resources Management: A Guide for Effective Practice*, ed. F.K. Foulkes. Englewood Cliffs, NJ: Prentice-Hall.

O'Toole, J. 1985. *Vanguard Management.* Garden City, NY: Doubleday and Company.

Pava, C. 1985. "Managing New Information Technology: Design or Default?" In *Human Resource Management: Trends and Challenges*, ed. R.E. Walton and P.R. Lawrence. Boston: Harvard Business School Press.

Piore, M.J. and C.F. Sabel. 1984. *The Second Industrial Divide*, New York: Basic Books.

Pollock, M.A. and A. Bernstein. 1986. "The Disposable Employee is Becoming a Fact of Corporate Life." *Business Week* (December 15):52–56.

Port, O. 1987. "The Push for Quality." *Business Week* (June 8):130–143.

Port, O. and J.W. Wilson. 1987. "Making Brawn Work with Brains." *Business Week*, (April 20):56–60.

Porter, M.E. 1980. *Competitive Strategy*. New York: The Free Press.

Quinn, J.B. and C.E. Gagnon. 1986. "Will Services Follow Manufacturing Into Decline?" *Harvard Business Review* (November-December):95–103.

Reich, R.B. 1983. *The Next American Frontier*. New York: Times Books.

Russell, G. 1987. "Rebuilding to Survive." *Time* (February 16):44–45.

Saporito, B. 1987. "Cutting Costs Without Cutting People." *Fortune* (May 25):26–32.

Schendel, D. and C.W. Hofer. 1979. "Introduction" in *Strategic Management: A New View of Business Policy and Planning*, ed. D. Schendel and C.W. Hofer. Boston: Little, Brown.

Schlesinger, J.M. 1987. "Costly Friendship: Auto Firms and UAW Find that Cooperation Can Get Complicated." *Wall Street Journal* (August 25):1.

Schuler, R.S. 1987. "Personnel and Human Resource Management: Choices and Corporate Strategy." In *Readings in Personnel and Human Resource Management*, 3rd ed., ed. R.S. Schuler and S.A. Youngblood, St. Paul: West Publishing.

Schuler, R.S. and S.E. Jackson. 1987a. "Linking Competitive Strategies with Human Resource Practices." *Academy of Management Executive* (August):207–219.

———— 1987b. "Organizational Strategy and Organizational Level as Determinants of Human Resource Management Practices." *Human Resource Planning* 10, 3:125–141.

Schuler, R.S. and I.C. MacMillan. 1984. "Gaining Competitive Advantage through Human Resource Management Practices." *Human Resource Management* (Autumn):241–255.

Tichy, N.M., C.J. Fombrun, and M.A. Devanna. 1982. "Strategic Human Resource Management." *Sloan Management Review* 23, 2:47–60.

Treece, J.B. 1987. "U.S. Parts Makers Just Won't Say Uncle." *Business Week* (August 10):76–77.

Volard, S.V. 1982. "Lincoln Australia: Philosophy and Practice." *The Practicing Manager* (October):19–28.

Wagel, W.H. 1987. "Keeping the Organization Lean at Federal Express." *Personnel* (March):4–12.

Walton, R.E. 1985a. "Challenges in the Management of Technology and Labor Relations." In *Human Resource Management: Trends and Challenges*, ed. R.E. Walton and P.R. Lawrence. Boston: Harvard Business School Press.

_____. 1985b. "From Control to Commitment in the Workplace." *Harvard Business Review* (March-April):77–84.

_____. 1986. "A Vision Led Approach to Management Restructuring." *Organizational Dynamics* (Spring):4–16.

Weisz, W.J. 1985. "Employee Involvement: How It Works at Motorola." *Personnel* (February):29–33.

Work, C.P., J.A. Seamonds, and R.F. Black. 1986. "Making It Clear Who's Boss." *U.S. News and World Report* (September 8):43–45.

Zager, R. 1978. "Managing Guaranteed Employment." *Harvard Business Review* 56, 3:103–115.

Zuboff, S. 1984. "The Revival of Productivity." *Business Week* (February 13):92–100.

_____. 1985. "Technologies That Informate: Implications for Human Resource Management in the Computerized Industrial Workplace." In *Human Resource Management: Trends and Challenges*, ed. R.E. Walton and P.R. Lawrence. Boston: Harvard Business School Press.

_____. 1987. "Downsizing Has Peaked." *New York Times* (August 23): Business Section, 1.

_____ ◆ _____

❖

1.2

Human Resource Planning and Strategy

James A. Craft

Some form of HR planning currently appears to be accepted and generally well-established in most medium-sized and large organizations.[1] As usually practiced, HR planning includes those plans, programs, and processes designed to meet future organizational HR needs. It frequently entails the use of some form of HR inventory, personnel forecasting, and the development of specific personnel programs. While sophisticated modeling and statistical procedures exist, the evidence suggests that qualitative and judgmental approaches are most widely used.[2]

As it has evolved, HR planning is pragmatic in nature and is not grounded in theoretical constructs. It has emerged as a practical response to organizational problems, such as shortages of skilled personnel, excessive turnover, problems of executive succession, and legal requirements for affirmative action.[3] As a result of this applied and responsive orientation to the unique problems of individual firms, HR planning systems currently do not rigorously follow any standard model or procedure. Experience shows that these systems vary greatly in the scope of employee coverage, processes used, forecasting methods employed, planning horizons selected, and results expected.[4]

Framework for Integrating HR Planning and Strategy

With the growth and acceptance of HR planning as a legitimate organizational activity, the cutting edge of thinking and practice has shifted. The focus has changed from designing technical approaches to forecasting HR needs and availabilities, and from integrating personnel functions to a broader concern for merging HR planning with the overall business objectives and strategic choices of the firm. In conjunction with this new focus, a growing interest has emerged regarding development of a framework for organizational HR strategy that will help coordinate and direct HRM and personnel activities toward the effective achievement of business goals.

Rationale for Integration

As with HR planning, this interest in integration of strategy seems to have developed for practical reasons. For example, the evidence suggests that most major firms already consider inventories of managerial talent and issues of managerial succession in their strategic business planning since these resources are perceived as important for smooth transitions in leadership, corporate renewal, and organizational momentum. Surveys show that HR executives and strategic planners wish to see even more HR information utilized in strategic planning activities.[5]

This desire emanates from a growing recognition that employees constitute useful sources of strategic opportunities or constraints and that inappropriate use of human resources can generate significant opportunity costs for a firm.[6] Ignoring human resources can result not only in loss of potential earnings, but in lower actual earnings and new costs as incomplete strategic decisions are rectified.

Interest has also grown in formulating HR strategies to guide organizational HR planning and programming in a way that "fits" the organization's mission, strategy, and structure.[7] A properly designed HR strategy which is aligned with the strategic objectives of the organization should help achieve these goals. Indeed, evidence shows that productivity leaders are managing their human resources strategically.[8]

An Explicit Framework

If HR professionals are to respond and build upon this emerging interest in integrating HR and strategic business planning, an explicit framework is needed. The framework should stimulate managerial thinking regarding human resources' contribution to, participation in, and response to organizational strategic planning.

Figure 1 offers an approach to integrating HR planning and business strategy. Along with showing the interaction among key elements, this framework can serve as a reference to illustrate how issues discussed in this chapter relate to the overall perspective.

Inputs and Responses

In particular, the model shows that HR planning, in addition to its traditionally responsive role, can provide useful inputs in organizational strategic planning. Indeed, strategic decision making requires key information on strategic competencies and competitive advantages related to available or prospective employees, policies, and HR programs. On the output side, HR planning requires an understanding of the business implications of formulated strategy and goals. This understanding is essential to the forecasting and interpretive activity involved in developing a meaningful HR strategy. The emphasis is on a strategically driven HR function to meet organizational objectives. The goal is to add value through HR activities which can provide a competitive advantage to the firm.

Process and Content

The model also shows that an integrated strategic HR system is a sequence of process and content elements. Process refers to the procedures, activities, and methods used to collect information, make decisions, or formulate programs and strategies. For example, HR planning is a process which includes environmental scanning and competitive analysis. Content, on the other hand, refers to the substance of plans, strategies, reports, and issues. The forecasted demand for employees in an HR plan or diversification goals in a strategic business plan illustrate content.

Organizational Influences

The framework identifies organizational culture, management philosophy, and political/power realities as factors influencing the HR planning and strategic activity. These pervasive organizational forces affect the processes and can shape the content of plans and strategies.

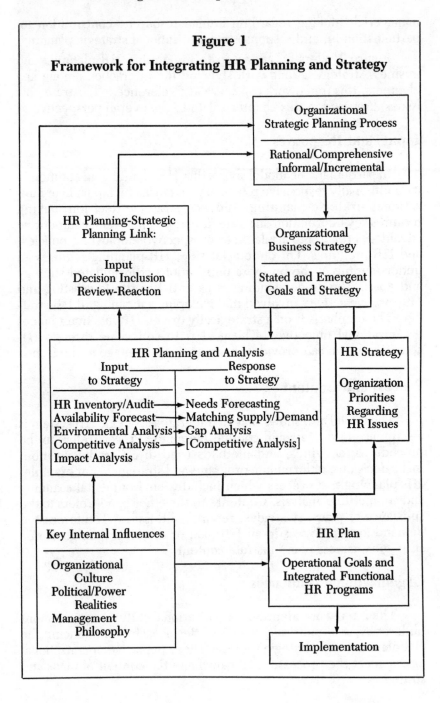

Figure 1

Framework for Integrating HR Planning and Strategy

Organizational culture refers to a pattern of values, mores, customs, and ideologies that are shared by organizational members and guide their behaviors and interactions. Each organization has a unique culture. For example, one large diversified electronics firm has a culture emphasizing a familial atmosphere, importance of the individual, entrepreneurial spirit, and pride in working for the firm. An old-line manufacturer of construction equipment has traditional values of paternalism and makes clear distinctions between managers and workers with limited communication between them. These diverse cultures certainly envision different roles for the HR function and its involvement in strategic planning.

With respect to management philosophy, top management generally has a set of values and beliefs that influence organizational activities. These values and beliefs often reflect the larger organizational culture, but can vary among executives in policy-making positions. Management philosophy may include beliefs about what motivates employees, the driving force of the business, the usefulness of delegation or centralized decision making, and so forth. These beliefs influence organizational management style, which in turn affects the HRM role and processes. Whether senior management views human resources as a necessary burden or an important management partner will definitely limit or facilitate the development of HR planning and its integration with strategic planning.

Finally, political alignments and power realities affect HR planning and its role in strategic business planning. Clearly, if the HR function does not play a significant role in the current power structure, any restructuring of internal responsibilities to allow HR planning greater input into strategic activities is likely to encounter substantial resistance. For example, in a financially driven and bureaucratically stable organization, a proposal to integrate human resources into strategic planning would likely threaten current power bases and portend a rearrangement of the control system. Established parties might foresee losing some of their influence in determining the organizational mission and strategy and their power and control over executive succession, rewards, and performance assessment. Therefore HR executives clearly have to become involved in organizational politics if they expect to participate in key decisions. In fact, some evidence suggests that the political skills of HR managers are important in the growth of HR planning.[9]

HR Planning and Organizational Strategic Planning

While a few progressive organizations seem to be moving ahead with more strategically oriented HR activities, the vast majority have yet to establish an integral relationship between strategic business planning and HR planning.[10] Even when information such as staffing forecasts is used in business planning, its value is limited by the omission of development activities and costs, two critical aspects of staffing strategies.[11]

Problems Hindering Integration

Several reasons account for the lack of integration between HR planning and strategic planning, and between HR strategies and business objectives. First, human resources have traditionally been taken as a "given" in the formulation and implementation of strategic plans. Planners often seem to assume that an adequate supply of labor will be available when needed and that employees are a highly flexible resource who can be recruited, trained, and laid off on reasonably short notice. This has worked against the vertical integration of HR planning into organizational strategic planning.[12]

Furthermore, over the last 20 years, the responsibility for business planning has typically rested with finance- and marketing-oriented executives. This context has fostered the perception that HRM does not contribute much to an organization's effectiveness and success. Top management and line managers have not been sensitive to HR issues in the absence of some dramatic event, such as a class-action lawsuit.[13]

Finally, HR managers have not been accustomed to thinking or behaving in strategic terms. They have often failed to demonstrate expertise in planning or an orientation to bottom-line business objectives. HR departments have often been reactive and transactional in nature, and HR planning has frequently been fragmented, technique-oriented, and relatively isolated in its operation. HR planning characteristically has been viewed as reactive rather than integral to organizational strategic planning.[14]

Strategy Formulation

If HR planning is to assume a more significant role in organizational strategic planning, HR professionals must develop a better understanding of the strategy formulation process. The nature of this process, which develops plans to align organizational resources with environmental opportunities and threats, affects the appropriateness and acceptability of HR planning activities and inputs. It also suggests possible linkages for HR planning. In general, strategy formulation can occur through either of two disparate processes: rational/comprehensive and informal/incremental.

Rational/Comprehensive Process

The rational/comprehensive process, frequently advocated in strategic planning texts and apparently by many practitioners, emphasizes purposeful activity through a logical formulation of goals, examination of alternatives, and delineation of plans prior to actions. It tends to have a long-term orientation and focuses on measurable forces affecting the firm, as well as on quantitative activities and procedures.[15]

Illustrative activities in this strategy formulation process include the following:

- Assessing the environment (for example, trends, competitors) to determine opportunities and threats to the organization

- Conducting an internal review to determine organizational strengths and weaknesses relative to these external circumstances

- Developing basic goals and objectives for the firm and its operating units

- Assessing how goals can be achieved given the current organizational situation (identify gaps, analyze issues)

- Generating alternatives and thoroughly assessing their likelihood of achieving goals (this may include special studies of alternatives and contingencies)

- Selecting an appropriate alternative based on its potential for achieving goals

- Developing programs and a budget for implementation

- Making a conscious effort to integrate the elements of the overall strategy to enhance synergy and mutual consistency (providing for a comprehensive and integrated whole)

■ Monitoring and evaluating progress and performance toward the goal

This approach to strategy formulation has important implications for HR planning. To fit, HR planning processes, activities, and data have to be consistent with this particular approach. This means longer-term planning horizons consistent with the firm's planning cycle, environmental scans and long-term trends as stimuli, quantitative and rigorously derived data, formal research reports and documents, and a power base predicated on personal expertise and legitimation by the formal organization. These and other implications are summarized in the left-hand column in Table 1.

Informal/Incremental Process

Incrementalism is another approach to the strategy formulation process. (See the right-hand column in Table 1.) Advocates of this approach argue that human cognitive limitations and unexpected changes make it impossible to formulate a comprehensive organizational strategy all at once. Moreover, their observations suggest that planning activity often occurs outside formal planning structures. The real strategy evolves through a stream of short-term remedial decisions made by organizational coalitions or a set of organizational subsystems. This approach posits that unexpected changes in a firm's environment or shifts in its internal power distribution can and do occur, necessitating piecemeal decisions. The pattern that develops from a set of crisis decisions becomes an organization's emergent strategy.

This type of strategy formulation is an iterative process that has a qualitative and interactive emphasis. Behavioral dynamics are important and there is a recognition that power relationships and influence processes affect strategic decisions. While personal power and group influence shape the basic decision processes, shifts of power within the organization also affect the direction of incremental decisions.[16]

For example, one analyst of the planning process suggests viewing organizations as coalitions of interested parties.[17] These parties negotiate membership in the organization, establish negotiated goals, and communicate in a self-serving and subjective manner. Decision making is the result of negotiation within the coalition. The relative power and influence of the parties obviously are key factors affecting the shape of the coalition's decisions.

Table 1

HR Planning Implications of Strategy Decision Processes

HR Planning Element or Process	Implications for HR Planning	
	Strategy Formulation Process	
	Rational/Comprehensive	Informal/Incremental
HR Planning Horizon	Long-term (based on firm's planning cycle)	Short-term (1 year or less)
Stimulus for HR Planning Activity	Environmental scan & monitoring long-term trends	Monitoring current programs/activity; unexpected change
Acceptable HR Planning Data	Hard data; emphasis on quantitative data, models and rigor	Experience, expectation and potential
Availability Analysis Focus	Development of internal HR and assess external supply given labor force trends	Inventory of current HR and assess outside supply for current challenge
Needs Analysis Focus	Quantity and mix of personnel needed to meet long-term organization changes	Quantity and mix of personnel to meet objectives defined at each interaction
Focus of HR Planning Coverage	Key jobs for continuity and organization transition	Jobs related to issue or current problems
Presentation of HR Planning Data	Formal research based reports, documents, files	Informal interaction with key managers, memos, summary findings
Focus of HR Planning Influence Efforts	Top management and members of strategic planning team	Managers of key subsystems and powerful organizational units
Source of HR Manager Influence	Personal expertise; legitimate power of HR Planning manager	Referent power, charisma, and legitimate power of HR planning manager

In this context, any strategic plan is really a deliberately imprecise document resulting from negotiations among the coalition members. It is based on current power and interests, along with the expectations of future coalition membership. In anticipation that decisions will be renegotiated, plans are intentionally ambiguous and imprecise to minimize injury to the coalition. Over time, there is informal give and take as the parties negotiate for their own personal and departmental best interests. The resulting flow of decisions leads to the operational organizational strategy.

The incremental approach to strategy formulation has some very different implications for HR planning from the rational approach. The planning horizon, for example, is likely to be relatively short term. In addition, the stimulus for HR planning activity will often come from monitoring current organizational programs and responding to unexpected changes rather than long-term external trends. The effective presentation of HR planning data will likely take place during casual interactions with key managers and through informal reports. Influence for the HR manager would derive from referential power (due to conformance to a powerful group's norms), personal charisma, and, to some degree, the legitimate power of office.

An Integrated Approach to Strategy Formulation

While the rational/comprehensive and informal/incremental models are quite different, both processes exist to some degree in the strategy formulation activities of many organizations. Firms with formal strategic planning often issue mission statements and attempt to formulate rational strategic plans to define and achieve objectives. Such comprehensive mission definition and planning is done intermittently, however, and in the interim, incremental decision processes are likely to shape, clarify, and more precisely define the strategic thrust.

In any particular organization, however, certain factors may move strategy formulation toward one particular model. For example, the stability of a firm's environment may influence strategic processes. In an unstable and dynamic environment, more activity and emphasis may be placed on incremental decision making than on formal rational processes. The age and growth rates of an organization may also be factors. An entrepreneurial fast-growing firm seems more likely to employ an incremental process, while a mature stable bureaucracy would utilize a more rational approach. An organization's culture and management style also appear to be relevant. Firms emphasizing participation, decentralization, and delegation are more likely to employ incrementalism than firms exhibiting centralization and controlled decision processes.

As a result, HR planning professionals must analyze and understand the strategy formulation process in their organizations if they hope to be involved in strategy development and to influence the content of strategic plans. For many HR planning professionals, this undoubtedly means going beyond formal planning processes and getting involved in the informal activities that shape and interpret rational programs.[18] The ideas presented in Table 1 can help analyze the types of tactics and approaches that can be adapted to a particular firm.

Linkages Between HR and Strategic Planning

Despite an increasing belief that HR planning should be linked to organizational strategic planning, uncertainty still exists regarding when and how such a linkage should be made. However, information from case studies of leading-edge companies and available survey data suggest at least three general types of linkages. As shown in Figure 2, these include input linkages, decision inclusion linkages, and review/reaction linkages.[19] It should be noted that these linkages are not mutually exclusive; many firms have multi-faceted linkages between HR planning and strategic planning.

Input Linkages

Input linkages focus on providing or inserting meaningful HR information into the strategic planning process either before or during the planning activity. This information may come from a specialized HR unit or it may be generated through a bottoms-up approach. At American Hospital Supply Corp., for example, the vice president of personnel receives input from both line and staff to formulate an annual personnel plan which is then passed along to top corporate executives.[20] Merck, in contrast, conducts an environmental scan which is compiled into a report and given to those involved in strategic planning.[21] (For a detailed analysis of environmental scanning see Chapter 1.3 of this volume.) In other firms, planning committees comprising HR staff, corporate planners, and line managers identify and analyze key HR issues.[22] In still other cases, HR information is included in strategic planning through the

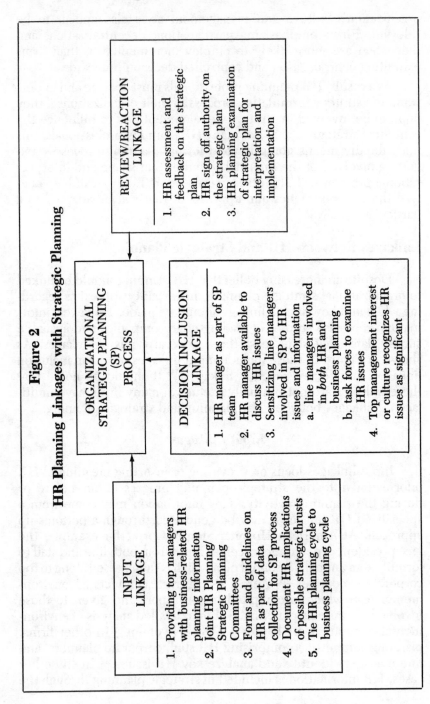

Figure 2

HR Planning Linkages with Strategic Planning

use of guidelines and forms that require managers to provide HR data along with other relevant planning material.

Another type of input linkage occurs during the planning process when the HR department is requested to document the personnel implications of proposed strategic thrusts and provide feedback to the planners. At Frito-Lay Inc., for example, the employee relations department links into the strategic process when it is "asked to anticipate internal and external threats to [the] business plan over the next five years and to develop solutions to these problems."[23] Finally, organizations such as Robbins and Myers Inc. have deliberately tied the HR planning cycle to the business planning cycle. This has focused line managers' attention on HR issues as they are doing business planning. In addition, it has piggybacked HR planning on an already legitimized process and has helped establish relationships with the corporate planning manager.[24]

Decision Inclusion Linkages

Decision inclusion linkages involve human resources in the strategic planning process either directly or indirectly. For example, a senior HR official might serve as a full partner on the strategic planning team. He or she would introduce and monitor HR issues and implications, as well as participate in developing overall goals and strategies. Less fully, an HR executive might sit in on strategy sessions and participate only in discussions of HR issues or, alternatively, be called in when HR issues arise. In 1983, Honeywell Aerospace and Defense Business established a direct linkage that involves HR executives, general management, and business planners in developing the business plan. The HR plan is directly generated from the business plan in this way.[25] At Marriot Corp., the HR vice president reports to the president and CEO and each division HR manager reports to the divisional general manager. The various HR managers also attend decision-making sessions so as to raise HR issues and note implications regarding company plans.[26] Finally, at IBM, the business divisions include HR managers in the strategic planning process on an "as needed" basis.

Decision inclusion linkages have also been established in a less direct fashion. One way is to "sensitize" executives involved in business planning to HR issues; another is to make these managers partners in HR planning. Both methods increase the likelihood that HR information and issues will be considered in the planning process. Illustrative of such efforts are the activities at 3M Co., which attempts to "get line managers to think more like HR managers" and to "get HR managers to think more like line managers." In particular, line managers have been involved in a task force examining aspects of HRM so they will have a full partnership and "will enjoy a degree of ownership of the [HR] programs that are put into place."[27] Citicorp achieves sensitivity and integration by having line managers do both the business and HR planning.

In some companies, top management has created an indirect linkage, even though HR executives are not directly involved in the strategic planning process. For example, at Union Oil Co., the corporate executive committee began regularly reviewing each major division's succession and career development activities, as well as its performance in managing human resources.[28] Graphic Controls Corp. has developed a culture emphasizing the importance of HR issues. This culture is reinforced with continuing measurements of employee attitudes and feedback to employees, as well as the expectation that "managers [will] . . . incorporate human resources into their strategic plans and priorities."[29]

Review and Reaction Linkages

Review and reaction linkages provide HR managers with an opportunity to respond to a proposed or final strategic business plan. They may simply be requested to review and assess a plan in terms of its HR feasibility and desirability, or they may even have "sign off" authority. For example, at IBM, personnel managers are required to approve strategic business plans before they can be implemented. If disagreement arises, IBM has a procedure to move the dispute up the organization for resolution.[30] This clearly encourages operating managers to take HR issues seriously when formulating strategic plans. Another type of review and reaction linkage might include requesting that HR planners examine and interpret strategic plans to suggest HR issues for further study which could affect later implementation or operations.[31]

Developing a Linkage

While it is too soon to be definitive, early research and experience suggest possible organizational and environmental factors which may enhance the prospect for the growth of HR planning and the development of linkages with strategic business planning.[32]

Aspects of the HR function that appear to promote establishment of linkages include the following:

First, HR professionals have to know the business. This gives them the ability to do analyses, collect data, develop appropriate programs, and ask questions that pertain to the business mission and goals.

In addition, it helps if HR professionals have demonstrated competence and expertise to line managers. They must share their knowledge about personnel technology, have appropriate HR information available for making decisions, and use clear, business-oriented, and understandable methods to explain HR programs to operating managers.

Linkages are further facilitated when HR managers are able to integrate functional areas of the field to offer coordinated programs that initiate, focus on, and respond to potential strategic directions. HR managers also must be willing to take the initiative and to begin at the bottom in demonstrating how they can contribute to strategy. Involvement and success at lower levels may increase the likelihood of a linkage at top strategic levels.

Finally, HR professionals must be sensitive to the internal political/influence system when carrying out their activities and defining opportunities to contribute. Skills in facilitating change enhance influence and the likelihood of making an impact on the organization.

Developing linkages between HR planning and strategic business planning is a process that occurs over time. When and how fast this occurs depends on the organization's competitive circumstances, the perceived potential of human resources to play a significant role in the business, and the readiness of HR professionals to respond when opportunities arise. Linkages may begin as limited input or review/reaction contacts, and with success, evolve toward direct and intensive involvement in the entire strategic decision-making process.

HR Inputs and Responses

The HR planning linkage provides a channel for HR input into the strategic planning and direction of the firm. Meaningful HR data can establish a basis for evaluating the feasibility of current plans or defining them more clearly. It may also stimulate exploration of new business prospects or suggest modifications to the current business so as to gain a competitive edge. Appropriate and meaningful HR data are generated through availability analysis, environmental analysis, HR competitive analysis, and feasibility/impact analysis. These are summarized in Figure 3.

Availability Analysis

Availability analysis is concerned with identifying the quantity, quality, and skills of personnel available to the firm currently or at some future date. It may, and often should, include assessments of human resources available to the firm from both internal and external sources.

In conducting a current internal availability analysis, the firm's HR information system or an audit/inventory of organizational personnel can provide the following data:

- Number of persons available, both part-time and full-time

- Individual and/or group demographic information, such as age, sex, race, and education

- Company employment data, such as employment status, tenure, positions held, and performance ratings

- Pay information, such as salary grade and recent adjustments

- Career information, such as specific skills, professional interests, degrees and certifications, and potential and readiness ratings for promotion[33]

In addition, interviews and observation provide information on the styles (for example, risk taking, participative, or flexible) of available managers. The availability analysis can focus on a particular department or business unit, or it can provide an aggregate analysis of the entire organization.

Data for external availability analysis may come from any number of sources which help identify and define the current or future labor force availability. These sources include the following:

- Federal, state, and local government reports on employment and changes in relevant labor markets

- Census data on population and work patterns, industry surveys on turnover and accessions

Figure 3
HR Planning Inputs Into Strategic Planning

STRATEGIC
PLANNING
PROCESSES

HR PLANNING AND ANALYSIS

AVAILABILITY ANALYSIS	ENVIRONMENTAL ANALYSIS
HR Inventory and/or Audit Management Styles Labor Market Analysis HR Supply Forecasts HR Mobility Patterns	Complexity and Stability External Trends: Technical, Social, Legal, Economic
HR COMPETITIVE ANALYSIS	**FEASIBILITY AND IMPACT ANALYSIS**
Competence Profile Strategy/Competence Fit Assessment Define Comparative HR Advantage Identify HR Strategic Initiatives	HR Costs and Potential for Strategic Alternatives Assessment of Impacts in Terms of Growth, Employment and Distribution in Firm

- State job service statistics on available workers and employment activities

- Information from special interest groups (such as the Urban League or rehabilitation centers) on available clients and placement experience

Monitoring events such as plant closings and changes in the activity and structure of the local economy may indicate additional sources of personnel.

To determine future HR availabilities, projections or forecasts are made using time horizons related to planning goals and directions. Methods employed for such forecasts range from managerial estimates and replacement charts to sophisticated statistical procedures such as Markov models of human resource flows.[34]

Regardless of the methods used, the analysis should include key factors affecting labor supply such as attrition, internal mobility, and expected accessions. Attrition analysis focuses on personnel losses due to retirement, voluntary termination, and discharge. In addition, losses from death and disabilities may be relevant. Union Oil Co., while doing an analysis of its work force a number of years ago, found that of two critical kinds of engineers employed by the company, one group was rather old while the other was young. This finding had implications for internal executive recruitment and future staffing activity. It also identified the problems associated with cyclical recruiting. Through this analysis, the company was able to deal with the issue before it became a problem.

Organizational accession activity and employee internal mobility patterns are also important since they can provide data on the flow of personnel into and within the organization. Such information can be utilized to estimate future labor supply in specific occupational and organizational categories.

Environmental Analysis

Environmental analysis is a process used to identify key characteristics of a firm's environment and to monitor significant changes, developments, and trends that occur. These findings are researched and assessed with respect to their effect on employees and HR activities. This information serves as input to planners evaluating strategic choices and to managers making program design and implementation decisions. The following discussion covers a few selected points and issues related to the environmental analysis process. Readers should consult Chapter 1.3 of this volume for an in-depth treatment of environmental scanning.

In assessing environmental characteristics, two key issues are complexity and stability. The complexity of the environment can be viewed in terms of (1) the number and types of organizations with which the firm has HR dealings, such as government agencies, unions, and search firms; (2) the variety and nature of different labor markets in which it operates (for example, the scope and structure of markets for technicians, engineers, and executives); (3) the amount and intensity of competition for needed talent. Stability refers to the consistency and continuity of the environment, dimensions along which change is occurring, the rate at which change is occurring, and the predictability of change.

In addition, environmental analysis focuses on identifying and monitoring trends and events that might impact on the firm's environment in the future and consequently may alter a business strategy. The HR planner, with a knowledge of business objectives and plans, can identify key areas and issues for review. For example, if, over the next decade, the firm's strategic thrust depends upon hiring large numbers of electrical engineers, then the supply of these engineers is a strategic contingency. Analysts will want to focus on specific factors that might influence supply, such as student enrollments, immigration, and attitudes toward engineering as a profession, since they portend trends and changes in the availability of engineering talent.

General areas that the HR planning analyst may wish to scan include the following:

- Economic conditions, such as inflation rates, unemployment levels, and productivity

- Demographic trends, such as work-force age distribution, life expectancies, and population shifts between regions

- Sociocultural trends, such as life-style changes or career expectations

- Legal trends, such as proposed labor legislation, new employment taxes, or emerging regulations

- New technologies, such as robotics or computerization of work processes

One large diversified manufacturing firm creates a matrix listing its HR strategic contingencies in the columns and the key issues from its environmental analysis on the rows and then fills in the cells with likely implications, if any. This provides a framework for action in HR programming or for input into strategic planning.

HR Competitive Analysis

A firm's competitive advantage in the market comes through its strategy which may emphasize cost competitiveness, market focus, or differentiation of its product or service. However, either directly or indirectly, a business's competitive edge depends on its HR capabilities. For example, HR strategies, policies, and programs affect employee motivation, skill levels, commitment to corporate objectives, retention, cost of hiring, and the like. These elements are important to all firms and for some firms they are critical to competitive advantage. An HR competitive analysis can provide important information on HR strengths that strategic planners can use to establish competitive superiority. Such an analysis consists of four activities: developing a competence profile; evaluating HR competence/business strategy fit; making a comparative advantage assessment; and identifying possible strategic initiatives.

Developing a Competence Profile

Through an audit or review, a profile of principal HR capabilities, resources, and skills is developed. Factors identified might include a state-of-the-art assessment center for management evaluation, a highly favorable image among prospective employees, or a policy providing employment security for all employees. In addition to these strengths, current weaknesses in the HR system should be identified. This competence profile alone could be useful to strategic planners when considering the organizational infrastructure necessary for potential strategic thrusts.

Comparing HR Competence to Business Strategy

Next, the pattern of strengths and weaknesses is matched to HR requirements necessary to support the firm's business strategy. If an appropriate "fit" is lacking, then a current or prospective strategy may have to be modified or abandoned.

An example of an admirable fit between competence and strategy is provided by Lincoln Electric Co. This company has a long-time specific niche in the electrical products industry, arc welding generators and equipment, and provides a high-quality product along with excellent customer service. It has a secure market share and enjoys steady growth. Its personnel system is designed to select and develop people for long-term employment with the company. It relies on internally developed personnel so employees mature in the Lincoln culture that emphasizes business and customer values. Also, the famous Lincoln incentive system emphasizes high quality and quantity of output with substantial rewards for successful performance.[35]

Assessing Competitive Advantage

Next, a firm should compare its HR capabilities and activities to those of its major competitors. By making such comparisons, a business can determine distinctive HR competencies that may be employed or developed for a competitive edge. For example, a major accounting services firm such as Arthur Andersen and Co. undoubtedly gains a competitive advantage through its thorough training that provides thousands of staff with a solid understanding of its firmwide methodology. IBM seems to enjoy a particular advantage from its reputation as a leader in HR practices, employment security, and potential for career growth. Conversely, HR deficiencies which could limit competitive effectiveness may become apparent.

To make a competitive assessment, intelligence about competitors can be gathered in a variety of ways including observing their recruiting patterns, watching key personnel movements and career changes, reading articles and case studies about the companies, carrying out legitimate recruiting and interview activity, and reviewing publicly available information from government and professional sources.[36]

Identifying Strategic Initiatives

Finally, with an understanding of current HR practices among competitors, an analyst can assess the prospects for a strategic initiative that might give the firm a particular competitive advantage.[37] For example, in an industry with high turnover, a company might consider implementing an employee stock ownership plan that could enhance worker commitment and subsequently reduce turnover and training costs. In an industry with traditionally adversarial labor relations, a firm might consider initiating a cooperative relationship with the union to reduce lost time due to strikes and to improve productivity through acceptance of employee participation programs. Such initiatives may allow the firm to take control of the strategic behavior in the industry and force its competitors to respond. In addition, if competitors are slow to respond because of bureaucratic inertia, need to reconfigure resources, or lack of expertise, the initiating firm gains additional advantages.

Feasibility and Impact Analyses

During the organization's strategic planning process, HR planning can offer valuable input through feasibility and impact analyses of proposed alternatives. Feasibility analysis reviews strategic options in terms of HR costs and availabilities.[38] Cost assessment focuses on the anticipated outlays associated with hiring, motivating, developing, and retaining the employees needed to implement a plan. It should also include less direct costs, such as the cost of assuming unfunded pension liabilities in a proposed acquisition. Clearly, an option is not feasible if expected costs exceed allowable outlays. Also, a strategic alternative may not be practicable if analysis predicts a scarcity in the human resources necessary to meet staffing goals.

Impact analysis examines the probable HR impact of implementing a proposed strategic alternative. One analyst has suggested three areas for assessment: direct employment impact, distribution impact, and growth impact.[39] Direct employment impact assesses the effects of a strategy on the total employment and occupational mix of the firm. This considers changes in the number and stability of jobs over time, shifts in the quality and mix of positions, and the extent to which available human capabilities would be used. Distribution impact analysis assesses the effects of a strategy on the distribution of jobs, job opportunities, and human capabilities in the firm. Factors of concern are changes in patterns of geography, minority employment, career opportunities, and skill availabilities. Finally, growth impact analysis looks at an option's effect on the firm's ability to grow in the future. Some issues of concern include the future availability of managerial and other key talent, anticipated flexibility of human resources, and capability for technological change.

HR Response to Organizational Strategy

As the content of an organization's strategic plan becomes more clearly defined, its HR implications must be determined. At a minimum, this entails a forecast of future HR needs and a gap analysis to determine how current supplies of personnel match up to these requirements. This information assists in the formulation of an organizational HR strategy and provides an important operational basis for developing an HR plan to implement the organization's strategic plan.

Needs Forecasting

Needs, or demand, forecasting basically translates the defined thrusts and directions of the strategic business plan into more precise quantitative and qualitative personnel requirements. While current practice is more of an imprecise art than a rigorous science, needs forecasting is recognized as a necessary component in carrying out additional HR planning activities. Some experts have suggested that this type of forecasting may be particularly important for firms experiencing rapid change or introducing new technologies or processes, and for those companies whose success requires an adequate supply of managerial, professional, and technical capabilities.[40]

Forecasting HR needs from strategic business plans may involve long-range time horizons. However, more immediate and middle-range forecasts may be appropriate to deal with current operating and transition needs as the organization moves toward meeting its strategic objectives.

Estimating future HR needs for all types of employees in an organization, even when possible, is probably not necessary or desirable. HR managers should focus instead on those skills and positions most significant to successful implementation of the organizational strategy. Experience suggests that strategic planners show relatively strong agreement on the identification of these key human resources.[41]

Forecasting Methods and Choice

A variety of forecasting methods are available to project expected organizational needs. They range from sophisticated quantitative techniques such as regression analysis and computer simulations, through more judgmental and intuitive methods such as delphi and managerial estimates, to the more traditional administrative methods of replacement charts, manning tables, and the like.[42] In choosing among these alternatives for use in their own organization, HR planners consider the following questions:

What are the assumptions about stability and certainty in the environment, the technology, and the organization? Consistency, certainty, and stability favor use of quantitative extrapolations since past experience provides a good basis for estimating the future. Long-term projections may be not only possible, but also reasonably accurate. The greater the turbulence and uncertainty, the more appropriate judgmental or administrative approaches will be to assess organizational needs.

How available, accurate, complete, and quantifiable are records and HR data? Generally, sophisticated modeling and statistical methods require a substantial data base of complete, accurate, and relevant information for effective forecasting. Judgmental or administrative methods require less complete and specific data.

How many persons or positions are the focus of the forecast? If the numbers are quite small, the sample size might be deficient or the processes might be too cumbersome to employ highly sophisticated probability models. On the other hand, if very large numbers are involved, statistical methods and simulations might prove to be reasonable and efficient forecasting approaches.

What quantity and what kind of resources are available for forecasting HR needs? Considerations may include the availability of staff to collect and organize needed data, computer time to perform data analysis, money to hire necessary consultants, time of managers at various levels to assist efforts, and so forth. A shortage of these resources can restrict choices of forecasting methodology.

What is the credibility of the method to line managers? If the method has low credibility or is not understood by those who must use the results, it is likely to have low impact. Sometimes the sophisticated methods advocated in textbooks have low credibility to the ultimate user, resulting in limited value to the HR planning forecaster.

What are the forecasters' levels of sophistication and capability? Obviously, if the forecasters have limited competencies in skills required by various methodologies, it would be foolish to attempt to outstrip these capabilities with a "state-of-the-art" approach.

Finally, is the time horizon of the forecast long term, intermediate, or short term? While this is clearly related to the first question, nevertheless, certain methods simply do not lend themselves to long-term forecasts. Replacement charts are one example. Other methods, such as the delphi method, may provide long-term forecasts under varying degrees of certainty.

Current Practice

Survey data indicate that most companies do some type of demand forecasting.[43] The majority of these firms rely on administrative methods, such as manning tables and replacement charts—most likely in conjunction with short-range (one year or less) planning horizons.

However, indirect evidence suggests many firms apparently utilize multiple methods. This seems to be the case even if forecasting efforts are limited to administrative or judgmental procedures. Firms employing more sophisticated methods often cluster in certain industries (that is, transportation, communications, utilities) and are particularly concerned with avoiding layoffs and in meeting equal employment opportunity/affirmative action goals.[44] In addition, these firms are likely to have medium- to long-range planning horizons and employ HR staff with economics training. Finally, research suggests that even those organizations using sophisticated methods continue to use replacement charts and other nonquantitative approaches.[45] This may suggest an evolutionary approach through which firms build upon their experience with simpler techniques and gradually develop more sophisticated approaches. It also may reflect the uncertainty of any one method and the importance of using both quantitative and qualitative forecasting approaches to determine the degree of "convergent validity."

HR Gap Analysis

A new business strategy signifies change and necessitates a needs forecast on the probable quantity, quality, and mix of human resources required to meet the new strategic thrust. At best, a needs analysis only suggests what HR policies and programs will be necessary to achieve and maintain forecast estimates. A more complete picture entails undertaking a gap analysis.

Gap analysis involves assessing the effects of current HR strategies, policies, and programs and then comparing these data to the forecasted HR needs of the new business strategy. This comparison over the relevant planning horizon identifies HR deficiencies, shortfalls, excesses, and performance problems that will likely occur if HR activity remains unchanged. The degree of difference between future HR needs and what current HR focus and activities will provide is the "gap" or challenge that must be addressed.

In conducting a gap analysis, the HR planning professional can draw upon information and procedures used earlier for input into the strategic planning process. Data and procedures from the availability and competitive analyses described earlier may be useful.

For example, data from an availability analysis on current HR quantity, quality, and skill mix can provide the necessary projections for the new business strategy. The HR competencies, strengths, and weaknesses identified in a competitive analysis form the basis for personnel programming and decision making, and thus provide estimates as to how the resulting HR position would fit the performance and availability needs of the new strategy. In other cases, information from HR environmental and impact analyses may assist in determining gaps between HR need and availabilities.

The goal is to state HR alternatives or options for closing these gaps. Options may be stated in terms of policies or programs relating to staffing, development, compensation, utilization and deployment, control and assessment, or union relations. The articulation and evaluation of options provides information on which to base an appropriate organizational HR strategy.

HR Strategy

An organizational HR strategy is the set of priorities a firm uses to align available or potentially available resources and its personnel policies and programs with its strategic business plan. The broad objective of the HR strategy is to facilitate implementation of the strategic business plan. An HR strategy defines the orientation and thrust of the firm in carrying out its HRM activities. It provides the basis for developing more specific plans to integrate and focus personnel policies and functional activities. As with business strategy, an HR strategy may be formally and directly articulated through a rational or comprehensive planning process, or it may simply evolve through incremental decision making.

Central Features of HR Strategies

Efforts to explore and more fully understand organizational HR strategy are still in the initial phases. It seems clear, however, that the main purpose of an HR strategy is to enhance the firm's business strategy by finding ways to gain competitive advantages through better HRM. Key goals of HR strategy involve such areas as managing labor costs (for example, increasing employee productivity or controlling compensation levels), enhancing employee morale,[46] and facilitating employee innovation. (For an in-depth discussion on strategic HRM consult Chapter 1.1 of this volume.)

A recent empirical study of 129 strategic business units from Fortune 1000 and 50 companies found that a business-level HR strategy can be described in terms of the following factors:[47]

- *Domain*, which encompasses the critical employee groups and the critical personnel activities

- *Deployments*, which encompass work-force competencies (for example, quality, potential skills), work-force performance (for example, productivity, labor costs), and the level of investment in HR decisions (for example, size of personnel budgets and direction of budget commitment to personnel)

- *Synergy*, which derives from the linkage between HR decisions and strategic business decisions, the ability to anticipate and respond to HR trends that have strategic business implications, the degree of functional cooperation, and the relative competence of key employees

- *Competitive advantages*, which relate to the flexibility and responsiveness of HR systems, their image and reputation, the skills available to support external aspects of strategy, and the skills available to support internal or operational aspects of strategy

Thus, research suggests that these may be common elements of HR strategy across organizations. If so, specific HR strategies can be examined in terms of these dimensions to facilitate comparison and analysis.

Factors Shaping HR Strategy

Organizational HR strategies vary among companies—even among those in the same industry. Variations can be found, for example, among firms in the airline, steel, and other industries in response to recent changes in competitive structures. Factors that seem to be influential in shaping an organization's HR strategy include the organizational business strategy, internal organizational factors, the external environment, and the life-cycle stage of the firm.

Organizational Business Strategy

Business strategy defines the competitive thrust of a firm and provides the basis for aligning resources, including human resources, to meet strategic objectives. Variation in business strategies creates differing HR needs, gaps, problems, and challenges from which unique HR strategies emerge. Indeed, the available conceptual and empirical work seems to support this conclusion.

For example, one study tested the hypothesis that an organization's HR strategy is directly affected by its business strategy.[48] Through examining a large diversified company with 22 business units in a variety of industries and tracking its strategic movement over the past year, the research found each business unit utilized one of three basic strategies: growth, profit, or stabilization. By exploring the impact of each business strategy on the "employee utilization and allocation" dimension of HR strategy, the study identified patterns of differences across the three business strategies in such areas as quantity of managers, performance and potential of managers, and importance of functional areas to solve business problems.

A more extensive study statistically examined the relationship between six business strategies, ranging from "profit" through "strategic turnaround" to "expansion," and the earlier described dimensions of HR strategy: domain, deployments, synergy, and competitive advantage. It found a significant but moderate relationship—strong enough that given the HR strategy of a firm, its business strategy could generally be identified.[49]

While these studies and other data suggest that business strategy significantly affects the design and emphasis of HR strategy, this clearly is not the sole determinant; other factors have some impact as well.

Internal Organizational Factors

Internal organizational and managerial factors are logical candidates for influence, as suggested earlier in this chapter. In addition, such factors as organizational structure (for example, centralized, decentralized, or functional); the availability or absence of slack in the system; employee attitudes; the dominant organizational value (for example, entrepreneurship, and cost control); and others have potential to shape the characteristics and content of HR strategy.

Consider organizational culture. An HR strategy that is consistent with a prevailing culture will likely encounter little difficulty in gaining acceptance and implementation. For example, at AT&T before the break-up of the Bell system, the culture emphasized lifelong careers, consensus management, promotion from within, customer service, and operational skills and competence. Not surprisingly, its HR strategy emphasized employee development for both managers and craftsmen, investment in HR activity, and the image of AT&T as a high-quality, stable employer.

Syntex USA, Inc., a large pharmaceutical firm, recently formed a new division to focus on cancer and developmental biology. The business strategy for the new division focused around a long-term (10 year) research plan and use of the latest technology and facilities to develop a differentiated anticancer drug that could compete in the rapidly growing market for this type of product. The HR strategy to support this business plan built on current competence and the creation of an innovative and motivated research group led by a respected scientist. Implementation focused on reallocating some current research personnel, maintaining high motivation, and selecting an established scientist to lead the division. The firm's culture facilitated this through emphasizing collegial values, mutual trust, research managed by researchers, and the opportunity for current staff to move to new projects. Eighteen internal researchers formed the nucleus of the new division and a faculty member from Stanford University was hired to lead it.

External Factors

An organization's external environment also plays a role in shaping HR strategy. This premise guides the environmental analysis activity discussed earlier in this chapter. For example, a trend toward more aggressive enforcement of equal employment opportunity laws could affect an organization's HR strategy, even if it had no impact on business strategy.

External factors can indicate the need for a new HR strategy or influence the relationship between a particular HR activity and the company's competitive posture. For example, Caterpillar Tractor Co., an established manufacturer of construction equipment, maintained a traditional HR strategy during the 1970s based on its dominant competitive position and on traditional assumptions about its employee and union relations. The advent of competition from Komatsu, Ltd. forced a reexamination of its business and HR strategies. Reformulation of its HR strategy was shaped not only by competitive factors, but also by the firm's adoption of new technology and its perceptions of changing attitudes and expectations in society and among its workers.[50]

The paucity of research makes it impossible to say with certainty which environmental factors might be the most important determinants of HR strategy. Indeed, a factor's importance is likely to vary across types of firms, industries, and organizations, and within these, across time. However, one study examined the major determinaints of HR strategy in 11 Canadian companies located in four industries and found the following factors: "the nature of the external labor markets (especially the availability of needed talent), labor unions (especially their perceived attitude toward productivity improvements and their perceived strengths), and, to a lesser extent, legislation."[51] Other environmental factors that might influence HR strategy include external economic stability (market, industry, or region), competitors' HR strategies, societal values, and life-style changes.

Life-Cycle Factors

Analysts suggest that firms may progress through at least four life-cycle phases: start-up or embryonic, rapid growth, maturity, and aging/decline.[52] Each of these phases imposes its own peculiar HR requirements as a result of changes in such factors as organizational flexibility, control systems, performance expectations, emphasis on innovation, and information requirements. Even if an organization pursues a consistent competitive strategy, such as "low-cost price competitiveness," throughout its life cycle, transitions from one phase to another will likely be accompanied by changing HR requirements and patterns of acquisition, utilization, development, and motivation.

Start-up phase. In the start-up phase, risk characterizes most operational aspects. Market share is volatile and there is substantial uncertainty regarding the future. An organization must display great flexibility and respond quickly to problems. Minimal controls are exercised over activities and operations, and informal relationships with minimal status barriers predominate. The business strategy emphasizes entrepreneurship and getting the product or service to the market. The HR strategy emphasizes immediate acquisition of necessary talent, flexible utilization of available skills, and motivation of employees through deep involvement and equity rights in the future business. At this point, little, if any organized HR planning occurs.

Growth phase. The growth phase is characterized by an increasing market share, a larger number of competitors, and less differentiated products or services as market rivals copy successful efforts. Organizational structure reflects functional activity with increased financial, operating, and personnel controls. The business thrust is to improve market share and increase sales. The HR emphasis focuses on external acquisition of necessary skills, motivation through high pay for performance (sales, production), development of certain organization-specific and key skill mixes, and more specialized use of available human resources. Interest develops in forecasting managerial and personnel needs to meet production and marketing objectives. Management succession planning is likely a programmatic effort.

Maturity stage. At the maturity stage in the business life cycle, most of the market has been tapped, the firm has a relatively fixed market share, and the number of competitors stabilizes. Obtaining a competitive advantage through product or service differentiation becomes increasingly difficult. The organization emphasizes stability and hierarchy, more formal procedures and relationships, and well-articulated control systems for financial, operating, and personnel activities. The business thrust stresses competitiveness to maintain the firm's own market share and to encroach as much as possible on rivals' shares. The HR emphasis centers on internally developing employees who know the business and the industry, motivating productivity through incentives, enhancing employee commitment to the organization, and specializing positions of technical and lower-level skills with broader lateral moves for managers. At this stage, the organization becomes more committed to forecasting personnel flows, developing career systems for employees, and establishing programs for management succession.

Decline phase. The aging or decline phase is marked by a saturated or declining market and concentrated competition through the loss of marginal competitors. The organization is likely to be centralized for direct and consistent decision making. The business stresses cost cutting to maintain cash flow for survival and an extensive set of control procedures are employed to monitor performance and outlays. The HR thrust is to keep labor costs down and minimize the impact of personnel problems resulting from organizational downsizing and job loss. Minimal new hiring takes place, but increasing effort goes toward moving current employees out of the organization, and the remaining employees are flexibly utilized. Planning concerns downsizing, succession, and effective allocation of employees.

Clearly, each phase of the organizational life cycle leads to differing pressures and unique circumstances that influence the nature of HR strategy.

HR Strategy, Plans, and Implementation

While strategy formulation and content are important, they have little operational significance without effective implementation. Despite increasing recognition of the role HR strategy plays in effectuating a business strategy,[53] regrettably little research has been conducted on this issue.

Nonetheless, the HR plan is a key element in both processes since it provides an operational statement of what is to be achieved and how it is to be achieved (see Figure 4). More specifically, the HR plan identifies distinct HR goals (regarding such matters as quantity of employees, types of skills, talent mixes); specifies the planning horizon for attaining these goals; and outlines a set of coordinated programs (in such areas as staffing, utilization, and development) to promote achieving the goals.

Development of the HR plan relies largely upon information from the analyses conducted as input and/or responses to the business planning process. It also derives guidance from the organizational HR strategy. The analyses provide specific data (for example, HR availabilities, expected needs, gaps, and the like); competitive information (for example, advantages or disadvantages of HR activity compared with competitors); and other information (for example, environmental trends and impact analysis) useful in setting operational goals and in assessing programmatic alternatives. The HR strategy articulates the priorities (labor-cost reduction, employee innovation, and so on), based on the strategic business plan, that will guide development of programs and policies to carry out the implementation activities.

HR Programs and Strategy Implementation

Specific personnel programs provide the means to effectuate HR aspects of strategy. Generic programs include the following:

- Staffing, such as recruitment, acquisition, internal movement

- Appraisal, such as performance assessment and evaluation of employee potential

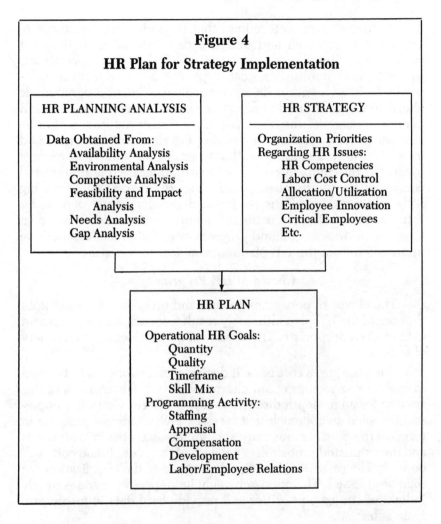

Figure 4

HR Plan for Strategy Implementation

HR PLANNING ANALYSIS

Data Obtained From:
Availability Analysis
Environmental Analysis
Competitive Analysis
Feasibility and Impact
Analysis
Needs Analysis
Gap Analysis

HR STRATEGY

Organization Priorities
Regarding HR Issues:
HR Competencies
Labor Cost Control
Allocation/Utilization
Employee Innovation
Critical Employees
Etc.

HR PLAN

Operational HR Goals:
Quantity
Quality
Timeframe
Skill Mix
Programming Activity:
Staffing
Appraisal
Compensation
Development
Labor/Employee Relations

- Development, such as career planning, training, and organization development

- Compensation, such as pay, nonfinancial motivational factors, and perquisites

- Labor/employee relations, such as negotiations, appeals procedures, and fair employment actions

Through selecting and organizing specific program alternatives from these activities, a coherent thrust emerges that is consistent with the goals of the HR plan. Consider an organization which, from its HR strategy, has determined that it needs a creative corps of engineers to research and design a new product over the next several years. Building on past experience and current expectations, the HR plan establishes a goal of placing 300 engineers in new-product research within three years. Several broad programmatic alternatives can be used to design the operating elements of an HR plan. For example, the objective may be achieved from within by increasing compensation, enhancing development activities, and fostering internal mobility without performing additional recruitment. Or, the company could decide to emphasize recruitment and compensation to attract engineers from the market while placing little additional emphasis on internal developmental or transfer activity. The choice and nature of the programs would be based on strategic priorities, skill and program availability, and competitive information from the HR planning and analysis efforts.

Choice of HR Programs

The choice of personnel policies and programs that constitute the core of the HR plan ultimately result from managerial judgment as to what is appropriate. The choices may be influenced by a variety of factors.

For example, a cost/benefit decision framework might be used to evaluate various program alternatives. (See Chapter 1.4 of this volume for an in-depth discussion of this.) Xerox Corp. has implemented such an approach that assesses each personnel program in terms of the possible monetary and nonmonetary benefits and costs and the estimated probability that each of the benefits and costs will occur.[54] The relative value of each program to the organization can then be assessed. This approach might help specify programs clearly in light of strategic priorities and provide hard data to justify program selection.

An overriding value or thrust can also exert a strong influence. As an illustration, a firm committed to reducing operating costs would make this a key factor in all decisions. This would in turn guide the selection of programs.

Whether these programs are seen as complementary and consistent with other programs could influence the selection process. If a pay-for-performance compensation system is proposed to meet business objectives, then the performance appraisal system must represent the types of measures necessary to determine specific performance.

In addition, factors such as feasibility of implementation, past experience with programs, and available expertise among managers might affect the choice of programming packages.

Addressing Business Needs

If the HR plan is to have any chance of successful implementation, line managers must see it as useful in addressing business needs. Or, as one executive put it, [T]he manager's first concern with human resource planning is simply whether it is helping him/her to do what he/she is committed to do. . . ."[55]

Certainly, a variety of actions can enhance the perceived business relevance of HR plans. However, experience suggests that direct involvement of the users, the line managers, in the HR planning process may be most effective. This can include line managers' involvement in task forces to assess the significance of human resources (for example, costs or productivity) in meeting profit goals, to help define HR planning goals, to select programs, or to monitor programmatic effectiveness.

In addition, keeping HR plans direct, uncomplicated, clear, and action-oriented can enhance their attractiveness to line managers.[56] Measuring outcomes of HR plans in terms relevant to users may facilitate both the implementation and evaluation processes.

The Need for a "Fit"

As noted earlier in the chapter, HR planning practices vary substantially across organizations. This suggests that for successful implementation, an HR plan must fit or be congruent with key elements of its context. It must, for example, be consistent with the beliefs, practices, and values of the organizational culture. Illustrative of this is the HR plan implemented by IBM during 1986 to reduce costs when it experienced sharply declining profits. Immediate reductions were constrained by IBM's long-standing commitment to full employment and avoidance of layoffs. Its operational HR plan called for significant staff reductions through a generous early retirement program, strict limits on hiring, and the shifting of more than 5,000 administrative and headquarters staff into the marketing operations. This HR plan enabled the corporation to pursue its strategic business priorities without changing its culture.

An HR plan must also be congruent and synergistic with other functional plans. If the marketing department is attempting to increase sales of current products through new distribution procedures, pricing formulas, advertising programs, and market territories, then the HR plan needs to fit with this effort. The operational HR plan might include such things as needs projections and staffing programs to assure the availability of salespersons, career planning to develop needed skills, training for new sales employees, and development of appropriate reward systems.

Other factors that influence the fit of the HR plan include current management styles, political and power realities in the organization, and organizational structure. If a poor fit exists between the HR plan and the significant elements in an organization, implementation will be difficult and superficial at best. The plan will create resistance and conflict in the system and will have generally negative effects.

Conclusion

A decade ago, a sizable number of HR scholars and professionals were calling for the widespread establishment and use of HR planning in private and public organizations. The response appears to have been significant. Current evidence suggests that most medium-sized and large organizations have some type of HR planning activity in place.

Today, an equally compelling voice, raised with the same passion and logic as heard with the earlier HR planning advocacy, is calling for the integration of HR considerations and strategic business planning activities. This new integration effort aims, in large part, to promote an overall organizational perspective among those with HRM responsibilities and to give HR issues a voice in the formulation and design of business objectives, plans, and programs. Indeed, this chapter has synthesized some leading-edge experiences and state-of-the-art analyses and research to stimulate thinking and suggest an approach for such an integration. This new emphasis appears to offer extended vistas and exciting new opportunities for HR practitioners. While this seems desirable for the profession, some words of caution are appropriate.

First, the movement to integrate HR planning with strategic business planning may attempt to go too far too fast given the current state of practice. Evidence indicates that HR planning, as practiced in many firms, may not yet be generally accepted as the critical and significant activity that many of its advocates profess. HR planning often has a limited scope, such as being restricted to management succession planning, and remains relatively unsophisticated in methods and approach.[57] It may not be realistic or beneficial to attempt to tie an activity into organizational strategic planning that, in many firms, has yet to define its own purpose or gain acceptance from operating managers.

It also is unclear whether HR professionals currently are able or willing to enter the political fray caused by any meaningful effort to increase their influence in setting organizational direction. Coming from a staff function that traditionally has had low clout and has depended upon the goodwill of others, the HR manager may not enjoy a substantive power base for a significant new role in strategic business decisions. In addition, possessing functional expertise may provide few skills in the politics of strategy formulation or implementation where broad knowledge may be valued and the allocation of substantial resources is at stake.

Another point to consider is that strategic planning is a relatively new management activity. During the current period of industrial soul searching, some firms have raised serious questions about the role and future of strategic planning. However appealing integration may sound, HR professions may wish to consider carefully whether "the linkage of the human resource management activities to strategic planning has a danger of becoming a cart hooked up to a not so healthy horse."[58]

These admonitions are not meant to cast a pall over current enthusiasm for HR planning and strategy. Rather, they are simply intended to suggest areas of caution as HR professionals explore ways in which their contributions can better assist the business in achieving its long-term goals.

◆

Notes

1. For an excellent critical survey of HR planning, see Milkovich, Dyer, and Mahoney.
2. Nkomo; Alpander and Botter.
3. Craft.
4. Milkovich, Dyer, and Mahony; Butensky and Harari; Marshall-Miles, Yarkin-Levin, and Quain-tance; Mills.
5. Tichy, Fombrum, and Devanna, pp. 22–23.
6. Cassell, Juris, and Roomkin; Dyer (1982).
7. Galbraith and Nathanson; Miles and Snow.
8. Misa and Stein.

9. Schwartz.
10. Nkomo, p. 80; Alpander and Botter, p. 196.
11. Mills, p. 103.
12. Alpander and Botter, p. 191; Cassell, Juris, and Roomkin, pp. 20–21.
13. Burack; Angle, Manz, and Van de Ven.
14. Groe; Tichy, Fombrun, and Devanna, p. 25; Alpander and Botter, p. 193.
15. For useful discussion of the rational/comprehensive process, see Frederickson, and Hofer and Schendel.
16. For reviews of the incremental process, see Frederickson, and J.B. Quinn.
17. James.
18. Dyer (1983).
19. For a somewhat different classification of linkages, see Dyer (1983 and 1984a).
20. Marshall-Miles, Yarkin-Levin, and Quaintance, p. 39.
21. Dyer (1984a), p. 81.
22. Nkomo, p. 80.
23. Bronson, p. 47.
24. Leigh.
25. Wheaton and Smith.
26. Erlich, p. 41–44.
27. Angle, Manz, and Van de Ven, p. 60–62.
28. Bright.
29. Mirvis.
30. Dyer and Heyer; Tichy, Fombrun, and Devanna, p. 25.
31. Dyer (1984a).
32. The discussion in this section draws heavily upon the following sources: Dyer (1984a); Golden and Ramanu-

jam; Milkovich, Dyer, and Mahoney; Burack.
33. Walker, pp. 107–109.
34. For useful descriptions of various supply forecasting models and procedures, see Dyer (1982), and Walker, pp. 117–143.
35. Zager.
36. For a discussion of HR competitive analysis, see Gould, and Henn. For a broader review of competitive analysis, see Porter.
37. Schuler and MacMillan.
38. Dyer (1983), pp. 261–267.
39. Boynton.
40. Walker, p. 104.
41. Dyer (1984), p. 262.
42. For discussion on needs forecasting methods, see Walker, pp. 122–143; and Dyer (1982), pp. 56–60. For a critical assessment of forecasting activity, see Craft, pp. 43–47.
43. Nkomo, pp. 79–80.
44. Fiorito, Stone, and Greer.
45. Ibid.
46. Dyer (1984b).
47. De Bejar and Milkovich (study 1).
48. Wils and Dyer.
49. De Bejar and Milkovich (study 2).
50. Mirvis.
51. Research by Christiane M. LaBelle reported in Dyer (1984b), pp. 163–164.
52. Smith; Hax.
53. Tichy, Fombrun, and Devanna, pp. 23–24.
54. Cheek.
55. Cashel.
56. Ulrich.
57. Rowland and Summers; Nkomo.
58. Tichy.

◆

References

Alpander, G.G. and C.H. Botter, 1981. "An Integrated Model of Strategic Human Resource Planning and Utilization." *Human Resource Planning*, no. 4: 189–203.

Angle, H.L., C.C. Manz, and A.H. Van de Ven. 1985. "Integrating Human Resource Management and Corporate Strategy: A Preview of the 3M Story." *Human Resource Management* 24 (Spring): 51–68.

Boynton, R.W. 1979. "Design Elements for a Human Resource Impact Statement." *Human Resource Planning*, no. 2: 103–109.

Bright, W.E. 1976. "How One Company Manages Its Human Resources." *Harvard Business Review* 54 (January-February): 81–93.

Bronson, J.S. 1985. "Frito-Lay Achieves Objectives Through People." In *Productivity and Quality Through People*, eds. Y.K. Shetty and V.M. Buehler. Westport, CT: Quorum Books.

Burack, E.H. 1985. "Linking Corporate Business and Human Resource Planning: Strategic Issues and Concerns." *Human Resource Planning*, no. 3: 133–145.

Butensky, C.F. and O. Harari. 1983. "Models vs. Reality: An Analysis of Twelve Human Resource Planning Systems." *Human Resource Planning*, no. 1: 11–24.

Cashel, W.S., Jr. 1978. "Human Resource Planning in the Bell System." *Human Resource Planning*, no. 2: 59.

Cassell, F.H., H.A. Juris, and M.J. Roomkin. 1985. "Strategic Human Resources Planning: An Orientation to the Bottom Line." *Management Decision*, no. 2: 16–28.

Cheek, L.M. 1973. "Cost Effectiveness Comes to the Personnel Function." *Harvard Business Review* 51 (May-June): 96–105.

Craft, J.A. 1980. "A Critical Perspective on Human Resource Planning." *Human Resource Planning*, no. 2: 39–52.

De Bejar, G. and G.T. Milkovich. 1986. "Human Resource Strategy at the Business Level, Study 1: Theoretical Model and Empirical Verification." Paper delivered at the Forty-Sixth Annual Meeting of the National Academy of Management, Chicago, August: 1–22.

————. 1986. "Human Resource Strategy at the Business Level, Study 2: Relationships between Strategy and Performance Components." Paper delivered at the Forty-Sixth Annual Meeting of the National Academy of Management, Chicago, August, 1–21.

Dyer, L. 1982. "Human Resource Planning." In *Personnel Management*, eds. K. Rowland and G.R. Ferris. Boston: Allyn and Bacon.

————. 1983. "Bringing Human Resources Into the Strategy Formulation Process." *Human Resource Management* 22 (Fall): 257–273.

————. 1984a. "Linking Human Resource and Business Strategies." *Human Resource Planning*, no. 2: 79–84.

————. 1984b. "Studying Human Resource Strategy: An Approach and an Agenda. "*Industrial Relations* 23 (Spring): 154–169.

Dyer, L. and N.O. Heyer. 1984. "Human Resource Planning at IBM." *Human Resource Planning*, no. 3: 116.

Erlich, C.J. 1985. "Marriot Benefits by Linking Human Resources With Strategy." In *Productivity and Quality Through People*, eds. Y.K. Shetty and V.M. Buehler. Westport, CT: Quorum Books.

Fiorito, J., T.H. Stone, and C.R. Greer. 1985. "Factors Affecting Choice of Human Resource Forecasting Techniques." *Human Resource Planning*, no. 1: 1–18.

Frederickson, J.W. 1983. "Strategic Process Research: Questions and Recommendations." *Academy of Management Review* 8 (October): 565–575.

Galbraith, J.R. and D.A. Nathanson. 1978. *Strategy Implementation: The Role of Structure and Process*. St. Paul: West Publishing.

Golden, K.A. and V. Ramanujam. 1985. "Between a Dream and a Nightmare: On the Integration of Human Resource Management and Strategic Business Planning Processes." *Human Resource Management* 24 (Winter): 429–452.

Gould, R. 1984. "Gaining a Competitive Edge Through Human Resource Strategies." *Human Resource Planning*, no. 1: 31–38.

Groe, G.M. 1980. "Legitimizing Human Resource Planning." *Human Resource Planning*, no. 1: 11–14.

Hax, A.C. 1985. "A New Competitive Weapon: The Human Resource Strategy." *Training and Development Journal* (May): 75–82.

Henn, W.R. 1985. "What the Strategist Asks From Human Resources." *Human Resource Planning*, no. 4: 193–200.

Hofer, C.W. and D. Schendel. 1978. *Strategy Formulation: Analytical Concepts*. St. Paul: West Publishing.

James, R.M. 1980. "Effective Planning Strategies." *Human Resource Planning*, no. 1: 1–10.

Leigh, D.R. 1984. "Business Planning Is People Planning." *Personnel Journal* 63 (May): 44–54.

Marshall-Miles, J., K. Yarkin-Levin, and M. Quaintance. 1985. "Human Resource Planning, Part 2: In the Private Sector." *Personnel Journal* 64 (September): 38–44.

Miles, R.E. and C.C. Snow. 1981. "Designing Strategic Human Resources Systems." *Organizational Dynamics* 13 (Summer): 36–52.

Milkovich, G., L. Dyer, and T. Mahoney. 1983. "HRM Planning." In *Human Resources Management in the 1980s*, eds. S.J. Carroll and R.S. Schuler. Washington, DC: BNA Books.

Mills, D.Q. 1985. "Planning With People in Mind." *Harvard Business Review* 63 (July/August): 97–105.

Mirvis, P.H. 1985. "Formulating and Implementing Human Resource Strategy: A Model of How to Do It, Two Examples of How It's Done." *Human Resource Management* 24 (Winter): 396–404.

Misa, K.F. and T. Stein. 1983. "Strategic HRM and the Bottom Line." *Personnel Administrator* 28 (October): 29.

Nkomo, S.N. 1986. "The Theory and Practice of HR Planning: The Gap Remains." *Personnel Administrator* 31 (August): 71–84.

Porter, M.E. 1980. *Competitive Strategy: Techniques for Analyzing Industries and Competitors.* New York: Free Press.

Quinn, J.B. 1980. *Strategies for Change: Logical Incrementalism.* Homewood, IL: Irwin.

Rowland, K.M. and S.L. Summers. 1981. "Human Resource Planning: A Second Look." *Personnel Administrator* 26 (December): 73–80.

Schuler, R.S. and I.C. MacMillan. 1984. "Gaining Competitive Advantage Through Human Resource Management Practices." *Human Resource Management* 23 (Fall): 231–255.

Schwartz, R.H. 1985. "Practitioner's Perception of Factors Associated With Human Resource Planning Success." *Human Resource Planning*, no. 2: 55–66.

Smith, E.C. 1982. "Strategic Business Planning and Human Resources: Part I." *Personnel Journal* 61 (August): 606–610.

Tichy, N.M. 1983. "Managing Organizational Transformations." *Human Resource Management* 22 (Spring/Summer): 54.

Tichy, N.M., C.J. Fombrun, and M.A. Devanna, eds. 1984. "The Organizational Context of Strategic Human Resource Management." *Strategic Human Resource Management.* New York: John Wiley & Sons.

Ulrich, D. 1986. "Human Resource Planning as a Competitive Edge." *Human Resource Planning*, no. 2: 41–50.

Walker, J.W. 1980. *Human Resource Planning.* New York: McGraw-Hill.

Wheaton, W.F. and L.M. Smith. 1984. In "An Interview With Wheaton and Smith. *Human Resource Management* 23 (Summer): 181–182.

Wils, T. and L. Dyer. 1984. "Relating Business Strategy to Human Resource Strategy: Some Preliminary Evidence." Paper delivered at the Forty-Fourth Annual Meeting of the National Academy of Management, Boston, August, 1–19.

Zager, R. 1978. "Managing Guaranteed Employment." *Harvard Business Review*, 56, 3: 103–115.

1.3

Environmental Scanning

Lorenz P. Schrenk

The world has clearly become a complex and rapidly changing place in which to live and work. Virtually all facets of organizational life—social, demographic, technical, political, and economic—are shifting at an unprecedented and accelerating rate. Anticipating and understanding these changes well enough to succeed in managing both their short-term and long-term implications is a major challenge. By meeting this challenge organizations are in a better position to avoid or minimize problems and to capitalize on opportunities.

Environmental scanning provides one way to meet the challenge of anticipating and understanding external changes. Briefly defined, environmental scanning is a process of systematic surveillance and interpretation designed to identify relevant events and conditions. Although such scanning may be done in a variety of ways, this chapter focuses on methodology that has been tested in practice and found effective in HRM applications. Regardless of technique, the primary purpose of environmental scanning is to answer the question, "What's coming and what will it mean to us?" This then becomes the basis for a more informed approach to HR planning and management.

The Context of Environmental Scanning

The primary context of environmental scanning lies in the business environment, which is increasingly global and fast moving. Evidence of this appears every day in the newspapers and on television. Fundamental changes are occurring and creating new business challenges and opportunities. A business, or an HR function, that lacks sensitivity to these changes is very likely suddenly to discover that it faces serious difficulties.

A second context of environmental scanning is an organization's business planning process and the business strategies that emerge from this process. To succeed, an environmental scanning activity must be consistent with both the method and timing of the relevant business planning activity. In addition, business strategies determine which trends and implications are of concern to an organization. For example, a growing software company might be greatly troubled by an anticipated shortage of programmers, while a similar company that is phasing out of business would not care about such a development.

The Evolving Role of HR Managers

Just as the world at large has been undergoing significant change, so the HR function has evolved through several clearly identifiable stages. Some years ago, the HR function emphasized "administrative activities," such as keeping records, processing payrolls, handling terminations, and the like. In the next stage, HR efforts focused on "employee relations," and the function became more involved in such activities as negotiating labor contracts, developing compensation systems, and running training courses. More recently, an emphasis on "human resources" has emerged that promotes more of a management perspective—one that has a more proactive role, takes a broader, forward-looking view, and is more involved with all aspects of HRM. (See Chapter 1.1 for a comprehensive discussion on the strategic perspective of HRM.)

This more central and more strategic role for the HR function is driven in part by a growing recognition that labor costs consume a very large part of the total operating budget for many companies. At the same time, competition, especially from overseas, has become tougher. Poor or inattentive management of people resources can compromise an organization's competitive position.

Other factors have also contributed to the increasing importance of the HR function. These factors include technological developments; legislation and regulations; mergers, acquisitions, and divestitures; an aging work force; more two-worker families; more women in the labor force; and higher demand for participation in management. All of these have complicated managing the people side of businesses and brought about an increasing need for effective strategic HR planning. An environmental scanning activity is an important part of this picture.

Integration of Environmental Scanning and HR Strategy

To succeed in this emerging context, management must pay increasing attention to long-term internal factors and external trends that may create issues for an organization. Many solutions may require several years or more to implement, especially if these changes are to be effective and cause minimal cost and disruption to the organization. The earlier a need for action can be seen, the more options will usually be available and the more proactive the HR function can be. Environmental scanning can help provide this long-range perspective.

Environmental scanning can also help the HR function achieve a closer, more effective partnership with line management. It helps HR managers and professionals achieve a greater knowledge of the business and its direction, and a better understanding of the language of business planning and management. It also provides a means through which they can participate actively with line management in running the business. By becoming an expert on environmental trends, the HR function can provide valuable information and perspective to other members of the management team. This, in turn, can help the team make better long-term business and HR decisions.

Finally, the HR function can provide greater coordination of existing data collection efforts. Few organizations have an effective integrated scanning process in place. Instead, what commonly exists are somewhat independent activities that follow selected areas. For example, the marketing function may track market trends and competitive developments, the public affairs function may follow key legislative activities, the finance function may monitor economic trends, and so on. This often results in significant gaps in coverage and restricted dissemination of the information gathered. Since the HR function must deal with all these areas, plus others, it can easily become a focal point for gathering and distributing external trend data on a more general basis.

Environmental Scanning Concepts

To expand on the brief definition of environmental scanning given earlier, a key concept is that scanning is a data-oriented activity. It is a process that looks for specific events, developments, and/or trends to identify strategic issues and then attempts to inter-pret these so as to help manage human resources more effectively.[1] It does not try to predict the future in any specific way, nor does it, of itself, prescribe action. However, an important measure of a scan-ning process' value is whether it leads to action.

Forecasting Approaches

A basic premise is that environmental scanning provides a rational basis for action by anticipating future conditions. Forecast-ing is an integral part of the process but there are many different approaches to forecasting.[2]

At one extreme is prophecy. This is a forecast based on indi-vidual, and usually mystical or intuitive, knowledge. The basis for the prophecy is normally unverifiable and often the resulting fore-cast is of a very specific, dramatic event or condition. Prophecy has a poor reputation for accuracy, but sometimes, as fiction, it may serve to trigger constructive, unconventional, creative thinking. As a regular technique, however, it lacks credibility.

At the opposite extreme is extrapolation. This forecasting approach is firmly grounded in data but usually assumes a continua-tion of whatever trends are revealed in the data. For example, extrapolation of past employment trends would forecast that every-one in the nation will eventually be employed by the federal govern-ment. This points up an obvious problem with extrapolation: It usually does not provide for discontinuities or natural limits. In addition, its emphasis on data may create an unjustified sense of precision.

Somewhere between prophecy and extrapolation is prediction. Prediction is more data-based than prophecy and less mechanical than extrapolation. Prediction, however, usually forecasts only a single situation or series of events. Much of the work of people known as "futurists" is of this type.[3] Such projections can be useful, but experience tells us that the world is too uncertain to rely on forecasts of single futures.

Forecasting Techniques

What is needed, then, is a general method for creating credible and useful forecasts that convey an appropriate appreciation of the lack of precision involved. There are many techniques for accomplishing this. Some are highly individual, others are group-oriented, some emphasize free thinking, and others are very analytical and structured. Each may have its place. Examples of techniques include the Delphi method for combining expert opinion,[4] the measurement of newsprint as advocated by John Naisbitt,[5] issue analysis as done by certain public affairs groups,[6] the creation of alternative scenarios,[7] and the projection of unexpected events by experts in given fields, such as the Club of 1,000's "Project Outlook."[8]

The forecasting approach recommended in this chapter emphasizes the use of objective data—especially trend data. To this extent, it resembles extrapolation. It adds, however, a strong measure of expert judgment. But unlike prediction, it does not rely on the use of specific scenarios. Instead, it recommends the drawing of implications, which may suggest multiple and even inconsistent pictures of the future. It also recommends explicitly prioritizing the various implications so that the most critical ones receive first consideration for action. Finally, for numerous reasons, the process is structured so as to involve several people who can contribute varying viewpoints and degrees of expertise.

Forecasting Assumptions

All forecasting techniques are based on assumptions, whether or not they are made explicit. Three areas of assumptions are fundamental: the data base used to make the forecasts, the model used to interpret the data, and the criteria used to determine what is important and unimportant to the enterprise. Obviously, a degree of interdependence exists among the three. The view taken here is that the more explicit the underlying assumptions, the more relevant, credible, and useful the scanning activity is likely to be.

Another view emphasized here is that environmental scanning must always fit the needs and operating style of a particular organization. The process is still fairly new and much remains to be learned; consequently, there is no single, correct approach.

Planning Strategic Issues

The term HR planning suffers from an imprecise meaning and can refer to many different processes, including succession planning, skills inventories, computerized workforce "flow" modeling, and strategic issues planning.

Strategic issues planning incorporates several planning approaches that focus on identifying emerging HRM concerns and developing plans to resolve these concerns. Figure 1 illustrates one proven approach to strategic issues planning and shows how environmental scanning is a key element in the process of identifying strategic issues.

Since this chapter is primarily concerned with the application of environmental scanning to strategic issues planning, it is necessary to define what is meant by a strategic issue. First, a strategic issue can be either a problem or an opportunity. A mistaken assumption is that an issue must be negative; that is, a problem or barrier. It can just as well present an important opportunity. Unless this two-sided aspect is recognized, an issue-oriented approach to environmental scanning may miss much of its potential power.

Second, a strategic issue poses a major question relating to the success or failure of an activity or business. This means that the issue is so important that a failure to recognize, understand, and resolve it could result in the activity or business failing to achieve its objectives (or vice versa). In simple terms, a strategic issue is one that could easily keep an HR director or general manager awake at night. This restricted definition of a strategic issue makes it much more likely that the issue will receive the attention necessary for effective action, and that the end result will make a positive, significant difference. If this can be achieved, the planning process, and environmental scanning, will have made a worthwhile contribution to business success and, in the process, will have established its credibility.

Framework for Environmental Scanning

The following discussion covers procedures for implementing an environmental scanning process. First, preliminary considerations, such as which time frame and categories to use in the scanning process, are reviewed. Then, the phases of implementation, from data collection to documentation, are covered step by step. Finally, practical obstacles that can arise during implementation are considered, along with suggestions for overcoming these barriers.

Figure 2 illustrates a logical nine-step process that can be used to do environmental scanning. Although the illustration suggests a

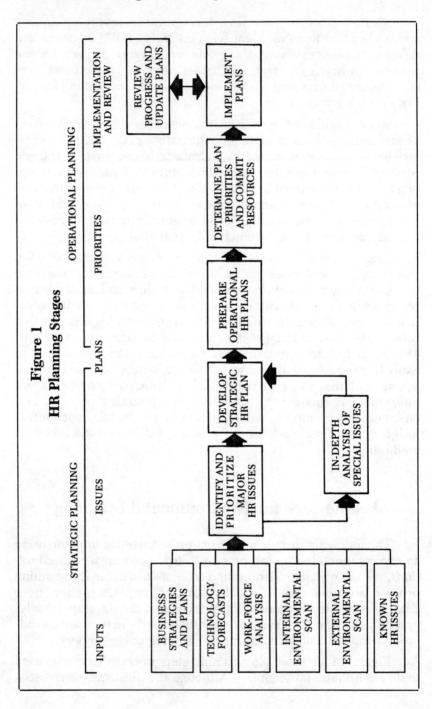

Figure 1
HR Planning Stages

Figure 2
A Process for Environmental Scanning

PLANNING STAGES

Select Time Frame
- ☐ Projection Period
- ☐ Timing of Scan
- ☐ Frequency of Scan

Choose Categories

DATA COLLECTION

☐ Quality	☐ Time Frame
☐ Source	☐ Time Span & Measurement
☐ Relevance	☐ Presentability
☐ Recency	

DATA ANALYSIS

Define Trends
- ☐ Data Inspection
- ☐ Statistical Analyses
- ☐ Graphic Presentation

Project the Future
- ☐ Data Extrapolation
- ☐ Limiting Factors
- ☐ Best-Case, Worst-Case

Predict Consequences
- ☐ Key Organizational Concerns
- ☐ Cross Impact Analysis

Prioritize Implications
- ☐ Likelihood of Occurrence
- ☐ Magnitude of Impact

Identify Issues
- ☐ Input from Decision Makers
- ☐ Cite Examples
- ☐ Pose as Questions

Rank Issues

Document/Disseminate Findings

simple linear process, in practice the various steps usually involve a number of iterations.

Selecting a Time Frame

Once a decision has been made to do environmental scanning, a specific approach must be worked out. An important consideration is the time frame, which comprises three inter-related aspects. The first is the time horizon. Should it be one year, three years, five years, or ten years? An obvious option is to use the same time horizon as the business' strategic and operational planning processes. From a practical standpoint, a very short planning horizon is likely to provide relatively little help since many strategic HR issues require some years to develop, address, and resolve. Conversely, a planning horizon that is too distant will seem irrelevant to immediate business issues and decisions. A three- to five-year horizon is often a suitable period.

A second aspect of time frame concerns the timing of the scanning process. Specifically, when in the planning cycle should the scan be provided? Since a scan should help identify issues for strategic HR planning, the results ought to be available early in the planning process.

The last question concerns the frequency of updating, and this question has no simple answer. One extreme would be to prepare the scan annually, with brief quarterly updates. This requires continuous effort and a commitment of resources that few organizations are prepared to make. The other extreme would be to prepare a scan only once every three to five years, with no intermediate effort or update. This infrequency is likely to undermine the currency and validity of the scan's findings, as well as to assure a lack of continuity and a loss of knowledge that would be detrimental to the overall effort. A major update every one or two years is probably most useful.

Choosing Categories

The first step in a suggested scanning process is to decide which categories or topic areas to select for analysis. Topic areas are broad categories of trends, such as demographics or economics, that are largely defined by conventional technical disciplines. This step facilitates data gathering, analysis, and reporting.

The initial selection of topic areas is probably best done by considering some known issues and making "best guesses" as to important trends in conventional categories. With experience, the initial set of topic areas may be modified if conventional ways of categorizing knowledge fail to match an organization's needs.

While there are many possible topic areas, the following have been found serviceable, at least as a first cut:

- Work-force demographics
- Economic conditions
- Technological developments
- Work-force social trends
- Legal and regulatory environment
- Regional and local characteristics and
- Human resource management

The last area, human resource management, deals with responses to other trends rather than a set of independent trends. It is included, however, because of its special relevance to strategic HRM and the need to stay abreast of competitive developments.

Each topic area might include a number of selected trends and address both national and international considerations. Alternatively, a separate category labelled "international developments" might be established.

Collecting Data

The second step in the environmental scanning process is to gather data. There are an enormous number and variety of possible data sources. They differ drastically in quality, and some of the most useful ones are not well known. Therefore, the primary problem at this step is deciding what information to use and what to ignore or discard. While a number of factors may help to guide this decision, the following offer useful screens.

Quality

Are the data valid or reliable? Two key guides to data quality are the source of the data (discussed below) and the method of collection. Does the report describe how the data were gathered and analyzed? If so, this can help in evaluating their validity and reliability.

Source

Is the source a reputable organization or authority with expert knowledge in the field? Is it an original or secondary source? Since secondary sources may not report the data accurately or completely, primary sources are preferable.

Relevance

Do the data really go to the heart of the condition or trend of concern? Since an overwhelming amount of information is often available, marginally relevant material should be bypassed.

Recency

Are the data really current? Even though many trends evolve relatively slowly, conditions sometimes change very rapidly. Up-to-date information is more credible for planning purposes.

Time Frame

Do the data, especially trend data, fit reasonably with the time scale of the organization's planning horizons?

Time Span and Measurement

A single data point does not establish a trend. Within limits, the larger the number of data points that have been measured or gathered in the same way, the clearer the trend is likely to be and the easier it may be to spot important changes.

Presentability

Are the data easily understood and assessed? Do they tell a story and is it convincing? The ultimate objective of the scanning process is action. Some forms of data and some methods of presentation—usually simple and direct ones—seem almost to demand action. Others seem more to obscure and confuse the picture.

Defining Trends

The third step is to define trends from the data that have been gathered. Trend definition abstracts and simplifies the data. It facilitates further analysis and communication, but the data invariably lose detail. Thus, it can conceal as well as reveal.

Sometimes, simple inspection of the data will show the trends. More complex techniques may be used, but many of these would probably be "overkill." A variety of statistical methods, for example, can determine lines of best fit, define confidence bands, or separate out the effects of two or more interacting factors. However, for environmental scanning, such mathematical precision is usually not needed or even appropriate. Graphic analysis and presentation normally will suffice.

Projecting the Future

Difficulties occur in projecting trends into the future. Some trends have obvious constraints, but the point at which these limits will be reached is not always clear. Sometimes the form of measurement itself imposes constraints. For example, the mathematical limit on the percentage of the work force that can be female is 100 percent, but, of course, practical economic and social factors will keep that limit from being reached. The question is how to determine and represent the limit.

Answering this question usually involves educated guesswork. Good trend data will often show changes, such as a tapering off, that can help suggest ultimate limits. However, real-world data are almost always "noisy" and contain fluctuations that may obscure underlying trends. Furthermore, real-world trends often interact in complex ways, so that simple extrapolations, whether straight-line or otherwise, may not be valid.

In light of these difficulties, the manner of presenting trend data can be important. One technique is to show confidence bands around the data when they are presented graphically. Projections might be represented in "best case, worst case" fashion, along with any known natural limits, and/or alternative scenarios. The point is, there are a variety of techniques that can be used to represent uncertainties and limits when making projections and care should be exercised to select the most appropriate one.

Finally, when using graphs or other forms of pictorial representation to show data and trends, good principles of presentation should be followed to avoid misleading the user. A common example of faulty presentation is a bar graph that lacks a zero base or does not clearly show that the vertical scale has been truncated and therefore exaggerates differences or degree of change over time.

Predicting Consequences

Once good data have been obtained and trends established, significant implications or likely consequences must be defined. This is a step where experience, creativity, and multiple views can all play a role. While some trends may have general implications and consequences, the real key is to specify the important implications for the organization involved. Implications for a particular organization will vary as a function of geographic location, business conditions, strategies, work-force characteristics, and a host of other factors. Therefore, this task cannot be safely left to uninvolved persons or organizations, such as consultants, scanning associations, or newsletters, although they may provide very good ideas and insights. The remoteness of such external sources may explain why the implications they suggest sometimes seem relatively trivial, even though they may be accurate.

As an example, consider the well-publicized trend of migration in the United States from the industrial Northeast to the South and Southwest. The implications obviously are quite different for a company in Boston than for one in Phoenix. Furthermore, differing implications can occur for two companies in Massachusetts that have different skill requirements or growth rates.

A complicating factor is that trends do not operate in isolation. As they interact, their consequences may be amplified, diminished, or transformed. It may or may not be worthwhile to evaluate the probable results of such interactions. One approach that may prove useful is "cross-impact analysis."[9] This is simply a matrix or grid that shows judgments regarding possible significant interactions between trends. However, because of the complexities and uncertainties involved, any more elaborate method is not likely to add much value, and may, in fact, cause confusion. Also, since a "trend" is really an abstraction and simplification of something that may be quite complex, defining and evaluating interactions among these abstractions moves the analysis one step further away from the underlying reality.

Prioritizing Implications

Once significant implications or likely consequences have been defined, the next step is to prioritize them. It often is easy to create long lists of possible consequences, but unless such lists are pruned, they will bury the process in excessive detail or trivia. Eliminating irrelevant or relatively unimportant implications basically is a matter of judgment, but several factors help guide these decisions.

A basic consideration in prioritizing implications is the likelihood of occurrence. Since environmental scanning addresses future implications of current conditions or events, the process is inherently uncertain, and this uncertainty should be made explicit. Otherwise, the implications reported will likely take the form of prophecies or definite statements about some future condition and thus can appear either foolish or misleading. The question is how best to convey this uncertainty. It could be done descriptively, graphically, or numerically, but the method should avoid making overly precise statements about the degree of uncertainty since this can also mislead.

In addition to likelihood, priorities may also be based on the magnitude of potential impact and the estimated time frame in which the impact will be felt. These additional factors can be explicitly addressed as part of the priority-setting process; exactly how is a topic that will be addressed later in this chapter.

Since judgment is involved in determining priorities, using some form of group process may prove helpful. This provides multiple viewpoints and may also educate the participants; both of these features will facilitate follow-through during plan implementation. A possible framework for prioritizing implications is described later.

Identifying Issues

The sixth step in environmental scanning is to define issues. An issue may arise from a single implication or a combination of them. Here again, judgment is a key ingredient.

Strategic HR issues were defined earlier as involving either problems or opportunities of organizational significance. The question at this point is: How does one select the most important issues and develop issue statements? This is a critical step, since it forms the foundation for much of what occurs in strategic issue planning. It is also one that, in the author's experience, tends to be done poorly.

Three reasons may explain this. One is impatience. Managers typically are busy, action-oriented people who have many areas of responsibility calling for their attention. They want to get on with things and tend to focus on steps to resolve an issue rather than take sufficient time to be sure that the nature of the issue is really understood.

A second apparent reason is a presumption that the words used to define an issue mean the same thing to all concerned. For example, an issue might be characterized during a meeting as "shortage of management talent," and the general manager and his or her staff might all nod their heads in agreement. Yet one person might be recalling the problem experienced in filling a field sales manager slot in a large city, another might be thinking of a shortage of back-ups to the general manager's position, and a third might be considering the poor performance of last year's college recruiting program. Each of these might reflect quite different causes and implications. Obviously, a lack of common understanding about the nature of the issue will impede effective action to address it, especially if the action requires integrated effort by different persons or functions.

A third difficulty in issue definition, related to the second, is a superficial understanding of an issue. It is not unusual for an issue to be something other than appears on the surface. The difficulty of filling the field sales manager position mentioned above might relate not to a shortage of candidates, but to the high cost of housing, or to local economic conditions that make the area an unpromising location, or to the tyrannical reputation of the hiring supervisor.

A number of steps can be taken to minimize these problems and improve the quality of issue definition. The following discussion highlights several which are particularly critical.

Include Key Decision Makers

Since, by definition, a strategic HR issue is of major importance to an organization's success, a number of key persons and functions will inevitably be involved in its resolution. Therefore, it is important that these persons and functions agree on the nature and importance of the issue and the steps necessary to address it. The best way to achieve this is to have key people directly involved in the process of issue definition, perhaps through one or more group meetings.

Cite Examples

To ensure that an issue is commonly understood, it is useful to list specific examples or data that illustrate its existence and potential effect. By the time six to a dozen examples or data points have been brought out, the issue usually is more clearly delineated and understood. The issue also may begin to take on a different character than it seemed to have originally. For example, difficulty in filling an opening for a manager in a large city, when no similar situations exist elsewhere, may indicate that the problem relates to conditions unique to that one location. And even if several similar situations can be listed, the causes might be unique to each. On the other hand, a problem could be generic; for example, promising candidates may see greater opportunities in moving to other organizations at a particular point of their careers.

Pose Issues as Questions

Another step that can facilitate common understanding is to write the definition of an issue in the form of an action-oriented question. This does several things. It describes the essence of the issue more completely than a short phrase could. It captures the definition of the issue developed by the group to serve as a reference for the future. Finally, it provides a natural transition into defining strategies to address the issue. For example, if the issue is "supply of management talent," the question might be, "How can we assure an adequate number of qualified candidates for each opening at the director level and above over the next five years?"

Worked to this level of understanding, it could take an hour or so for a general manager and his or her staff to agree on the definition of a single issue and to write one such question. In fact, if the process takes much less time, it may indicate that the issue did not receive adequate consideration.

Ranking Issues

The next step in environmental scanning is, once again, to prioritize. If a number of potential issues have survived to this point, some further culling and prioritizing will likely be required. It is not unusual to pare an initial list of one or two dozen issues by 50 percent or more. Although the rejected items may merit attention, they often are clearly of lesser priority or can be handled on a routine basis.

Once the initial list is reduced, the remaining issues should be put in priority order. All the various processes that might be used for this purpose rely on management judgment and share the same ultimate goal—namely, to identify a few really key issues for action. A point to keep in mind is that the external environment is only one source of possible HR issues.

Documenting and Disseminating the Findings

The final step in environmental scanning is to document the process and results and disseminate them to planners, managers, and other users. Options range from a very simple summary that shows the trends that led to the selected issues to a comprehensive reference document or even a set of parallel documents matched to different user groups. (More is said about the format and content of presentations and reports later in this chapter.)

Whatever the level of detail, it is always useful to list key assumptions underlying the effort. All too often, basic assumptions are not articulated or self-evident, even to the persons developing the scan. Some examples of assumptions include the following:

- The organization will continue with its present mission and structure.

- No major discontinuities will occur in relevant aspects of the environment.

- The organization will continue to operate under the current set of business strategies.

- Certain trends were considered and judged unimportant to the strategic HR planning process and therefore are not addressed.

When assumptions are documented, users of the scan report have a better picture of why certain trends and implications are presented and can better judge the significance of results. This perspective may also prove helpful the next time the scanning process is conducted. Furthermore, if some scan users disagree with one or more of the assumptions, documenting scan assumptions can reveal such differences of opinion.

For some purposes, it will suffice to carry the documentation only through the implications stage. For example, a basic scan that will be used by several different groups or divisions may offer implications in the form of examples and suggestions, since each individual organization ultimately must define and prioritize its own specific implications and issues.

Practical Concerns

When implementing the environmental scanning steps just described, a number of practical considerations need to be taken into account. The following discussion addresses some of these issues and the specific ways in which they affect the scanning process.

Form and Content

The process and results of scanning can be presented in many different ways and in varying degrees of depth. The choices basically depend on audience and use.

Form. Most scanning efforts result in some form of document, oral report, or both. Sometimes findings are presented in two, three, or even more versions, such as separate domestic and international documents with or without executive summaries, supplemental slide or overhead transparency presentations, or even a videotaped report.

Content. With respect to content, or questions of scope and level of detail, the options range from very simple to great detail. The former involves only a brief summary of key facts, while the latter includes extensive material on each trend, issue, and implication, including specific references to sources.

Obviously, a connection exists between form and content. Written reports can be either simple (for example, executive summaries) or detailed (for example, documented scan reports). Videotaped and oral presentations, however, of necessity must be kept simple.

Audience. Executives generally prefer conciseness over complexity; thus, brief executive summaries or presentations with "just the facts" are particularly appropriate for them. For example, each trend might be stated in a single sentence, followed by a few key implications and issues, perhaps with an indication of probable timing and consequences. The executives' staffs, however, may require further detail in case questions arise. For both groups, the general rule is to begin with the "bare bones" and introduce more detail over time as experience is gained with scanning and planning processes.

When HR specialists constitute the intended audience, scan reports are called for, and these should provide greater detail and document sources more thoroughly than usually would be the case for either executives or their staffs.

If a scan is to serve other staff functions, such as public affairs or finance, it will need both greater breadth and depth. Inviting specialists from these other functions to participate in the design and implementation of the scanning process helps to ensure that the scan contains relevant issues, clear implications, and suitable report format and content.

Use. Along with audience, a scan's intended use must be considered when choosing format and content. For example, a scan intended primarily to support an annual planning process should include only basic data that can serve as "homework" reading for the planning meetings. A scan intended to have year-round use, on the other hand, should be more complete and may require multiple oral presentations, as well as thorough written documentation. Each use, however, may involve only excerpts from the more extensive report.

As is probably evident, all of the foregoing considerations are interrelated. The important point is to consider each approach when planning an environmental scan and again after each run-through. As experience is gained, modifications will no doubt occur in response to successes and failures, and to changes in users' needs over time.

Information Sources

Given the innumerable potential sources of data for environmental scanning, it is necessary to be judicious and selective in choosing the most helpful ones. A major consideration, as noted earlier, is whether to rely on primary or secondary sources. Primary sources report original data and findings which the authors themselves usually have gathered or measured. Secondary sources summarize or interpret original data that have been reported elsewhere.

Primary sources have the advantage of giving direct access to original data. From this standpoint, they have greater credibility than secondary sources. On the other hand, secondary sources may yield a broader, more integrated perspective on some event or trend. In other words, each type of data source has its strengths and weaknesses. The bottom line is that the persons responsible for environmental scanning must evaluate each source on its merits and relevance to the purpose at hand.

There are no simple rules for doing this. In general, one must consider the credibility, expertness, and possible biases of the source. Factors internal to the data or information, such as the methodology used, may also indicate its reliability. With experience, it also becomes possible to judge the credibility of a source by comparing its consistency to other sources of similar data. However, unconventional findings should not be discarded just because they are unconventional. They may, in fact, prove to be among the most useful.

While relevant data may be found in many places, Appendix 1 of this chapter lists some sources which have been found, through experience, to be particularly useful.

Information Extraction

Once decisions regarding format, content, and information sources have been made, there still is the matter of how best to filter and integrate raw data into the desired information base. This process is one of selection and refinement and can be accomplished in several ways.

Internal options. One approach is to provide internal staff to gather, evaluate, and extract data. This, of course, can be costly. In addition, it may not be feasible to assemble a staff with expertise in all areas of a broad-based scan. Given time, however, one person may become sufficiently knowledgeable to handle a full range of topic areas. Another possibility is to use one person, probably part-time, to gather information, but conscript various staff members to do most of the filtering and evaluation of the data. An advantage of an in-house scanning expert is that this person can maintain up-to-date files with material on each topic area of interest. These files can then serve as an ongoing reference source for the organization when more current or in-depth information is required.

A second approach is to establish an internal network of experts to gather, interpret, and disseminate refined information. This develops and maintains internal expertise with no staff increase. It also facilitates understanding and use of the scan by actively involving more people in the organization. Any sizable organization will likely have individuals who routinely follow developments in most, if not all, of the selected topic areas anyway. Since these individuals may hold differing viewpoints and use inconsistent methods, a focal person or group is needed to manage the process, prepare or edit reports, and ensure that the total effort fills the needs of the HR planning process.

External options. Another approach is to go outside by hiring a consultant or buying into a scanning service. The trade-off here likely entails gaining expertise while losing relevance and/or increasing cost. Consultants or organizations specializing in environmental scanning may have well-developed data sources and analytical capabilities. On the other hand, an "off-the-shelf" scan report may not fit the needs of a specific business or organization. Sometimes outside experts can customize the scan, but usually at additional expense. Further, an organization that purchases a scan loses the benefit gained by having its own people work through the data, and thus forfeits an important educational opportunity.

Several businesses may join together to sponsor or conduct environmental scanning activities, thereby pooling resources, sharing expertise, and reducing the out-of-pocket costs of any one member. This is the approach of the Environmental Scanning Association, for example, whose members have included such companies as Atlantic-Richfield Co., Boise-Cascade Corp., Champion International Corp., Chase Manhattan Bank, GTE Service Corp., Honeywell Inc., International Paper Co., Merrill Lynch & Co., Northrop Corp., Westinghouse Electric Corp., and Xerox Corp. A major benefit of such a consortium is the sharing of differing views regarding the significance of trends, implications, and issues, as well as the merits of proposed strategies. Relying on a consortium to prepare a scanning document, however, has the same drawbacks as the "off-the-shelf" approach.

While each organization must decide on its own approach, experience has shown that a combination of methods can work particularly well. For example, an organization might establish an internal network that feeds information to one designated person, perhaps a graduate student, who maintains current scan files on a part-time basis. At the same time, the organization might participate in a cross-industry scanning group.

Priority Setting

As previously indicated, prioritizing implications and issues is usually necessary to focus attention on only the most important ones. One particularly useful method uses likelihood, impact, and timing as criteria for setting priorities.

Likelihood. This approach first asks: How likely is it that a suggested implication or issue will, in fact, occur? Answering this question requires some way of indicating the degree of likelihood or uncertainty.

One way is to provide an explicit indication of the estimated degree of uncertainty associated with each specific implication or issue. This might be done through qualifying statements, a numeric scale, or a verbal scale. If a scale is adopted, it is probably wise to limit the scale to a few broad categories, rather than to try more refinement than the process may warrant. A simple three- or five-point ordinal scale might do very well, as long as users agree on the meaning or definition of the various points on the scale.

Impact. A second consideration in setting priorities is the anticipated magnitude of impact. Some consequences may be quite minor, while others could threaten the very existence of the business. Here again, a simple three- or five-point scale may suffice, although, as before, it needs to have agreed-upon definitions of the chosen categories. For example, a high-impact implication or issue might mean one that threatens the long-term survival of the business or, alternatively, provides a rare and significant opportunity to enhance the prospects of the business. At the other end of the scale, a low-impact implication or issue might be one that, however unusual, can be handled in a routine manner.

Time. Implications and issues that meet likelihood and impact criteria should also be evaluated on yet a third dimension—time. Some implications and issues need to be addressed immediately, others may require only contingency planning but no immediate action, still others may need nothing more than monitoring. An agreed-upon set of categories for sorting implications and issues according to time urgency can facilitate this process.

Cross-evaluation. Figure 3 illustrates a simple matrix for establishing priorities. Likelihood and impact are both ranked simply as high, medium, or low. The time dimension is scaled according to when action needs to be taken—immediate (for example, this year), mid-term (for example, next year), or long-term.

If only immediate implications or issues are considered, they fall into one of nine cells. High-impact implications or issues that have a high or intermediate likelihood of occurring clearly should be addressed in the current planning cycle. Likewise, intermediate-impact implications or issues that are very likely to occur also need attention fairly soon. Implications or issues of intermediate likelihood and impact might simply require monitoring or low-level contingency actions. At the other extreme, implications or issues judged low in both likelihood and impact can probably be dropped from top-level planning, and left to lower levels of the organization to address. The same will likely hold true for implications or issues with low impact but intermediate or even high likelihood.

Action on implications or issues with intermediate or long-term time frames can perhaps be postponed, but here again, preparatory activity or monitoring may be needed. Part of this decision depends on the lead time required for effective action. In some cases, lead time may span years, so that even implications or issues that will not become critical for several years or longer may require some current action.

Implications or issues that have low likelihood but high impact constitute special cases. Research on decision making has demonstrated that people tend to treat highly improbable events as though they will never occur. While this tendency makes the world easier to deal with, it can literally be fatal. Thus, in environmental scanning, it is wise to address any implication or issue that is categorized as high impact but unlikely with special consideration. Some form of preventive action, contingency plan, monitoring process, or other measure might be a good idea.

As suggested earlier, prioritization usually is needed at several stages of the scanning process. For example, even after issues have been prioritized and a few are selected for attention, resources may limit the actions that can be taken to deal with them. This may indicate a need for different strategies, for deferral of action, for assigning additional or different resources, or even for reprioritizing the issues. The overall scanning and HR planning process, therefore, like most planning processes, needs to be iterative.

Figure 3
Issue Prioritization Matrix

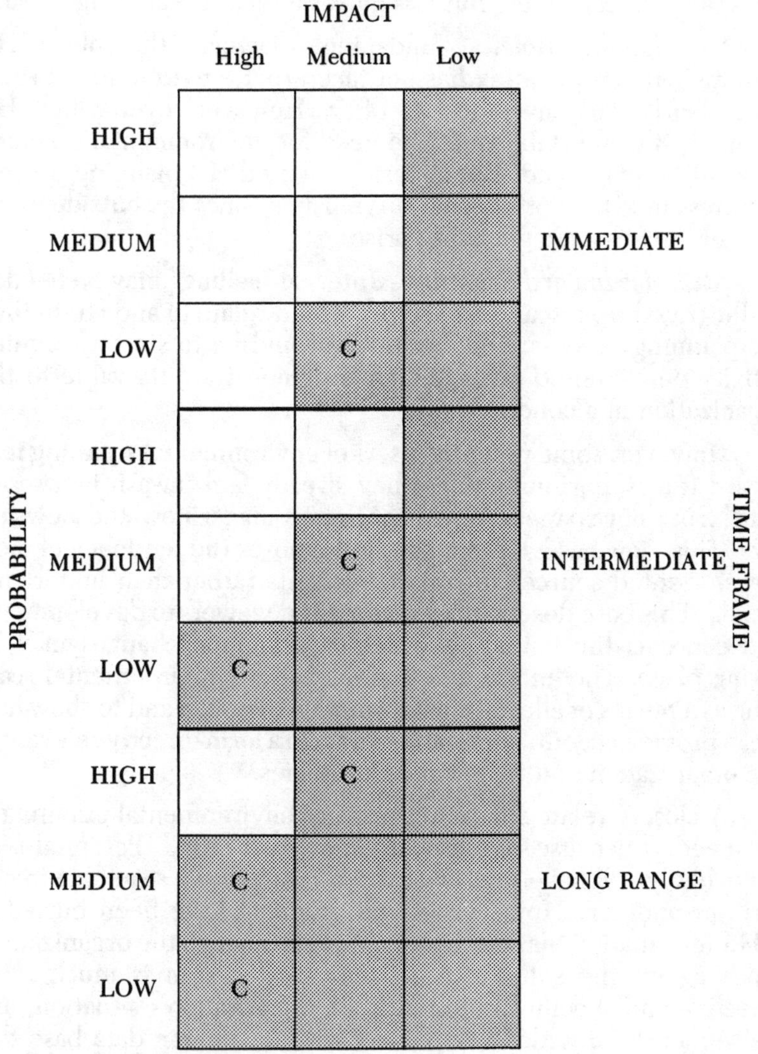

C = Consider contingency plan

Additional Considerations

Another practical aspect of environmental scanning relates to the readiness of the organization to accept and use it. To some extent this is a "political" issue, but this makes it no less real or significant.

HR Planning Role. A fundamental factor is the role of HR planning. If HR planning has not taken root, environmental scanning clearly will have little to offer. However, even when HR planning is well established, the need for environmental scanning may not be perceived. But an issue-oriented HR planning process requires some type of external surveillance, since the outside world is where many strategic issues arise.

Attitudes toward Scanning. Internal "selling" may be needed to illustrate how a scanning activity would relate to and strengthen the planning process. One approach would be to start a scanning activity on a limited basis and thus demonstrate its value to the organization in a concrete way.

However, some potential users of environmental scanning may regard it as superfluous since they already feel "awash in a sea of data" from newspapers, television, news magazines, and newsletters. This view has a lot of merit, but ignores the tendency of most news-oriented sources to report incidents rather than underlying trends. This both desensitizes readers and viewers to developments and conceals the extent to which fundamental changes may be taking place. The antidote is to demonstrate environmental scanning as a means of alleviating information overload and to show how it can provide cogent, summarized data in a form directly relevant to the organization and its business strategies.

A closely related view argues that environmental scanning is not needed because "we already know that stuff." Potential scan users likely will have previously seen much of the scan data in one form or another. However, it will probably have been buried in other information that had little or no relevance to the organization. Once again, the solution is to show that a scan is much more selective and specifically tuned to an organization's situation, and consequently provides key players with a common data base that facilitates decision making. It is important, of course, that the data base and related thinking not become too "inbred."

Short-term Orientation. Industry's well-publicized tendency to focus on short-term actions and results also can inhibit interest in environmental scanning. Shareholders, especially institutional ones, want immediate results and business executives feel pressured to produce results this quarter, next quarter, and certainly within the year. However, environmental trends and their implications usually evolve over years, not months. As a practical matter, there may be relatively little that can be done to resolve this obstacle, except to show how some current problems might have been avoided or more easily resolved through recognizing and addressing trends.

Indirect Outcomes. Another factor concerns the position of scanning in the planning chain. The problem here is that no direct results are likely to be attributable to environmental scanning. Instead, scanning is one element in a series, each step of which must be successful to achieve results. In brief, the process is as follows: A scan helps identify major issues, initial planning determines what action to take on these issues, the plan must be implemented, and, finally, desired outcomes must follow. The obvious conclusion is that scanning in absence of the other steps cannot be very useful. Therefore, attention needs to be given to achieving success at each of the steps.

Time Span. One final consideration is the matter of continuity and time. An environmental scanning activity probably cannot be very effective unless it is carried out over a matter of years. It takes time to build up a data base, to establish scanning as a routine part of the planning process, and to build user understanding and facility in employing scanning data. It is important, therefore, to allow sufficient time for the necessary learning and development to take place.

A Real-Life Example

The following discussion of an actual case may prove useful in illustrating how one company developed an environmental scanning process. The company is Honeywell Inc., which identified a need for HR planning and developed an issue-oriented process during the early 1980s. Early in this development, Honeywell recognized the necessity of including some form of external environmental scanning in the planning process.

Start-up Phase

A small team undertook to explore alternative approaches to environmental scanning and to select the one which seemed most suitable. Through reviewing many different articles and scanning approaches, the team defined broad subject categories to be monitored and identified specific important trends within each category. The company then hired a graduate student on a part-time basis to identify data sources, perform the actual gathering of data, establish and maintain a set of data files on each trend, and respond to inquiries about scan data. Given the importance of these functions, the student was hired for a long-term position.

Data Collection Process

The scanning process used was a simple one. Planning team members voluntarily reviewed various publications, such as *The Wall Street Journal*, on a continuing basis. Any especially relevant information or article was clipped or copied and sent to the student aide who simply placed it in the appropriate file folder. Meanwhile, the team developed further data sources through subscriptions to selected publications, such as the *Monthly Labor Review*, which likewise were reviewed for significant articles. The review process emphasized hard data—especially data which revealed important trends—and knowledgeable interpretations of the data, whether singly or in combination.

Over a period of months, a very useful data base developed. A quick review of the topic files easily revealed which ones were accumulating too much data and required some culling, and which ones called for library research or pursuing alternative sources to round out the data base.

Document Design

When the team began to develop an environmental scan document, a good file of data and implications had accumulated on most of the trends, and often the information included differing viewpoints. Different members of the planning team took responsibility for drafting a section of the scan document, a process made much easier by the availability of a solid base of data. Drafts were circulated among planning team members and then were discussed in review meetings that provided a forum for reassessing the trends, key implications, and priorities. By this time, incidentally, the planning team members had become fairly expert on the status of important trends and were usually able to move quickly to a consensus that was well grounded in facts.

The question of format received considerable attention. After various approaches were proposed and debated, the end decision was to publish two versions of a scan report: a detailed document and a shorter executive summary. The same format was used in both reports and included a short statement, boxed at the top of the page, that described the trend and important implications or consequences.

Below the trend statement, a graph or diagram presented the objective information, including its source, which served as the basis for the trend statement or at least confirmed the existence of the trend. Next, there were a series of implication statements, sometimes accompanied by additional data, that were designed to be both significant and suggestive. Rather than lay out all of the implications, or even all of the major ones, the intent was to trigger the users' thinking. This reflected the view that for implications to have real meaning, they had to be defined, evaluated, and planned for by local organizations throughout the company. To facilitate more detailed study, references were given at the end of each trend description.

Within the scan document, related trends were grouped together under a topic category (e.g., demographics), each separated by a tab. A summary table at the front of the document further assisted easy reference. The entire design was intended to facilitate the use of the scan material. For example, a quick overview could easily be performed by skimming through the document and focusing only on the boxed statements. The graphic presentations gave an easy-to-read picture of the trend, its magnitude, and its rate, as well as objective data confirming the trend statement.

Figure 4 shows the organization of the scan report and lists the specific trends that were covered. An example of a trend description is given in Figure 5.

Dissemination and Use

The report was published internally and distributed to senior executives, heads of operating units, key HR staff members, and various corporate staff functions. External distribution was limited since some of the data and implications were directly relevant to the company's business directions and strategies.

As intended, a number of operating units used the report in generating their HR plans. In some cases, planners made specific reference to trends and drew division-specific implications. The

Figure 4
Environmental Scanning Report

Example: TABLE OF CONTENTS

Figure 4 continued

VII. U.S. Regional/Metropolitan Characteristics
    7.0 Overview
    7.1 Local Variation in U.S. Labor Costs
    7.2 Regional Variations in Labor Supply
    7.3 State Political-Economic Climates

VIII. International Factors
    8.0 Overview
    8.1 International Labor Costs
    8.2 The Shift to a World Economy
    8.3 Collective Bargaining
    8.4 Trans-Border Data Flow
    8.5 Japanese Competition
    8.6 European Economic Community (EEC)
    8.7 International Business Policy Organizations
    8.8 International Labor Union Activity

IX. Human Resource Management
    9.0 Overview
    9.1 Flexible Compensation
    9.2 Work Force Stability
    9.3 Productivity Programs/Quality Programs
    9.4 Quality of Work Life

Source: Reprinted with permission from Honeywell, Inc., *Human Resource Trends*, 1982.

trends report also served as background for the development of a corporate-wide HR strategies document. Somewhat surprisingly, the environmental scan document became a reference for purposes not originally considered. For example, company executives used it as a source of data for some of their presentations to external audiences.

Since publication of the first scan report, revised versions have been prepared and issued almost yearly, with modifications taking place in off years. Several separate "international scan reports" have also been published, and recently, the company issued a single document covering both domestic and overseas trends and implications. More recently, Honeywell has begun to rely more on scan reports prepared by various consulting organizations under the sponsorship of a scanning association which Honeywell helped to initiate.[10] These reports are then modified and distributed internally.

Figure 5
Example of a Trend Report

2.2 FEMALE PARTICIPATION IN THE LABOR FORCE

Women have been entering the labor force at a faster rate than men. Projections show the growth rate of women in the labor force for the next ten years to be twice that of men. This will intensify the significance of concerns such as career development, flexible benefits, working hours, and relocation of two-worker families.

SUPPORTING DATA

FEMALE PARTICIPATION RATE
AND FEMALES AS A PERCENTAGE
OF THE TOTAL LABOR FORCE,
1970–1990

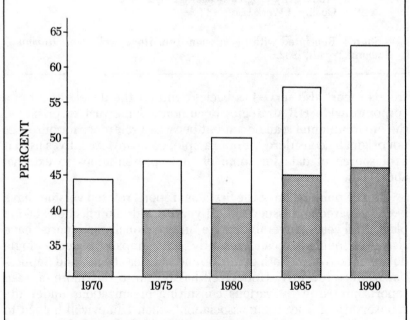

☐ = FEMALE PARTICIPATION RATE
▦ = FEMALES AS A % OF TOTAL LABOR FORCE

Figure 5 continued

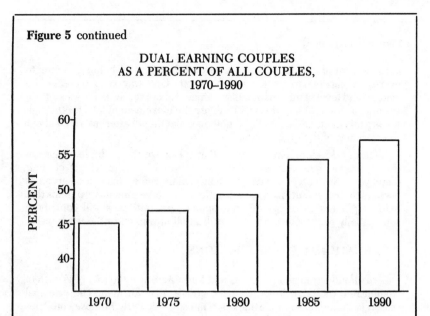

DUAL EARNING COUPLES
AS A PERCENT OF ALL COUPLES,
1970–1990

IMPLICATIONS

Women's labor force participation is expected to continue to increase, accounting for two of every three additions to the labor force in the U.S. through 1995. Because of this, many of the issues raised by the increase of women in the work force during the 1970's will be intensified in the 1980's.

Married women are entering the labor force in ever increasing numbers at younger ages. The result may be better career opportunities and higher incomes as this segment of the work force matures.

Another aspect of this trend is the so called "baby echo." The baby echo refers to the increasing number of baby boom women in the work force who are having children. In order to alleviate long child-care interruptions in service that would prove damaging both to the employee's career and the organization's effectiveness, a number of alternatives to the normal work week are being utilized. These include "flex time" and the use of part-time schedules for professionals. Another approach is that of allowing the employee to work at the office half of the day to perform duties that must be carried out at the work place and at home the rest of the day. At present, the latter policy only appears to be used in the case of managers and professionals, but it is likely that such alternatives will become available to many women in the work force.

Women hold only a small number of the managerial and professional jobs (only 25 percent of all managers are women), and women managers earn on average only 55 percent of the amount earned by men in management. There will be pressure to change institutional structures which thwart the

Figure 5 continued

advancement of females. There are several strategies for helping women to overcome barriers to female advancement. One way is to increase the amount and level of information disseminated about the available jobs within the organization. Doing this will facilitate the movement of females through the organization, and should also help to make them better informed about the workings of the organization.

Career development programs that recognize the multiple aspects of career success will help organizations better utilize the talents of their employees. Stereotypical attitudes concerning women have also served as barriers to their full utilization. Educational and experimental programs that help employees to recognize and modify these attitudes will contribute substantially to the more effective utilization of women in the work place.

INTERNATIONAL CONSIDERATIONS

In all industrialized countries and Latin America, the rate of growth of women into the labor force has been greater than for men. The principal reason is the increase in participation rates, particularly in those countries where rates are currently below 50%.

In Europe, female unemployment is likely to increase more than for men. The principal reason is that many of the jobs are part-time and, at a time of recession, it is the women's jobs which have been the first to go. By 1986, with the possible upturn in the economy and the reduced total number entering the workforce the situation should start to level out. One key factor is that fewer women are trade unionists and the unions' first loyalty is to the male employees. Nonetheless, female expectations remain and will impact employers when the economy picks up.

As in the U.S., trends will need to be reflected in career development programs, post-maternity retraining, provision of child day-care centers and, especially with the advent of the "office of the future," work at home. A further consideration will be resistance to relocation.

ADDITIONAL REFERENCES

Economist (The), June 13, 1981.

Management Review, July, 1981.

Personnel Administrator, October, 1981.

"Women in Management," U.S. Department of Labor, 1980.

"Working Wives and Mothers," *Monthly Labor Review*, September, 1981.

"More Young Wives Are Entering Work Force," *Minneapolis Star & Tribune*, August 16, 1982, p. 3.

Figure 5 continued

"Working Around Motherhood," *Business Week*, May 24, 1982, p. 188.

"The 1995 Labor Force: A First Look," *Economic Projections to 1990*, U.S. Department of Labor (BLS), March, 1982.

Source: Reprinted with permission from Honeywell, Inc., *Human Resource Trends*, 1982.

Conclusion

While a number of companies have conducted environmental scans to support HR planning for several years, the activity is still either very new or nonexistent in most organizations. On the other hand, environmental studies of external trends and developments is certainly not new, and different fields have developed a variety of approaches to anticipate future developments as a guide to current action. Although the HRM field has tended to lag in such efforts, it now appears that, for a number of reasons, environmental scanning will become an increasingly important part of strategic HRM in the future.

The dominant role of the United States in international business and commerce has clearly diminished in recent years. We now compete in a global marketplace and industrial production is shifting more and more to third-world countries. External forces have become increasingly important influences on business management decisions, including those pertaining to people management.

Given this condition, professional HR managers cannot afford to ignore external trends and consequences that relate to the people side of business. Environmental scanning can be a major vehicle for helping HR professionals to become knowledgeable about these external forces and their implications for strategic HRM.

While HR environmental scanning is still in the early stages of development, leading companies' experience has already demonstrated that such scans are both feasible and practical. A great deal of valuable information is available, along with effective ways of evaluating it to identify significant trends and HR implications. Properly used, environmental scans can add significant value to the HR planning process. The real challenge at this point is to make environmental scanning accepted and effective within the realities of a specific organization and its planning processes.

◆

Notes

1. Fombrun.
2. Kruzic
3. Fowles.
4. Linstone and Turoff.
5. Naisbitt.
6. Brown.

7. Wack.
8. Enzer (in various issues of *New Management*).
9. Gordon and Hayward.
10. Environmental Scanning Association.

Editor's Note: In addition to the References shown below, there are other significant sources of information and ideas on external environmental scanning.

Books
Aguilar, F.J. 1987. *Scanning the Business Environment*. New York: Macmillan.

Guth, W.E., ed. 1985. *Handbook of Business Strategy*. Boston: Warren, Gorham & Lamont.

O'Toole, J. 1985. *Vanguard Management*. New York: Doubleday & Co.

Organizations
Human Resource Planning Society, P.O. Box 2553, Grand Central Station, New York, NY 10163.

◆

References

Brown, J.K. 1981. *Guidelines for Managing Corporate Issues Programs*. Conference Board Report No. 795. New York: The Conference Board.

Environmental Scanning Association, % Peter Miller, Champion International Corp., One Champion Plaza, Stamford, CT 06921.

Enzer, S., ed. "Project Outlook." *New Management* (various issues). New York: John Wiley & Sons.

Fowles, J. 1978. *Handbook of Futures Research*. Westport, CT: Greenwood Press.

Gordon, T.J., and H. Hayward. 1968. "Initial Experiments with the Cross-Impact Method of Forecasting." *Futures*, Vol. 1, No. 2 (December): 100–116.

Kruzic, P.G., 1978. "Forecasting Modeling" in R.K. Jain and B.L. Hutchings, eds., *Environmental Impact Analysis: Emerging Issues in Planning*. Chicago: University of Illinois Press.

Linstone, H.A., and M. Turoff, eds. 1975. *The Delphi Method: Techniques and Applications*. Reading, MA: Addison-Wesley.

Naisbitt, J. 1982. *Megatrends*. New York: Warner Books.

Wack, P. 1985. "Scenarios: Shooting the Rapids." *Harvard Business Review*, Vol. 63, No. 6 (November-December): 139–150.

————— ♦ —————

Appendix 1

Some Environmental Scan Data Sources

American Demographics
Appliance Manufacturer
Assembly Engineering
Bureau of the Census reports
Business Conditions Digest
*Business Week**
Computerworld
Conference Board reports
Datamation
The Economist
Electronics Business
Employment and Earnings
Engineering Manpower bulletins
Federal Reserve bulletins
Forbes
Fortune
Future Survey
The Futurist
Harvard Business Review
HR Planning Newsletter
*Human Resources Network**
*Human Resource Planning**
IEEE News
Industry Week
Information
Iron Age
The Kiplinger Washington Letter
Management Review
*Monthly Labor Review**
*New Management**
The Numbers News
Occupational Outlook Handbook
*Public Opinion**
Psychology Today
Technology
Technology Review
U.S. News & World Report
*Wall Street Journal**
Work in America Institute reports

*Most useful publications

❖

1.4

Utility Analysis

John W. Boudreau

What do HRM decisions contribute to organizational objectives? Are organizational investments in HRM programs—pay for knowledge, enhanced employee benefits, and the like—justified by their returns? Are human resources, the costs of which can exceed 50 percent of total operating expenses,[1] being managed with the same accountability, rationality, and care as the plant, equipment, and marketing resources? Is such management even possible with human resources, or are the "people issues" facing organizations simply too ill-defined and unpredictable to be managed systematically?

These important questions face any HR manager, whether a line executive or a staff professional. Most managers, and certainly most HR professionals, would readily agree on the importance of human resources in terms of dollar expenditures and effects on organizational goals. Yet, management often regards the HRM function as a "cost center" or as an "overhead budget item" and devotes little systematic attention to its contribution to organizational goals. Indeed, the question of its contribution to corporate profit still generates debate in professional circles.[2]

With increased competition and growing evidence from the United States and abroad that competitive companies manage their people differently, organizations are paying more attention to their HRM decisions. HR managers are finding it increasingly difficult to justify very large year-to-year HR programs solely because they are "good for human relations," "done by everyone else in the industry," or "done in Japan and Korea." Instead, the HRM function is being required to justify its existence and to account for its contributions. Even though the HR department oversees the single largest resource in most organizations, personnel managers may have trouble responding when asked to justify a million-dollar training program. What can a personnel manager say when top management proposes cutting 30 percent of the HRM programs in an effort to reduce "excess overhead"? How can an HR manager justify increasing budgets for training and outplacement when the organization is reducing staff levels to cut costs?

Even when budgets are tight, HRM programs can produce lucrative returns. But because the costs of such programs are often more visible and measurable than their benefits, decision makers may be tempted to "cut the overhead" without considering lost program benefits. In contrast, decisions about programs in other management areas (for example, marketing, finance, accounting, and plant operations) often consider dollar estimates of program benefits as well as the costs. Yet, decisions about million-dollar HRM programs are routinely made with little explicit consideration of their effects on product quality or cost. For example, a program to train 1,000 employees can easily incur costs of $1,000 per trainee, considering course development, instructor time, travel and lodging, but training results often go unmeasured. Unless a systematic analysis of the training program's returns is performed, a top manager might view such a million-dollar HRM program as more expendable than programs in other management areas.

Cost-benefit, or utility, analysis, provides a decision-support framework that explicitly considers the costs and the benefits of HR decisions. Utility analysis provides formulas for computing the dollar value of HR programs, but it involves more than formulas. It provides a way of thinking about HR decisions that makes facts, assumptions, and beliefs behind decisions more explicit, systematic, and rational. It supports HR decisions even when information is unavailable or uncertain, it translates statistics into useful decision information, and it helps determine whether more information is needed.

Although utility analysis models can be complex and detailed, the focus here is on their managerial implications. Algebraic formulas will be minimized to emphasize the findings and implications of various utility models. Several case studies will further illustrate how utility analysis models can encompass progressively more realistic and complete HRM decisions.

Alternative Approaches vs. Cost-Benefit Analysis

Decision makers concerned with how to invest resources in HRM programs have several types of information available to support those decisions. This section will examine how cost-benefit analysis compares to other decision systems.

Cost Reduction

Organizations could make HRM decisions based on costs or attempts to minimize them. Since every HRM activity incurs expenses, reducing costs often means reducing the number or scope of HR activities. Another typical cost-reduction technique involves reducing presumably costly employee behaviors such as turnover.[3] However, reducing HR activities or presumably costly employee behaviors may also reduce organizational effectiveness. HR activities or employee behaviors that at first appear costly may actually enhance effectiveness, such as when turnover of marginally qualified employees creates opportunities to hire those that are more qualified.

Informal Analysis of Benefits

Organizations might consider HRM benefits without using an explicit framework or system, but the sheer complexity of these benefits can lead to unsystematic shortcuts. For example, a recruitment program could be assessed in terms of filling vacancies, while a selection test could be evaluated in terms of whether competitors use such devices or whether it meets equal employment opportunity requirements. Without a systematic approach, unrelated factors, such as unsubstantiated beliefs, personal influence or political power, may dominate the decisions, and, as a result, the programs may not achieve organizational goals.

Cost or Head Count Ratios

Decision makers can use a variety of ratios designed to analyze HR costs or staff levels. For example, an organization might compute the ratio of total employees to HR staff employees, or the ratio of sales to HR costs, or the ratio of training costs to the number of trainees.[4] Comparing such ratios over time or to competing organizations can help direct attention to staff levels or costs, but the figures alone provide no framework for interpretation or decision making. If the cost ratio exceeds last year's, or a competitor's ratio, what decision does that suggest? Are high or rising HR staff-to-employee or HR cost-to-sales ratios always bad? If the programs and activities provided through such cost or staff levels produce high organizational returns, the higher ratio need not cause concern. Thus, cost and head-count ratios must be interpreted within a decision framework to be useful in guiding HR decisions.

Audits

A fourth approach involves auditing HR activities.[5] These audits, which can be quite systematic and detailed, demonstrate whether HR programs are being implemented as planned. However, audits provide only limited information because they rarely address whether the plan was appropriate in the first place. Managers will find little consolation in knowing that an ill-conceived program was implemented as planned, incurred costs at the budgeted level, or served the projected number of employees. A decision system should address costs and benefits before activities are implemented, as well as provide an evaluation framework after they have been implemented.

Formal Evaluation

This approach involves conducting formal statistical studies to determine the effects of HR programs. Examples include validation studies reporting the statistical relationship between test scores and performance ratings, and experiments comparing the statistical difference in output levels between groups receiving different training programs. However, statistics alone are often not very useful to HR managers when debating how to invest their limited resources to achieve the greatest benefit. Scientific studies rarely even mention dollar values, let alone report results in terms of investments and returns.

Advantages of a Cost-Benefit System

A full-blown cost-benefit analysis involves identifying alternatives, drawing up a list of all the factors to be considered for each alternative, measuring the factors on a common scale (such as dollars), and then computing the benefits less the costs to determine the net value of each alternative. The best alternatives, or those with net values (or returns on investment) exceeding a minimum standard, would be implemented. The problem with this approach is that some of the decision factors cannot be evaluated with precision and certainty. Moreover, measuring everything may prove quite costly. Still, the cost-benefit approach, if efficiently applied, offers a number of advantages compared to other approaches.

Explicitness

Identifying and evaluating costs and benefits makes the assumptions, beliefs, and facts more visible to all. They can be discussed, questioned, and corrected, thus reducing the chance that incorrect or counter-productive information will go undetected.

Consistency

Without a system for making complex HR decisions, HR managers and strategic planners could easily make different decisions based on differing sets of issues. For example, a personnel manager might choose recruitment programs based on low cost and probability of filling vacancies,[6] but choose selection programs based on legal defensibility and tradition. Yet, all these factors are relevant to both decisions, and neither decision considers the productivity of those hired. A cost-benefit system encourages consistency by providing a list of factors to be explicitly considered before basing a decision on only a few of them.

Efficiency

A cost-benefit system promotes efficiency because it can be applied to many decisions. While each decision is different and may require some new analysis effort, organizing the most commonly considered factors in a cost-benefit system frees resources to focus on the factors unique to the particular decision. Moreover, a cost-benefit approach guides the use of information and information systems. By identifying the decision factors, a cost-benefit framework allows decision makers to set priorities in gathering and using information.

Communication

A cost-benefit system improves communication among decision makers because it offers a common language for decision making. An identified set of decision factors and a system for applying them allows managers to devote more resources to making decisions rather than identifying and locating information. Moreover, communication with other management functions is improved by expressing cost-benefit information in dollars, since organizations are measured, at least in part, by how well they use dollar-valued resources to achieve goals.

Cost-Benefit Decision Systems in HRM

The principal drawback of a cost-benefit decision system is that all the costs and benefits cannot be measured precisely; indeed, some cannot be measured at all. As a result, the variety of factors affecting HR decisions cannot be quantified into a single dollar value that expresses their contribution to the organization.

But is this really what a decision system must do? Anyone who has tried to forecast the stock market or predict the sales of a new product realizes that finance and marketing are not exact sciences. Yet, these functions typically express their programs' effects in dollar terms. The objective of a decision system is to focus on important factors, isolate ambiguous or uncertain factors, and systematically and explicitly address potential risk and uncertainty.

Unfortunately, the simplifications typically used in HR decision making (such as focusing only on costs, adopting programs because of tradition, and ignoring HR benefits because of uncertainty), can have undesirable effects. A cost-benefit decision system offers a way out of this bind. It simplifies the decision situation and proposes a set of variables to describe HR program consequences, but it also efficiently summarizes a great deal of important information about HR programs in an explicit, consistent, and systematic way. It does not require measuring everything. To the contrary, cost-benefit techniques can help to pinpoint important information, and thus reduce the data collection effort.

Utility Analysis in HR Decisions

Utility analysis is the term for a set of cost-benefit models originally developed by industrial psychologists concerned with selection, and recently extended to other HR programs and decisions. "Utility" simply means usefulness, and the aim of these models is to predict, explain, and improve the usefulness of different HRM decisions.

Utility analysis, like other decision systems, requires a *problem*, or a gap between what is desired and what is currently achieved; a set of *alternatives* to address the problem; a set of *attributes*, or the variables that describe the important characteristics of the alternatives (such as effects on productivity, costs, and employee attitudes); and a *utility function*, or a system to combine the attributes into an overall judgment of each alternative's usefulness. Utility analysis is generally employed once the problem and alternative solutions have been identified. Utility models suggest a set of attributes for each proposed solution and a utility function for combining attributes into an overall usefulness value, usually expressed in dollars.

Units of Analysis: HR Programs

Utility analysis models focus on decisions about HR programs. An HR program, which may be called an intervention by industrial psychologists or an activity by HR professionals, is simply a set of activities or procedures that affects HR value. Examples include selection tests, training courses, recruiting techniques, compensation plans, and job redesign. Decisions about such programs provide a vital link between broader HR strategies and the day-to-day operational decisions made by HR managers.

Programs are more specific than strategies. HR strategies address broader issues such as staffing levels, dominant functional areas, and appropriate organizational structures. But strategy implementation does require decisions about HR programs. For example, a strategy to increase manufacturing employee flexibility requires choosing among competing programs in selection, training, and job design.

In addition, decisions about HR programs go beyond purely operational decisions about individual employees, such as which employee to hire, train, promote, or reward. For example, deciding which employee(s) to hire or promote requires a framework of HR programs that generate a pool of job candidates (such as college recruitment or job posting) and other programs that provide staffing information (such as selection tests or skill inventories).

Measures of Usefulness: Quantity, Quality, Cost

Decisions about HR programs have wide-ranging effects and are subject to the scrutiny of many constituents. No decision system encompasses all of these effects, but utility analysis focuses on three important factors: quantity, quality, and cost. HR programs have value when they affect many employee work behaviors over time, when they produce large improvements or avoid large reductions in the quality of those work behaviors, and when they minimize the costs required to develop, implement, and maintain the programs.

These three factors resemble those typically used in other management functions, and this similarity is not accidental. The quality or value of marketing, finance, and manufacturing operations' programs also depends on the extent to which they produce quantitative gains in productivity (such as sales or units produced) or qualitative improvements (such as reduced costs or increased quality) while minimizing the necessary cost or investment. The utility analysis models presented in this chapter reflect these similar priorities among managerial areas when deciding how to invest resources.

Influences on Utility Measures

In considering quantity, quality, and cost, different constituents may be concerned with different aspects of these three factors. For example, operating managers may focus on the program's short-term effects on unit revenues and operating costs, while the financial and accounting staff may be concerned with the program's impact on the unit's financial statements, and top management may care more about enhancing the long-term flexibility and productivity of the work force. Utility analysis can reflect these different perspectives, but each one implies a different way of measuring program payoff.

Utility analysis must also identify the mechanisms through which HR programs affect the organization. For example, organizations facing increasing product demand use enhanced employee productivity to increase output, while organizations facing cost pressures apply productivity improvements to reduce head counts and compensation costs. Utility analysis can encompass each of these effects, but the analyst must carefully define and measure the payoff to reflect the appropriate effect. A common mistake in utility analyses is to measure whatever outcomes are convenient (for example, sales or absenteeism) even when such outcomes have little relevance to organizational goals.

Utility analysis models clearly omit some decision factors. They emphasize productivity-related outcomes and ignore other potentially important factors such as employee attitudes, union relationships, government or public relations, and political considerations. Utility analysis represents one valuable decision support tool in the arsenal of HR decision makers. It does not provide answers to all HR decisions any more than a financial analysis alone fully addresses a decision about whether to build a nuclear power plant. What utility analysis models do provide are methods to summarize a great deal of productivity-related information, which can then be compared to these other important factors.

Ways to Address Imprecision

Although all utility analysis models are based on three simple concepts of quantity, quality, and cost, they are nonetheless complex. This complexity can give the incorrect impression that utility analysis is impractical. Some of the variables cannot be measured precisely, others cannot be measured at all, and those that can be measured are often uncertain and prone to change over time or in different situations. Finally, some variables that could be measured precisely are simply very expensive to measure.

These measurement limitations and uncertainty, while legitimate and important concerns, should not prevent systematic analysis of HR programs. After all, uncertainty about stock prices or inability to measure consumer preferences precisely does not prevent systematic analysis of financial investments or marketing strategies. Management recognizes the limitations and costs of information, and established methods have been developed to address these problems.[7] Simply put, information will prove useful if it serves the following purposes:

- The information is likely to correct decisions that otherwise would have been incorrect.

- The corrections are important and produce large benefits.

- The cost of collecting the information does not outweigh the expected benefit of the corrected decisions.

In other words, information gathering is itself an investment decision. Rather than abandon systematic analysis because of uncertainty, decision makers should use methods that identify the sources of uncertainty, how, or whether, the uncertainty affects decisions, and when to invest in better information. This approach differs from common practices that focus only on the most measurable information, such as costs, or base decisions on inexplicit beliefs or opinions. Subsequent sections will illustrate how utility analysis models make HR decisions more systematic even in the face of uncertainty.

Types of HRM Programs and Effects

The components and concepts of cost-benefit analysis noted above can be applied to all HR program decisions, but the analysis will differ depending on whether the program affects employee stocks or flows.

Employee Stocks

Programs affecting employee stocks (such as training, compensation, performance feedback, and employee involvement) aim to increase valuable characteristics (such as skills, abilities, or motivation) among existing employees to improve their current job performance. In terms of quantity, quality, and cost, decisions affecting employee stocks enhance productivity more when they affect a broad range of employees and time periods, cause large average increases in the value of employee job behaviors, and achieve both effects at minimum cost. Thus, decisions affecting employee stocks "work" by improving employee behaviors in their existing assignments.

Employee Flows

Employee flows occur when employees move into, through, and out of an organization through selection, promotion, demotion, transfer, and separation. In terms of quantity, quality, and cost, decisions affecting employee flows enhance productivity more when they impact large numbers of employee flows and time periods, greatly increase the value of job behaviors through better person-job matches, and achieve these goals at minimum cost. Most research has focused on utility analysis for selection decisions, but the approach applies as well to other programs affecting employee flows, such as improved recruitment, job posting, or incentives that encourage employees to apply for jobs or promotions. Programs affecting employee flows "work" by improving the pattern of movements into, through, and out of the organization so that more valuable employees are placed in jobs or work roles.

Utility Analysis for Decisions
Affecting Employee Stocks

Utility models have been applied to performance feedback[8] and training[9] decisions, but such models can also guide decisions about other programs affecting employee stocks such as compensation and employee involvement. To illustrate utility analysis for such programs, the case of a large manufacturing organization faced with a choice between two training programs is discussed below. Although the organization has been disguised, this example is based on an actual utility analysis application conducted in 1986.

The Decision Situation

The decision involved a choice between delivering training for engineers through a traditional classroom system, or through a sophisticated audiovisual network. While some training staff believed the audiovisual system would be a good investment, cost pressures had convinced others that the network would prove too expensive. Table 1 describes the example in terms of quantity, quality, and cost.

Cost

The classroom program, conducted in 20 half-day sessions led by current employees, would cost $451,035 over five years. The audiovisual network, consisting of one broadcast studio and ten remote conference rooms, would cost $1,031,147 to build and staff over five years, with the largest portion occurring in up-front costs. To keep cost estimates conservative and ensure no unfair advantage to the audiovisual system, the entire cost of the system was charged to this one program, even though many programs would use the network if implemented.

Quantity

The target population for training consisted of 200 current employees, plus 20 new engineers added each of the next four years. Due to training capacity constraints, the classroom program could train only 40 employees per year, or 200 over the five-year target period. Audiovisual training could accommodate up to 200 persons

Table 1

Utility Analysis for Decisions Affecting Employee Stocks: A Training Delivery Decision

	Option 1 Classroom Training	Option 2 Audiovisual Training

Initial Information

Total Costs Over 5 Years:	$451,035	$1,031,147
Start-up Costs:	None	High
Employees Trained Per Year:	40	200 incumbents in Year 1, and 20 new hires in each following year

Utility Analysis Information

Leverage
(# of trained employees in work force)

Year 1	40	200
Year 2	80	220
Year 3	120	240
Year 4	160	260
Year 5	200	280
Total Leverage:	600 person-years	1,200 person-years

Quality

P_1: Dollar Value of the productivity increase from classroom training

P_2: Dollar Value of productivity increase from audiovisual training

Utility Computation

Utility = (Quantity × Quality) − Costs

$U_1 = (600 \times P_1) - \$451,035$ $U_2 = (1,200 \times P_2) - \$1,031,147$

Table 1 continued

Option 1 Classroom Training	Option 2 Audiovisual Training

Break-Even Analysis

$U_1 = 0 = 600(P_1) - \$451,035$	$U_2 = 0 = 1,200(P_2) - \$1,031,147$
$\$451,035 = 600(P_1)$	$\$1,031,147 = 1,200(P_2)$
$P_1 = \$451,035/600$	$P_2 = \$1,031,147/1,200$
$P_1 = \$752$	$P_2 = \$860$

Payoff Formula

$$U_2 - U_1 = (1,200 \times P_2) - (600 \times P_1) - (\$1,031,147 - \$451,035)$$
$$= [(P_2 - (.5 \times P_1)] - \$484$$

Decision Rules

1. If both P_1 and P_2 are less than break-even, do neither program.
2. If P_1 exceeds \$752, and P_2 is less than $(.5 \times P_1) + \$484$, do Option 1.
3. If P_2 exceeds \$860, and P_2 is more than $(.5 \times P_1) + \$484$, do Option 2.

per year, thus it could fully train the incumbent work force in the first year and easily accommodate the additional 20 new hires in each future year, for a total of 280 trainees over five years.

Cost per Trainee

Following its typical practice, the organization computed the accounting cost per trainee by dividing total costs by the number trained. Classroom training cost \$2,255 per trainee (\$451,035 ÷ 200) and audiovisual training cost \$3,683 per trainee (\$1,031,147 ÷ 280). These figures suggested that audiovisual training would need to demonstrate much higher per-trainee effectiveness than classroom training to be cost effective, and discussions concerning whether the program could achieve this result had reached no definite conclusions. Some managers believed that spending over one million dollars on a training delivery system for 280 engineers could not possibly prove cost-effective. Moreover, some believed that performing a cost-benefit analysis to measure the program's effects on performance would require a costly and complex experimental study.

Utility Analysis Application

Evaluating training programs solely on the basis of cost-per-trainee is like evaluating a manufacturing plant in terms of the amount of raw materials it consumes rather than the number of finished goods it produces. The impact of each program on productivity should also factor in the decision equation.

The first step in determining program effects on productivity is to examine the number of trained engineers each program would place into the work force over the five-year period (shown in the middle portion of Table 1). Because engineer tenure averaged more than five years, turnover did not affect these figures. Audiovisual delivery trains more people earlier (the first 200 trainees are productive for the entire five-year period), so it affects 1,200 person-years of productivity over the 5-year period (that is, 200, + 220, and so on). Classroom training trains a total of 200 employees, but only 40 each year, so the work force does not reach 200 trained employees until Year 5. Still, even classroom training affects 600 person-years of productivity (that is, 40 + 80, and so forth). This measure of quantitative impact, known as the leverage of the two programs, demonstrates how faster training can substantially increase the program's effect. Leverage occurs because HR programs affect many employees who affect productivity for a long time.

Quality

Typical of many organizations, little information was available to help estimate the effects of the two training programs on employee quality, and certainly none that could forecast the dollar value of improved performance. Rather than ignore this uncertainty, the unknown average productivity increase per-trainee, per-year was simply given an explicit symbol: P_1 for Option 1 (classroom training) and P_2 for Option 2 (audiovisual training).

Payoff Formulas

Even without knowing how either program affects employee quality, the cost and leverage information proves quite useful in constructing the payoff formulas shown in Table 1. The total utility (usefulness) of classroom training (U_1) equals the leverage (600 person-years) times the unknown average program effect per person-year (P_1), minus the total cost ($451,035). The same formula shows the utility of audiovisual training (U_2): leverage (1,200 person-years) times the unknown average program effect per person-year (P_2), minus the total cost ($1,031,147).

The relationships are even clearer when charted graphically. Figure 1 shows the total payoff of either training program along the Y axis and various levels of average program effect per person-year along the X axis. The line showing the payoff from the classroom training delivery option rises by $600 for every one-dollar increase in average employee quality per person-year, offsetting its $451,035 cost. The line showing the payoff from the audiovisual training option rises by $1,200 for every one-dollar increase in average employee quality per person-year, offsetting its $1,031,147 cost.

These payoff functions suggest that even modest program effects might justify training expenses and that large improvements in employee value would produce quite sizable returns to the training investment. For example, an average productivity increase of $1,500 per person-year would produce total utility of $448,965 from classroom training and $768,853 from audiovisual training. This represents a 99.5 percent return on investment for the classroom program, and a 74.6 percent return on investment from the audiovisual training. At higher increases in average productivity, the relative advantage of the audiovisual training grows since it places trained employees into the work force more rapidly.

Break-Even Analysis

Of course, the $1,500 productivity increase used above was only a guess. As noted, little information was available to estimate the exact dollar increase in employee value per person-year from either training program. Break-even analysis provides a way to address this uncertainty without performing potentially costly studies attempting to measure this variable. Dividing the costs by the leverage gives values for the productivity increases that would cause each program's total payoff to equal (or "break even" with) its costs. These values are shown in Table 1. Classroom training costs would be covered if the program produced at least $752 per person-year ($451,035 ÷ 600), while the break-even value for the audiovisual training program equals $860 per person-year ($1,031,147 ÷ 1,200). In Figure 1, the break-even point corresponds to the point at which the line showing the average payoff per person-year (on the X-axis) for each program crosses the line of zero payoff (on the

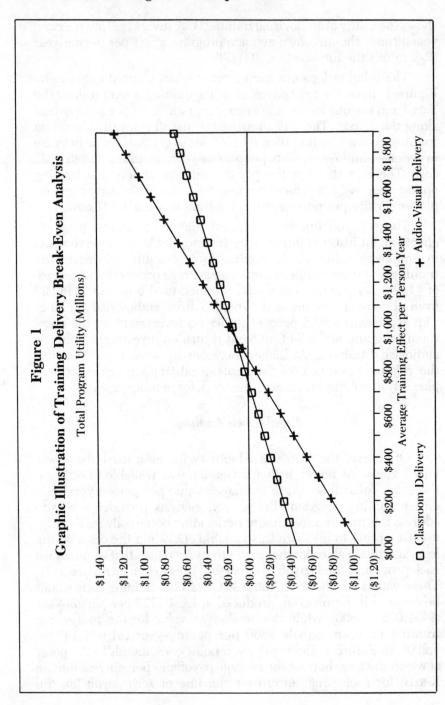

Figure 1

Graphic Illustration of Training Delivery Break-Even Analysis

Y-axis). Notice that these break-even values are much lower than the costs-per-trainee computed earlier. Relatively modest training effects could justify what had originally appeared to be a very large necessary training investment.

Program Comparisons

Since the break-even analysis treated each training option independently, it did not address the question of whether to substitute the more expensive audiovisual training for the less expensive classroom training. However, the same break-even logic could be applied by finding the values of the unknown classroom training effect (P_1) and audiovisual training effect (P_2) that would make the total utility of audiovisual training equal to classroom training.

The formula for these relative effects is found by subtracting the classroom payoff formula from the audiovisual payoff formula. This produces a payoff formula reflecting the difference between the two programs as shown in Table 1. By setting the difference $(U_2 - U_1)$ to zero, the resulting formula indicates the training effect (P_2) needed to make the audiovisual program's payoff exactly equal to the classroom program's payoff, given a certain classroom training effect $[P_2 = (.5 \times P_1) + \$484]$.

The decision rules implied by this break-even analysis are shown at the bottom of Table 1. For example, if the payoff per person-year from classroom training (P_1) is equal to \$2,000, then the payoff per person-year from audiovisual training (P_2) must exceed only \$1,484 $[(.5 \times 2,000) + 484]$ to justify its greater expense. If classroom training produces large productivity increases (greater than \$968 per person-year), investing in the faster audiovisual system will prove more cost-effective, even if it has a smaller average productivity effect per person-year than classroom training. The break-even formula provides a simple equation that shows when each program is the better investment. These relationships can also be seen in Figure 1, where the steeper payoff line for audiovisual training crosses the line for classroom training at a payoff of \$968 per person-year. Moreover, the computations can be further simplified using personal computers. [10]

This example demonstrates how the utility analysis concepts of quantity, quality, and cost can be applied to training programs. Similar applications are possible for other programs affecting employee stocks, such as compensation and employee involvement. Moreover, the example demonstrates how an explicit cost-benefit analysis can address uncertainty about program effects. Uncertainty is a fact of decision making. Break-even analysis is one method of addressing uncertainty explicitly, and reducing its detrimental effects on decision quality.[11]

Utility Analysis for Decisions Affecting Employee Flows

As noted earlier, employee flows occur when people move into, through, and out of organizational positions/jobs (for example, through selection, promotions, demotions, transfers, and turnover). HRM decisions that affect employee flows operate differently than those affecting employee stocks. Rather than enhancing the value of employees in their current positions, decisions affecting employee flows work by affecting which individuals will occupy those positions.

In general, three processes govern which individuals flow through the work force:[12]

- External recruitment/selection, which attracts a pool of job applicants from which individuals are hired

- External separation/retention, which affects the quantity and pattern of employee separations and, consequently, which employees are retained by the organization

- Internal staffing, which governs the quantity and pattern of employee movements between positions within the organization

Although organizations typically manage, evaluate, and plan employee flows as if these processes were independent, the three types of flows obviously are quite closely related. Effective management of each process depends on the quantity, quality, and cost effects of HRM programs that identify candidates for employment opportunities, that choose which candidates will fill employment vacancies, and that affect those who stay and leave the job.

Preliminary Attempts to Develop Selection Utility Models

Utility analysis models for selection enjoy a long history, but dollar values were only recently incorporated into these selection models. Understanding the early utility models shows why researchers and managers were compelled to develop utility analysis models for selection.[13]

The earliest index of selection value was the correlation (or validity) coefficient, which examines how strong a relationship, if any, exists between scores on a selection device (called a predictor) and subsequent performance levels.[14] If how applicants perform on the test matches their later job performance, then the validity coefficient, or predictive value of the selection test, increases. This statistical measure reflects one aspect of a test's value, but it overlooks the quantity of employees and time periods affected, fails to reflect any tangible quality index (such as dollars), and ignores testing costs.

A second index of selection usefulness was the success ratio,[15] or the probability that someone who passes the selection test would turn out to be at least minimally successful on the job. Under certain assumptions, the success ratio is improved by higher validity coefficients, by setting higher passing scores on the selection test, and when only about half of the applicant pool would produce adequate job performance if hired without the selection test. Although the success ratio measures more than the validity of a selection device, its value as a cost-benefit index is limited because it ignores the quantity of employees and time periods affected and testing costs. Moreover, the success ratio rates job performance in only two categories: minimally acceptable or unacceptable.

These early models laid the foundation and highlighted the need for selection utility models that present the value of selection investments in more tangible units, preferably dollars, and that reflect variations in acceptable job performance.

Current Selection Utility Models

The following sections develop utility models for decisions affecting employee flows. The models proceed from simple, with the first models focusing solely on external selection, to more complex, as enhancements are added to reflect and integrate the other employee flow processes. Table 2 summarizes the decision models, the features added by each one, and the decision addressed by each model. Model 1 focuses on choosing who to hire from among one group of external job applicants. Model 2 incorporates financial factors into the selection model so HRM decisions will be compat-

Table 2

Summary of Cost-Benefit Decision Models for Employee Flows

Decision Model	Added Features	Decision Addressed by the Model
Model 1: One-Cohort External Selection Utility Model (*Schmidt, et al., 1979*)		Deciding how to choose which external applicants should be hired in a particular time period.
Model 2: Financial One-Cohort External Selection Utility Model (*Boudreau, 1983a*)	Effects of taxes, interest rates, and costs of maintaining and improving employee performance	Financial value of deciding how to choose which external applicants should be hired in a particular time period.
Model 3: Financial Multiple-Cohort External Selection Utility Model (*Boudreau, 1983b*)	Effects of re-applying the selection program to subsequent applicant groups.	Financial value of deciding how to choose which external applicants should be hired in each future time period during which a selection program is applied.
Model 4: Financial Multiple-Cohort External Recruitment and Selection Utility Model (*Boudreau & Rynes, 1985*)	Effects of recruitment decisions on the outcomes of selection, and vice versa.	Financial value of deciding how to attract the applicant pool, as well as how to choose which external applicants should be hired in each future time period during which recruitment and selection programs are applied.

Table 2 continued

Decision Model	Added Features	Decision Addressed by the Model
Model 5: Financial Multiple-Cohort External Recruitment, Selection, and Separation/Retention Utility Model (*Boudreau & Berger, 1985*).	Effects of employee separation/ retention patterns on recruitment and selection, and vice versa.	Financial value of deciding how to attract the applicant pool, how to choose which external applicants should be hired, and how to manage employee separations/ retentions during each future time period during which recruitment, selection and separation management programs are applied.
Model 6: Financial Multiple-Cohort Internal/ External Recruitment, Selection and Separation/Retention Utility Model (*Boudreau, 1987b*)	Effects of recruitment, selection and separation/retention of employees moving between jobs within the organization on external staffing decisions, and vice versa.	Financial value of deciding how to attract the applicant pool, how to choose which external applicants should be hired, and how to manage employee separations/ retentions from the organization; as well as how to attract, choose and manage separations when employees move between jobs within the organization, during each future time period in which internal/external recruitment, selection and separation management programs are applied.

ible with the cost considerations typically applied to other investments. Model 3 extends the model to reflect the effects of reapplying selection programs over time. Model 4 incorporates the effects
of recruitment into the external staffing utility analysis. Model 5
adds the impact of employee separations (such as turnover, layoffs,
or resignations) into the recruitment-selection utility analysis.
Finally, Model 6 factors the effects of internal employee movements (for example, promotions, demotions, and transfers) into the
analysis, providing an integrated decision framework for the staffing
process. Thus, Table 2 provides an outline and summary for the
discussion that follows.

These utility models for employee flows are explored using a
case study. Although hypothetical, this example uses information
based on published studies and realistic assumptions. Readers may
find it useful to substitute values from their own experience to
produce illustrations that are more familiar to them. The important
point is not the numbers themselves, but the decision systems they
illustrate.

Throughout the discussion, break-even analysis will illustrate
how uncertainty can be explicitly and systematically addressed.
Readers should also keep in mind that although the computations
behind the models can become complex, computer analysis methods greatly reduce the computational burden.[16]

Case Study of Employee Flow Models

Consider a large organization employing 4,404 entry-level
computer programmers and 1,000 data system managers one level
above them. Table 3 contains a description of the characteristics of
the two jobs.[17] At the entry level, 618 programmers leave the
company each year and are replaced by 618 new hires. The organization experiences 100 separations per year in the upper-level managerial jobs, which are filled by promoting 100 entry-level computer
programmers in accordance with company policy. An additional 100
new hires fill the entry-level vacancies created by these promotions,
bringing the total number of new computer programmers hired per
year to 718.

HR managers in this situation face decisions about how to
recruit and select employees, how to manage their turnover, and
how to control their movements between the two jobs. How can

Table 3

Situation to be Analyzed

Cost-Benefit Information	Entry-Level Computer Programmers	Upper-Level Data System Manager
Current Employment	4,404	1,000
Number Separating	618	100
Number Selected	718	0
Number Promoted	100	100

Adapted from: Schmidt, Hunter, McKenzie, and Muldrow (1979) and Boudreau (1987b).

managers determine whether the outcomes of these activities provide sufficient returns to justify organizational investments? How much additional investment could be justified? How should resources be allocated between activities such as recruitment, external selection, and internal staffing? To illustrate how utility analysis addresses issues like these, the case study will consider four questions:

■ Should the current employment interview be augmented by an ability test?

■ Should the recruitment program be changed to attract higher-quality applicants?

■ Should the pattern of employee separations be changed to retain more of the good performers, and how much would such a change be worth?

■ Should an assessment center be used to promote programmers to system managers, and how much would such a program be worth?

Utility Analysis for Employee Selection

The first issue to address is the method used to select new employees. Selection test development and validation can be an expensive and time-consuming process, and HR managers may have to justify such costs. Several models have been proposed to address this question.

Model 1: One-Cohort External Selection

This model focuses only on one group (or "cohort") of employees hired with the new test.[18] In this model, the *quantitative* impact of the selection system is the person-years of productivity it affects found by multiplying the number of employees hired through the new system by their average tenure. The *qualitative* impact of the new selection system is the difference in the average annual productivity per person (measured in dollars) between those selected with the new system and those selected without it. The *cost* of the selection program is equal to the additional costs incurred to develop (or acquire) the new selection device and to apply it to one group of job applicants.

Quality is the product of three factors:

- The validity coefficient, or the difference between the validity coefficient of the proposed selection system versus that obtained without it, which reflects how accurately the system predicts later job performance

- The average standardized test score of those selected, which indicates how selective the organization is[19]

- The *standard deviation of applicant value*, usually symbolized as SD_y, which reflects the dollar value to the organization of obtaining applicants whose average selection test score is one standard deviation higher than other applicants

SD_y *Measurement Controversy*

The standard deviation of applicant value (SD_y) has become a controversial topic in industrial psychology, and requires some explanation. This variable is necessary because this utility model expresses both the selection test score and the validity coefficient, or the value of job behaviors predicted by the test, in standard deviation units. In the quality computation just described, the product of the validity coefficient and the average standardized test score equals the difference in productive value, measured in standard deviation units, between applicants selected with the device and those selected without it. To translate this difference into dollars per person-year, it is multiplied by SD_y, or the dollar value of one standard deviation in performance per person-year between applicants.

In general, SD_y will increase under the following conditions:

- When job performance is greatly affected by individual differences, such as when managers have great discretion over how they carry out their jobs and make decisions

- When the consequences of those selection decisions are important, such as when employees handle expensive raw materials

- When a high percentage of the applicant pool possesses job-relevant characteristics, such as when the pool of applicants for a managerial job contains recent college graduates as well as experienced former managers

Most utility analysis research by psychologists compares different SD_y measures.[20] Although different measurement techniques do indeed produce different SD_y values, none offer a convincing case for greater accuracy or validity. Considering the difficulties in measuring job performance differences between existing employees on *any* scale, it seems unlikely that one of these measures of dollar-valued performance differences among job applicants will become generally accepted.

However, this limitation does not threaten most utility analysis applications, and the models illustrated in this chapter will employ only one method.[21] The method used in the following examples measures SD_y by asking job supervisors to estimate the dollar value of an employee who outperforms 95 percent of the population, another who performs better than only 50 percent of the population, and a third whose performance surpasses only 15 percent of the population. Under certain assumptions, the highest and lowest estimates will differ from the middle estimate by the same number of dollars. That difference represents the value of one standard deviation.

Application of Model 1

The organization is considering using a written test of programming ability, the Programmer Aptitude Test (PAT), to select programmers. Table 4 shows the information needed to apply the

Table 4

One-Cohort External Selection Utility Model

Cost-Benefit Information	Entry-Level Programmers
Current Employment	4,404
Number Separating	618
Number Selected	618
Average Tenure	9.69 years

Test Information	
Number of Applicants	1,236
Testing Cost per Applicant	$10
Total Test Costs	$12,360
Test Validity	.76
Average Test Score	.80 SD
SD_y (per year)	$10,413

Utility Computation

Quantity = Average Tenure × Applicants Selected
= 9.69 years × 618 applicants
= 5,988 person-years

Quality = Average Test Score × Test Validity × SD_y
= .80 × .76 × $10,413
= $6,331 per year

Utility = (Quantity × Quality) − Costs
= (5,988 person-years × $6,331 per year) − $12,360
= $37.9 million

Adapted from Schmidt, Hunter, McKenzie, and Muldrow (1979).

one-cohort selection utility model. The model focuses on one group of applicants and one type of job, so here only the consequences of selecting 618 computer programmers are relevant. Costs equal $12,360, calculated by multiplying the cost of testing each applicant ($10) by the number of applicants tested (1,236). The quantity of employees and time periods is calculated by multiplying the average employee tenure (9.69 years) by the number of applicants selected (618) to produce 5,988 person-years. The quality per person-year, which equals $6,331, is the product of three factors:

- The increase in average standardized test score compared to random selection (.80, found through standardized tables),[22] times

- The validity coefficient (.76, estimated from previous studies), times

- The dollar value of a one-standard-deviation difference between job applicants (calculated to be $10,413 per year[23])

The validity coefficient, assumed to be .76, represents the increase in validity obtained by using the test versus not using it (that is, not using the selection test results in essentially random selection). Of course, the models can easily be modified to reflect comparisons between two selection systems with different validity.

Utility Computation

Multiplying quality ($6,331 per person-year) by quantity (5,988 person-years) produces an estimated benefit of $37,910,028 for the 9.69 years. Subtracting testing costs of $12,360 produces increased utility of $37.9 million over random selection, as shown in Table 4. The $37.9 million divided by the $12,360 increased testing costs represents a return of 306,634 percent! Not surprisingly, when these results were first published they caught the attention of psychologists and some managers because they were much higher than most people would have suspected.

Dealing With Uncertainty

These values certainly do not represent a perfect prediction of the dollar value of selection. Many of the parameters represent estimates, and thus contain various sources of bias, uncertainty, and error. However, as the break-even analysis of Table 1 showed, uncertainty should not prevent applying decision models. We can apply break-even analysis to this example as well.

SD_y *Uncertainty.* Considering the controversy surrounding measures of SD_y, the value used above might generate some uncertainty and skepticism. The payoff function can be rewritten to leave this value unknown:

$$\text{Utility} = (3{,}641 \times SD_y) - \$12{,}360 \quad \text{(Equation 1)}$$

Setting utility equal to zero and dividing $12,360 by 3,641 gives the value for SD_y that would make benefits exactly equal costs. This value is $3.39 per person-year, and is the lowest value for SD_y that would still justify the testing costs. Hiring superior applicants may be valued because it increases the amount of work, the quality of work, or allows the same work to be accomplished with fewer programmers. While many people might argue that the estimated SD_y value of $10,413 used in the first calculation may be too high, even these skeptics would agree that a one-standard-deviation improvement in employee value (for example, the difference between a superior programmer applicant and an average applicant) would be at least $3.39 per year. Thus, break-even analysis shows that the wisdom of investing in improved selection is not uncertain, only the magnitude of the positive returns to that investment is uncertain.

Uncertain Quality Measures. Break-even analysis can address even greater uncertainty. Suppose it is unlikely that using the test would increase selection validity by .76, or that selected applicants would attain an average standardized test score of .80 (which assumes that the top 50 percent of applicants will receive and accept job offers). Neither of these parameters is without scientific controversy.[24] By symbolizing the unknown effect on quality as *QUAL*, the utility formula can be rewritten in terms of quantity (5,988 person-years) and cost ($12,360):

$$\text{Utility} = (5,988 \times QUAL) - \$12,360 \quad \text{(Equation 2)}$$

The value for *QUAL* at which the testing benefits would break even with the testing costs is $2.07 per person-year ($12,360 ÷ 5,988). The question boils down to whether using the test instead of selecting applicants randomly will improve hiring decisions enough to raise the value of those new employees by an average of at least $2.07 per year (over 9.69 years).

Cost Uncertainty. Finally, consider the possibility that testing costs are uncertain. Suppose costs might be as high as $1,000 rather than $10 per applicant, implying a total expense of $1,236,000. Equation 2 can be reworked to reflect this as follows:

$$\text{Utility} = (5,988 \times QUAL) - \$1,236,000 \quad \text{(Equation 3)}$$

The break-even value for *QUAL* is increased by 100 times to $207 per person-year ($1,236,000 ÷ 5,988). Thus, even if costs are 100 times higher than expected, they will be offset by rather modest selection effects per person-year. This occurs because of the large leverage (5,988 person-years) affected by this selection program.

Model 2: Financial One-Cohort External Selection

The previous analysis provides a systematic framework that focuses attention on selection costs and benefits. One consequence of such a focus, however, is that it draws attention to the financial implications of HR investments. Line managers and those in other functional areas (such as finance, accounting, and marketing) frequently incorporate financial factors not usually considered by HR managers. What are the tax implications of increased productive value? Wouldn't hiring superior programmers require higher costs to attract and retain them? Is it appropriate to value productivity increases obtained next year equal to productivity increases obtained up to 10 years from now? HR managers unprepared to address such questions may find that their cost-benefit numbers lack credibility or even lead to incorrect conclusions.[25]

Financial analysis typically focuses on the value added by investments in programs. The financial model projects the value of resource requirements and program outcomes for each future time period. Such projections typically reflect the following considerations:

- *Service costs.* When productivity increases enhance the value of goods sold ("service value"), they often require increased "service costs" to maintain the higher productivity levels. These service costs are in addition to the direct costs of the productivity improvement program. For example, better testing that increases service value (for example, sales levels) by $105,000 per year may also require an increase in service costs (for example, inventories or sales commissions) of 4.75 percent, or $5,000. Thus, the net value of testing is $100,000 per year (that is, .9525 times $105,000).

- *Income Taxes.* When productivity increases enhance the organization's reported income or profit, the organization often must pay a portion of that increased income to federal, state, or local governments. Thus, the net income (service value − service costs and other costs) arising in any future period carries with it a tax burden equal to the organization's tax rate multiplied by the net income. For example, at a tax rate of 45 percent, a net profit increase of $100,000 per year carries with it a tax obligation of $45,000. Therefore, the after-tax net profit from the investment is only $55,000 per year (that is, .55 × $100,000).

Table 5
Financial One-Cohort Entry Level Selection Utility Model

	Entry-Level Programmers
Cost-Benefit Information	
Current Employment	4,404
Number Separating	618
Number Selected	618
Average Tenure	10 years
Test Information	
Number of Applicants	1,236
Testing Cost per Applicant	$10
Total Test Costs	$12,360
Test Validity	.76
Average Test Score	.80 SD
SD_y (per year)	$10,413
Financial Information	
Variable Costs	5 percent of increased service value
Corporate Tax Rate	45 percent of net increase in taxable profits
Corporate Interest Rate	10 percent of invested resources per year

Table 5 continued

Utility Computation

Unadjusted Quantity = Average Tenure × Applicants Selected
= 10 years × 618 applicants
= 6,180 person-years

Unadjusted Quality = Average Test Score × Test Validity × SD_y
= .80 × .76 × $10,413
= $6,331 per year

Adjusted Costs = Test Costs − Taxes
(after taxes) = $12,360 − (.45 × $12,360) or .55 × $12,360
= $6,798

	Unadjusted Quantity	×	Unadjusted Quality	×	Variable Cost Adjustment	×	Tax Cost Adjustment	×	Discount Rate Adjustment	−	Adjusted Costs
Utility =											
=	[6,180	×	$6,331	×	.95	×	.55	×	.614]	−	$6,798
=	$12.55 million										

Adapted from Boudreau (1983a).

■ *Discounting.* Benefits received (and costs incurred) sooner are worth more than those received (or incurred) later. This future devaluation occurs because benefits received sooner can be invested earlier, thus earning more interest than delayed benefits. Similarly, costs that must be paid earlier draw on resources that could have been invested longer, thus causing a greater loss of earned interest. The higher the interest rate that can be earned on invested resources, the greater the relative value of benefits received (or costs incurred) earlier rather than later. For example, at 10 percent annual interest, $50,000 received today will be worth $55,000 in one year (that is, $50,000 + 10 percent). Thus, the "discounted net present value" of $55,000 received in one year (at a 10 percent discount rate) is $50,000, reflecting the lost opportunity to earn $5,000 in interest. All things equal, investments that postpone costs and accelerate benefits have a higher discounted net present value. For example, the value of $55,000 received in each of the next 10 future years would be 6.14 × $55,000, rather than 10 × $55,000. Thus, the discount factor[26] is .614 (that is, 6.14 ÷ 10). To achieve a common basis for comparison, financial analysis computes the discounted present value of all future benefits and costs before combining them to evaluate investments.

Application of Model 2

Table 5 applies these financial considerations to the utility values derived in Table 4. Necessary additional information includes the proportion of variable service costs, assumed to be 5 percent of the increase in service value; the corporate tax rate, assumed to be 45 percent of reported increases in income; and the corporate interest or "discount" rate, assumed to be 10 percent per year.

Utility Computation

The financial considerations are incorporated into the utility computation by adjusting the program costs as well as the product of quantity and quality. Unadjusted program costs were $12,360 as noted in Table 4. These costs are adjusted to reflect the assumption that they partially reduce the organization's tax obligation by 45 percent of the cost amount. Thus, adjusted program costs are $6,798 (that is, $12,360 × .55).

Assuming a 10-year analysis period, then unadjusted quantity would equal 6,180 person-years as shown in Table 5. Unadjusted quality is $6,331 per person-year, as computed in Table 4. Thus, the unadjusted product of quantity and quality is $39.125 million. To reflect the effects of 5 percent variable costs, multiply this amount by .95. To reflect the effects of taxes, multiply this amount by .55. Finally, to reflect the effects of the 10 percent discount rate, multiply by a discount factor of .614. Multiplying $39.125 million by these three adjustments would result in $12.5519 million in after-cost, after-tax, discounted net program benefits, as shown in Table 5. Subtracting the after-tax initial testing costs of $6,798 produces an after-cost, after-tax discounted net utility of $12.55 million. While smaller than the results of Model 1, this return remains substantial and may be more credible to those accustomed to financial analysis.

Dealing With Uncertainty

Equation 2 can be rewritten to reflect the financial/economic factors shown in Table 5 as follows:

$$\text{Utility} = (1,983 \times QUAL) = \$6,798 \qquad \text{(Equation 4)}$$

Where 1,983 equals the unadjusted quantity of person-years (6,180) multiplied by the three adjustments (.95 for variable costs, .55 for taxes, and .614 for discounting). Thus, Equation 4 reflects the relationship between the unadjusted increase in value per person-year ($QUAL$) and the after-cost, after-tax, discounted utility level. This formula suggests that to justify the $6,798 after-tax testing cost, those programmers selected with the test must be $3.43 more valuable ($6,798 ÷ by 1,983) per person-year than programmers selected randomly. This value is higher than the $2.07 value obtained in Equation 2, due to the recognition that the benefits of improved testing must offset not only testing costs, but also increased taxes, service costs, and interest.

Model 2 can also explore uncertainty in the financial/economic factors, although these variables are typically estimated by the organization's financial experts and are relatively certain.[27] The point is that break-even analysis explicitly addresses uncertainty within a financial framework just as it did when using the non-financial model. Note that these same financial factors can also be applied to utility analyses for decisions affecting employee stocks discussed earlier.[28]

Model 3: Financial Multiple-Cohort External Selection

Utility models 1 and 2 reflect only the consequences of selecting one group of new hires—in this example, 618 programmers who stay on the job for about 10 years. However, evaluating only the effects of the first group hired is like evaluating a new production plant based only on its first production run. Selection programs are typically reapplied to new groups of applicants for several years. Testing costs obviously will increase as programs are reapplied. What may not be so obvious is that the leverage and potential benefits of selection programs also rise substantially as selection programs are reapplied. Model 3 is designed to address these concerns.[29]

In the multiple-cohort selection model, the selection program is reapplied for a chosen number of years. Thus, testing costs are incurred in each future year, rather than only once as in the one-cohort model. Each group of new hires presumably will stay for the same length of time and then leave. Consequently, as the selection program is reapplied, the work force gains a higher proportion of better-selected employees. For example, assuming no new-hires leave during the first three years of a selection program, the first better-selected group is joined by a second better-selected group in Year 2, and still a third better-selected group in Year 3. The multiple-cohort selection utility model considers both the increased costs of applying the selection program for several years and the benefits derived from having a greater number of more qualified employees on the job. Moreover, it continues to reflect the financial considerations discussed earlier.

Application of Model 3

Table 6 shows the results of applying Model 3 to the case study. The work-force size, number of applicants, testing costs, number selected, number leaving, tenure, test validity, and financial variables are assumed to be constant throughout the analysis. Thus, the test still costs $10 per applicant, and the value of those applicants

Table 6

Financial Multiple-Cohort External Selection Utility Model

Cost-Benefit Information	Entry-Level Computer Programmers
Current Employment	4,404
Number Separating	618
Number Selected	618
Average Tenure	10 years
Number of Applicants	1,236
Average Test Score	.80 SD
SD of Applicant Value (SD_y)	$10,413/yr.
Variable Costs	5%
Corporate Tax Rate	45%
Corporate Interest Rate	10%
Analysis Period	10 years
Test Application Period	7 years
Person-Years Affected	31,282
Leverage over 10 years	4,326
Ability Test	
Validity	.76
Testing Cost	$10/applicant
After-Cost, After Tax, Discounted Utility	Benefit − Cost
Increase over Random Selection Without the PAT (Millions)	$54.32 − $.04 = $54.28
Adapted from: Boudreau (1983b).	

selected is assumed to average $6,331 ($10,413 × .76 × .80) per person-year more than the value of applicants selected randomly. Other assumptions are that the program is applied for 7 years, that each group hired stays 10 years, and that the testing program is evaluated for 10 years.

In each of the first 7 years, 618 better-selected new hires are added to the work force, replacing 618 employees selected without the PAT. Because each cohort stays for 10 years, the number of better-selected programmers in the work force steadily increases by 618 employees each of the seven years. By the time the program ends in Year 7, 4,326 (7 × 618) out of 4,404 programmers have been selected using the PAT. All 4,326 programmers stay for the remaining 3 years of the 10-year analysis.

The increased leverage of the selection program is substantial. Over the 10-year analysis, selection affects 31,282 person-years of productivity (618 + 1,236 + 1,854, and so on) as noted in Table 6. This leverage concept is similar to the one illustrated in Table 1 for training programs. Moreover, the selection program's leverage over 10 years is far greater than the number of programmers selected (618 × 7, or 4,326).

Utility Computation

The utility values shown at the bottom of Table 6 were calculated by computing the cost-benefit consequences for each of the 10 years, and then summing them over all 10 years, adjusting for taxes, variable costs and interest rates. Comparing these values to those in Table 5 illustrates the substantial effects of reapplying the test as subsequent groups of programmers are hired. Testing costs indeed rise substantially to a discounted after-tax total of approximately $40,000. Selection benefits, however, are now $54.32 million (that is, the after-tax, after-cost discounted sum of the productivity effects over 31,282 person-years). The difference between the $54.32 million benefit and the $40,000 cost is $54.28 million in after-tax, after-cost discounted value (compared to selecting randomly). This value is substantially greater than the $12.55 million reported in Table 3, primarily because of the increased leverage gained by reapplying the selection program. Yet HR decision makers seldom even compute a leverage figure, let alone trace its effects on program costs and benefits.

Dealing With Uncertainty

Once again, break-even analysis can assist with uncertainty. Suppose some disagreement and uncertainty surrounded the increased value per person-year produced by using the test. The analysis above assumed it would equal $6,331 per person-year. However, one might question the assumed validity increase of .76, or the likelihood of hiring the top 50 percent of applicants, or the assumption that the value of those selected remains constant over time and as new programmers join the work force. The relationship between total utility and the increased value per person-year (symbolized $QUAL$) can be expressed as follows:

$$\text{Utility} = (8,580 \times QUAL) - \$40,000 \qquad \text{(Equation 5)}$$

where 8,580 equals the total benefit divided by the work-force value increase (\$54.32 million/\$6,331 per person-year), and reflects the 31,282 person-years of leverage as well as the financial considerations.

Applying break-even logic using this formula suggests that new-hire value must increase by only \$4.66 per person-year (\$40,000 ÷ 8,580) to break even with the \$40,000 discounted, after-tax testing costs. Once again, break-even analysis suggests that the program runs little risk of producing an effect small enough to make it a poor investment, since new-hire value needs to increase by only \$4.66 per person-year to offset testing costs. At the very least, such an analysis focuses debate on the decision, rather than on the measurement details behind a particular utility value. Moreover, because the relationships are mathematically explicit, personal computer programs using spreadsheets or other types of software can greatly reduce computational requirements.

Utility Analysis Integrating Selection and Recruitment

The analysis thus far has simply assumed that the same group of applicants would be considered regardless of the selection system used. However, selection programs are affected by characteristics of the applicant pool generated through recruitment activities.[30] A stringent selection process will still yield new hires of lower value if applied to poorly qualified applicants, and vice versa. So, the quality of new hires may be enhanced through investments in improved recruitment (such as recruiting at better-quality colleges), as well as investments in better selection.

Changes in selection activities also can affect the applicant pool even when recruitment activities remain the same. For example, polygraph or drug tests might actually reduce work-force quality if better-qualified applicants find them intrusive or insulting, and decide not to apply. When can changes in selection strategies actually reduce the quality of applicant pools? When are investments in improved recruitment cost effective? How can investments in recruitment and selection be integrated to create the highest combined return? Utility Model 4 (see Table 2) addresses questions such as these.

Model 4: Multiple-Cohort External Recruitment and Selection

In this model, the quantity of person-years in the recruitment-selection utility model reflects the same flow of employees into and out of the work force as assumed in Model 3 (Financial Multiple-Cohort External Selection Utility Model). The costs now reflect both selection and recruitment programs applied in each year of the analysis. Finally, in this model, the quality calculation is based on the average value of applicants produced by a random selection program plus the incremental value added by non-random hiring from that applicant pool. Whereas the utility values reflected in the first three selection utility models reflected only the *difference* in work-force value between selecting systematically versus randomly, the utility value calculated by this model reflects the expected work-force value of those hired using the recruitment-selection system during the analysis period. This value includes not only how well employees are selected from among the applicant pool, but also how valuable that applicant pool is in the first place.

Application of Model 4

In this model, the key strategic question is: "Should the recruitment program be changed to attract higher-quality applicants?" Table 7 shows how the utility model can estimate the selection program's returns when used in combination with one of two recruitment methods—recruitment advertising or a recruitment agency. Recruitment advertising should produce an applicant pool with diverse qualifications but a moderate average applicant value since advertising reaches a wide audience but provides little pre-screening. The recruitment agency should generate a less diverse applicant pool with a higher average applicant value due to the agency's screening of applicants before referral.

Variables that do not change as a result of recruitment include the number of new hires, tenure, number of applicants, testing costs, average test score, and financial considerations. Utility is assessed using the same 10-year application of the staffing program and employee flow pattern discussed earlier.

Table 7

Financial Multiple-Cohort
External Recruitment and Selection Utility Model

Cost-Benefit Information	Entry-Level Computer Programmers
Current Employment	4,404
Number Separating	618
Number Selected	618
Average Tenure	10 years
Number of Applicants	1,236
Average Test Score	.80 SD
Variable Costs	5%
Corporate Tax Rate	45%
Corporate Interest Rate	10%
Test Application Period	7 years
Person-Years Affected	31,282
Analysis Period	10 years

Work Force Utility Results

Staffing Variable	Recruitment Advert.	Recruitment Agency
Ability Test Validity	.76	.60
Testing Cost	$10/applicant	$10/applicant
Recruitment Cost/Hire	$ 2,500	$ 4,450
Avg. Applicant Service Value	$52,065	$60,000
Avg. Applicant Service Cost	$36,445	$40,000
Avg. Net Applicant Value	$15,620	$20,000
SD of Applicant Value (SD_y)	$10,413	$ 8,500
Value of Random Selection	$141.04	$180.50
Cost of Random Selection	−$ 4.55	−$ 8.10
Value Added by Testing	$ 54.32	$ 35.00
Cost Added by Testing	−$ 0.04	−$ .04
Total After-Tax, After-Cost Discounted Work Force Value (Millions)	$190.76	$207.45

Adapted from: Boudreau & Rynes (1985).

Table 7 also shows the variables affected by recruitment. Recruitment advertising costs $2,500 per hire, while the recruitment agency costs $4,450 per hire.[31] Recruitment advertising is expected to produce an applicant pool similar to the present one, so validity is .76 and SD_y is $10,413 as before. Because of the recruitment agency's pre-screening, these applicants will show less variability, reducing validity to .60 and reducing SD_y to $8,500 per person-year.

Since the recruitment agency identifies higher-quality applicants, agency-recruited applicants also should have a higher average service value. This value, estimated at $60,000, is offset by average service costs (including higher salaries/benefits to attract and retain them) of $40,000 per person-year. Thus, the net applicant value for agency-recruited applicants is $20,000 per person-year. The estimated average service value per person-year for advertising-recruited applicants is $52,065 per person-year (reflecting the lack of pre-screening), and is offset by service costs of $36,445 per person-year. This produces a net applicant value for advertising applicants of $15,620 per person-year, somewhat lower than that of agency-recruited applicants.

Utility Computation

The expected value of each new hire is the sum of two values: the value produced by random selection (that is, hiring average-value applicants) from the particular applicant pool, plus the incremental value produced by systematic selection from that pool. Thus, the average value of those hired through advertising is equal to the average value of the advertising-generated pool ($52,065 − $36,445 or $15,620 per person-year) plus the incremental value produced by using the test (.76 × .80 × $10,413, or $6,331 per person-year), totaling $21,951 per person-year. The value of those hired from the agency-generated applicant pool equals the average value of the agency-generated applicants ($60,000 − $40,000 or $20,000 per person-year) plus the incremental value produced by systematic selection using the test (.60 × .80 × $8,500, or $4,080 per person-year), for a total of $24,080 per person-year.

Once these quality levels are computed, total utility is computed precisely as before in Model 3: Average new-hire quality is multiplied by the number of new hires in the work force in each of the 10 years and summed over the 10-year analysis period. Next, total selection and recruitment costs are subtracted and the figure is adjusted for the discount rate, variable costs, and taxes. Once again, these computations are easily accomplished using a personal computer with spreadsheet software programmed to reflect the mathematical relationships.

The results are shown in Table 7. The after-tax, discounted value of random selection (hiring applicants of average value) from the advertising-generated applicant pool is $141.04 million, with a recruiting cost of $4.55 million. The after-tax, discounted value of random selection from the agency-generated applicant pool is higher at $180.50 million, but so are the costs of $8.10 million. The value added by testing the advertising-generated applicants is the same as before ($54.32 million incremental benefit minus $40,000 testing cost). However, testing the agency-generated applicant pool adds less value (because they are already pre-screened), producing incremental benefits of $35.00 million, with the same testing cost of $40,000.

If only selection utility is considered, the testing pays off under either recruiting strategy, although its payoff is smaller when applied to agency-generated applicants rather than to advertising-generated applicants ($34.96 million versus $54.28 million). However, the recruitment-selection model shows that the agency-generated applicant pool produces a much higher average value than the advertising-generated applicant pool ($180.5 million versus $141.04 million). When the effects of recruitment and testing are integrated, the advantage of combining agency recruiting with the selection test is clear. Agency recruits hired through the testing program produces a total work-force value of $207.45 million ($34.96 million + $172.4 million), while testing advertising recruits produces a total work-force value of only $190.76 million ($54.28 million + $136.48 million). Thus, sacrificing some testing effectiveness for an increase in average applicant quality makes sense, and agency recruitment proves to be more valuable than advertising. By systematically integrating the cost-benefit implications of recruitment and selection decisions, the recruitment-utility model identifies the conditions that lead to this outcome. Of course, the utility model could also be used to explore other implications of the recruitment-selection relationship.[32]

Dealing With Uncertainty

Break-even analysis once again offers a method of addressing uncertainty and risk. Suppose some doubt surrounds the estimate that the service value of agency-recruited applicants averages $7,935 more per person-year ($60,000 − $52,065) than that of advertising recruits. Agency recruiting costs more, its recruits require higher service costs to attract and retain, and the selection test is less useful when applied to agency-recruited applicants. Isn't it rather risky to switch to an agency given this uncertainty regarding the true difference in value between the applicants generated by each recruitment method?

One way to address this question is to determine how much higher the average net value of agency-recruited applicants must be in order to offset the reduced testing effectiveness and the increased recruiting and salary costs. Agency recruiting increases recruitment costs by $3.55 million over advertising ($8.10 million − $4.55 million) and reduces the selection test's incremental value by $19.32 million ($54.32 million − $35.00 million). This produces a total negative effect for agency recruitment of $22.87 million.

The value of random selection for advertising is $141.04 million with an average net applicant value of $15,620 per person-year, while the value of random selection for agency recruiting is $180.50 million with an average net applicant value of $20,000 per person-year. The net value of random selection increases by $39.46 million ($180.5 million − $141.04 million) when an average net applicant value rises by $4,380 ($20,000 − $15,620) per person-year. Because recruitment does not affect the other variables used to calculate the value of random selection, the formula for the value of random selection can be written as a function of the average net value per person-year in the applicant pool:

Value of random selection = (9,009 × net value) (Equation 6)

Where 9,009 equals the change in the value of random selection ($39.46 million) divided by the change in net value per person-year in the applicant pool ($4,380).

The next step is to solve this formula to find the change in average net value per person-year that will offset the negative effects of agency recruitment ($22.87 million) by increasing the value of random selection. This change in average net value equals $2,538 per person-year ($22.87 million ÷ 9,009).

So, the agency-recruited applicant pool must have an average net value of $18,158 ($15,620 + $2,538) or more per person-year to justify the more expensive agency recruiting effort. If service costs for agency-recruited applicants rise to $40,000 per person-year, then their service value must be at least $58,158 ($40,000 + $18,158) per person-year to offset the negative effects of agency recruitment. In the example, agency-recruited applicants have an assumed average service value of $60,000 per person-year, producing a sizable advantage for the agency recruitment method.

The complexity of the recruitment-selection utility underscores the advantages of cost-benefit analysis in permitting calculations to be computerized and in analyzing uncertainty systematically. Moreover, the sizable effects shown in Table 7 suggest that adopting an integrated approach to recruitment and selection programs may produce substantially more valuable HR decisions.

Utility Analysis Integrating Recruitment, Selection, and Employee Separations/Retentions

Integrating recruitment and selection enhances the utility model and, as shown above, can improve staffing program decisions. However, decisions about selection and recruitment programs affect and are affected by employee separations. If improved selection produces better-qualified new hires who leave sooner than less-qualified applicants, could the increased turnover costs nullify the advantages of improved recruitment-selection? How much should an organization invest in programs designed to retain the best performers, such as higher compensation or improved benefits? What is an "optimum" level of employee turnover, and how is it affected by recruitment/selection programs? Should investments in improved recruitment/selection be combined with investments in programs to retain the best performers? Answers to these questions require analyzing both the effects of employee acquisitions and the effects of employee separations (such as quits, resignations, or layoffs). Model 5 (see Table 2) provides a framework for such analysis.

Model 5: Financial Multiple-Cohort External Recruitment, Selection, and Separation/Retention

The previous models have assumed that each group of hires simply stays for a number of years (10 years) and then leaves. This is more realistic than focusing on only the first group hired, but it still vastly oversimplifies actual separation patterns. Hired employees do not actually stay together in one group, and then leave together. Rather, separations during each time period may include new, old, good, or bad employees. HRM decisions and programs affect the pattern of separations, which in turn affects the value of the retained work force. This is true for both selection/recruitment programs and for programs designed to manage employee separations more directly.[33]

Model 5 considers the effects of separations on work-force value; but rather than focusing on who is lost, the model focuses on who is retained. Consider the group of job incumbents before separations (the pre-separation work force) as a pool of employees with a certain average value to the organization. When employees separate, a subset of the incumbent pool stays with the organization. If more valuable employees separate, the retained work-force value is lower than the pre-separation work force value, and vice versa. Thus, the effect of employee separations/retentions on work-force quality can be analyzed by calculating the quality (that is, average net value per person-year) of the retained work force in each time period under different assumptions about who is retained. The cost of employee separations and retentions includes the cost of the separations themselves (such as exit interviews or severance pay), as well as the costs of programs designed to affect the pattern of separations (for example, retirement incentives). The quantity of person-years affected by the separation-retention pattern is the number of employees and time periods involved in the analysis. Decisions and programs that tend to retain more valuable employees produce higher work-force value, and vice versa.

To integrate employee separations and retentions with recruitment and selection, this model simply considers the effects of recruitment/selection on the value of employees added to the work force, and then the effects of the employee separation/retention pattern on the value of employees who are retained. Briefly, in any given time period, the value of the work force consists of (1) the quantity of employees retained times their average quality, plus (2) the quantity of new hires times their average quality, minus (3) the costs of acquiring the new employees (recruitment/selection costs) and releasing the separating employees (separation/retention costs). The utility model sums the work-force values in each time period, adjusting for taxes, variable costs, and the discount rate.

In concept, separation/retention is similar to recruitment/ selection. Recruitment/selection begins with an applicant pool from which certain individuals are chosen to join the organization. Separation/retention begins with an incumbent work force from which certain individuals are retained by the organization. Such systematic retention is quite apparent in layoff or dismissal decisions, where the organization decides who leaves and who stays. The concept also applies, although perhaps less apparently, when employees do the choosing (for example, in the case of quits or resignations). Here, those who remain are not directly "chosen," but HRM decisions (such as competitive compensation for star performers or pension rights that vest only after extended tenure) are certainly intended to manage these separations.

Application of Model 5

In their decision model, the key question asks: "Should the pattern of employee separations be changed to retain more of the good performers, and how much would such a change be worth?" Table 8 applies Model 5, the Financial Multiple-Cohort External Recruitment Selection and Separation/Retention Utility Model, to address this question.[34] The number of acquisitions and separations (618), the number of programmers (4,404), the financial/economic considerations, and the analysis period (10 years) all remain unchanged.

This model assumes recruitment through advertising, so the selection and recruitment parameters reflect the assumptions corresonding to recruitment advertising in Table 7. The validity of the test, number of applicants, standard test score, testing cost, average applicant service value, average applicant service cost, and SD_y remain the same as before. Each group of 618 acquisitions has an average value of $21,951 per person-year. This is the sum of the value of random selection ($15,620 per person-year) plus the incremental value added by systematic selection ($6,331 per person-year).

Each acquisition is assumed to cost $7,000 (reflecting such things as the $2,500 recruitment cost, relocation, orientation, and administrative activity) and each separation likewise is estimated to cost $7,000 (reflecting administrative activity, outplacement assistance, exit interviews, and severance pay).[35] Such costs are incurred regardless of the quality of the person joining or leaving. At

Table 8

Financial Multiple-Cohort External Recruitment, Selection, and Separation/Retention Utility Model

Cost-Benefit Information	Entry-Level Computer Programmers
Current Employment	4,404
Beginning Average Service Value	$52,065
Beginning Average Service Cost	$36,445
Number Separating	618
Number Selected	618
Acquisition Cost	$7,000
Separation Cost	$7,000
Number of Applicants	1,236
Average Applicant Service Value	$52,065/year
Average Applicant Service Cost	$36,445/year
Average Test Score	.80 SD
SD of Applicant Value (SD_y)	$10,413/yr.
Testing Cost	$10/applicant
Variable Costs	5%
Corporate Tax Rate	45%
Corporate Interest Rate	10%
Analysis Period	10 years

Work Force Utility Results

Staffing Variable	Option 1	Option 2	Option 3	Option 4
Test Validity	0.00	0.76	0.76	0.76
Separation Effect	$0	$0	$2,707	− $2,707
After-Tax, After-Cost Discounted Work Force Value (Millions)	$200.31	$242.10	$351.69	$132.50

Adapted from: Boudreau & Berger (1985a).

the beginning of the analysis, the work force is assumed to resemble the average of the applicant population (that is, average yearly incumbent service value is $52,065 and average yearly incumbent service cost is $36,445 for a net value of $15,620 per person-year).

These assumptions establish all the information needed except the pattern of separations. The separation pattern determines whether the organization keeps its better or poorer performers. Table 8 analyzes four contrasting situations:

- Random selection and retentions

- Valid selection with random retention, where those retained have the same average value as the pre-separation work force

- Valid selection while retaining the best, where those retained have an average yearly value of $2,707 greater than the pre-separation work force

- Valid selection while retaining the worst, where those retained have an average yearly value of $2,707 less than the pre-separation work force

Utility Computation

The results of the four selection and retention combinations are shown at the bottom of Table 8. Though the computations required to generate these values are complex, they were computed using a LOTUS 1-2-3 spreadsheet model reflecting the algebraic logic of the acquisition and separation utility model.[36] Computerization greatly reduced the calculation effort, and simplified the analysis. Under Option 1, where the organization experiences random selection (validity of zero) and random retention (zero separation effect), it will have a 10-year after-tax, after-cost discounted work-force value of $200.31 million. Under Option 2, where valid selection (validity equals .76) is introduced and retentions remain random, the work-force value increases to $242.10 million over 10 years. Option 3 shows that if the organization has high validity and also retains the best employees (that is, those retained are $2,707 more valuable per person-year than the pre-separation work force), it will attain the highest work-force value of $351.69 million. Finally, Option 4 shows that even with highly valid selection, if the organization retains its worst employees (that is, the effect of separations lowers the average programmer value by $2,707 per person-year), it will have a low 10-year work-force value of $132.50 million.

The interaction between separation and acquisition patterns has some important implications. If decision makers considered only the effects of valid selection, they would expect a $41.79 million increase in work-force value compared to random selection ($242.10 million minus $200.31 million). However, if improved selection is combined with improved retention, an additional $109.59 million ($351.69 million − $242.10 million) could be realized. By the same token, dysfunctional retention patterns can disrupt the effects of improved selection, as illustrated by the fact that valid selection combined with retaining the worst employees produces a work force value $67.81 million *lower* than random selection and retention (that is, 200.31 million − 132.50 million). While these effects are based on a specific set of assumptions, they suggest that integrating HR programs that affect selection and retention may produce substantial organizational benefits.

Dealing With Uncertainty

The analysis in Table 8 shows that the highest value from improved selection is achieved when the best employees are retained. Work-force value is $242.10 million when the separation effect is zero, $351.69 million when the separation effect is $2,707 per person-year, and $132.50 million when the separation effect is −$2,707 per person-year. Thus, work-force value changes by $109.59 million for each change of $2,707 in the separation effect. This suggests the following relationship between changes in the separation effect and total work force value:

Work-force value = 40,488 × separation effect (Equation 7)

where 40,488 equals $109.59 million divided by $2,707. Simply put, every dollar increase in the difference between the average value of the retained work force and that of the pre-separation work force is worth $40,488 in discounted, after-tax, after-cost value over 10 years.

Suppose managers disagreed about the likely effect of improved selection on the separation pattern. If the current selection and separation pattern is random with respect to job performance, then better selection will produce better-qualified new hires. However, if better-selected employees are more likely to leave (for example, due to better job opportunities), could this reduce the value of the work force enough to offset the selection improvement? Taking the difference between the total work-force value for Options 1 and 2 suggests that improved selection produces an additional work force value of $41.79 million ($242.10 million − $200.31 million), assuming the separation pattern remains random. Solving Equation 7 for the separation effect necessary to reduce work-force utility by $41.79 produces a break-even separation effect of −$1,032 per person-year (that is, $41.79 million ÷ $40,488). As long as improved selection causes a separation pattern where the retained work-force value is greater than the pre-separation work-force value minus $1,032 per person-year, then improved selection will produce a higher total work-force value than random selection with random retention. Thus, this model does not require a certain value for the Separation Effect. In fact, it enables the implications of uncertainty to be tracked more precisely by making more explicit the relationships between recruitment, selection, and separations/retentions.

Effectiveness clearly requires more than filling all vacancies, using valid selection, or keeping the turnover rate comparable with others in the industry. It is the *patterns* of employee acquisitions and separations, expressed in terms of quantity, quality, and cost, that produce results. The integrated utility model provides a framework for considering how these patterns and relationships can produce substantial improvements in work-force value and organizational performance.

Utility Analysis Integrating Internal and External Staffing Decisions

The separation-retention utility model integrates selection and recruitment with employee separations and retentions, but it still leaves an important gap—it deals with only one job. Decisions that affect selection and separation in one job often affect and are affected by how employees move between jobs within the organization. If you select and retain highly qualified employees in lower-level jobs, do they also make good promotion candidates, or does their narrow focus make them poor performers in upper-level jobs? When is it better to select employees based on their potential to perform in higher-level jobs rather than their qualifications for entry-level jobs? If you promote your best technical performers into management, are you decreasing work-force value by reducing valuable technical performance or building organizational value with strong technical managers?

External and internal staffing are closely linked. The pool of promotion candidates is partially determined by external hiring and separation. Downsizing may involve layoffs, but it also often involves some redeployment or rebalancing in job assignments by moving employees between jobs. Moreover, internal staffing is important independent of external staffing. Organizations devote substantial time and resources to promotions, demotions, and transfers, even if no external staffing takes place. The final utility model (Model 6) presents a framework for integrating the consequences of decisions that affect not only how employees enter and leave the work force, but how they move between jobs.

Model 6: Financial Multiple-Cohort Internal/External Recruitment, Selection, and Separation/Retention

Internal staffing involves employees moving between jobs within the organization, and includes promotions, demotions, and transfers.[37] HR planning has focused on the *quantity* of internal movements between jobs[38] using Markov or other models to predict this quantity.[39] Such planning identifies gaps between desired and projected quantities of employees in various jobs. Some have recognized that internal movements affect the efficient allocation of labor resources,[40] but have not proposed a framework for analyzing the productivity consequences of internal movements. A decision model for internal employee movements should consider the effects of internal staffing on not only the quantity of employees, but also their quality and cost.[41]

For jobs that receive employees, internal movement is very much like external selection, except that the applicant pool consists of current employees, whose characteristics will be determined in part by their current and previous work experience in the organization. Whereas external selection decisions might use test scores to predict future performance, internal selection decisions might consider seniority, performance, or assessment center scores.

For jobs that supply employees, the effects of internal movements are similar to external separation/retention, except that the pattern of separations is determined by internal staffing decisions, instead of by dismissals, layoffs, or quits. Internal staffing decisions usually emphasize filling vacancies with qualified candidates. Yet, as Model 6 shows the effects of internal movements on the jobs that supply candidates can be as serious as the effects of employee separations, and may not always be offset by improved performance in the receiving job.

In the utility model, the value of the work force in any job at a particular time is found by first calculating the quantity times the quality of the following:

- Employees retained when external separations take place
- Employees added through external recruitment/selection
- Employees retained when internal separations take place (that is, employees move out of the job into other jobs)
- Employees added through internal selection

These figures are then totalled and the costs of external and internal selection and separation activities are subtracted to obtain work-force value. The model establishes the value of the work force in each job at the beginning of the analysis, and then changes that value in each time period to reflect the effects of internal and external employee movements. The resulting utility value is the sum of the work-force values in the jobs analyzed during the time period analyzed, adjusted for taxes, interest rates, and variable costs.

Application of Model 6

The final issue in the case study concerns whether investing in an assessment center for internal promotions is cost-effective. Table 9 presents the results of applying Model 6 to the current example. In Table 9, the external staffing variables for the programmer job are the same as before, except that instead of 618 new hires to replace external separations, this example requires 718 new hires to replace the 618 separations and the 100 promotions. The financial considerations and 10-year analysis period are the same for both jobs.

For illustration, this case will consider the effects of 100 internal promotions from programmer jobs into vacancies at the data system managerial level. Each separation from the manager job costs $8,000, slightly higher than the $7,000 cost for programmers, regardless of the quality of those retained. Each promotion from programmer to manager also costs $8,000 (including relocation, orientation, and administration). Internal selection uses an assessment center, which, at an average cost of $380 per tested applicant,[42] produces a total cost of $1.44 million per year to assess all 3,786 promotion candidates.

Notice the symmetry between the external staffing variables considered in the programming job and the internal staffing variables considered in the managerial job. The applicant pool for promotions is the group of 3,786 programmers (4,404 − 618)

Table 9

Financial Multiple-Cohort Internal/External Recruitment, Selection, and Separation/Retention Utility Model

Cost-Benefit Information	Entry-Level Computer Programmers	Upper-Level Data System Managers
Current Employment	4,404	1,000
Beginning Average Service Value	$52,065	$57,272
Beginning Average Service Cost	$36,445	$40,000
Number Separating	618	100
Number Selected	718	0
Number Promoted	100	100
Acquisition Cost	$7,000	NA
Separation Cost	$7,000	$8,000
Promotion Cost	NA	$8,000
Number of Applicants	1,436	3,786
Average Applicant Service Value	$52,065/yr.	1.10 times average Programmer value
Average Applicant Service Cost	$36,445/yr.	1.10 times average Programmer cost
Average Test Score	.80 SD	2.32 SD
SD of Applicant Value (SD_y)	$10,413/yr.	$11,454/yr.
Testing Cost	$10/applicant	NA
Assessment Center Cost	NA	$1.44 million/yr.
Variable Costs	5%	5%
Corporate Tax Rate	45%	45%
Corporate Interest Rate	10%	10%
Analysis Period	10 years	10 years

Total Work Force Utility Results

HRM Activity	Options			
	1	2	3	4
Programmer Selection Validity	0.00	0.76	0.76	0.76
Programmer Promotion Effect	$0	$0	$0	−$625

Table 9 continued	Options			
HRM Activity	1	2	3	4
Manager Promotion				
Validity	0.00	0.00	0.35	0.35
After-Cost, After-Tax,				
Discounted Total				
Work Force Value				
(Millions)	$249.86	$296.90	$302.51	$278.68

Adapted from: Boudreau (1987b).

available in each year after external separations take place. This figure assumes that all programmers are promotion candidates, but it could easily be adjusted for situations in which only a limited number of programmers are eligible or tested. With 3,786 applicants for 100 job openings, the organization can be quite choosy, so the average standard test score of those promoted is 2.32 standard deviations above average. Performance differences among managers should have larger consequences, so SD_y among promotion candidates is $11,454 (about 10 percent higher than the $10,413 SD_y for programmer applicants).

Because the managerial job involves more discretion and responsibility, the average service value of promoted employees (that is, the value obtained through random promotions) is assumed to be 10 percent higher than they had produced as programmers. Their average service cost also rises by 10 percent when promoted, reflecting higher salaries. As the value of the programmer work force increases (through valid external selection and beneficial separations and retentions), programmers' value as promotion candidates also increases. Thus, decisions that improve the programmer work force produce an added benefit by improving promotion candidates for manager jobs, and vice versa. The model could also reflect smaller or larger performance relationships between programmers and managers.

Utility Computation

The bottom of Table 9 shows the effects of different internal and external staffing patterns. The values shown represent the after-tax, after-cost discounted value of the programming and managerial work forces, summed over the 10-year analysis period. While the computations are rather complex, the mathematical utility model is explicit enough to program on a personal computer with spreadsheet software. The values in Table 9 were generated using such a spreadsheet program.[43]

Option 1 depicts random external and internal staffing. Under such a system, the average value of each job's work force remains constant as internal and external movements occur, producing a total 10-year value of $249.86 million. Option 2 introduces valid external selection using the selection test with a validity of .76. This enhances the value of programmers, which in turn augments the value of the managerial work force when programmers are promoted, producing a total work force value of $296.90 million. Option 3 analyzes internal staffing in the typical manner. It acknowledges the validity of the assessment center (validity equal to .35) for the managerial job, but it still assumes that promoting highly qualified programmers has no effect on the quality of the programmer work force. Under these assumptions, total work-force value increases to $302.51 million. Option 4 considers the possibility that internal promotions will pull high performers from the programmer work force, reducing the average value of the retained programmers by $625 per person-year. This produces a total work-force utility of $278.68 million. Although the assessment center validly predicts future job performance for managers, its negative impact on the programmer work force costs the organization $12.22 million compared to random internal staffing (Option 2).

While assessment centers are not always poor investments, this example illustrates the value of a decision framework that incorporates the effects of internal staffing decisions on both entry-level and managerial jobs. It also demonstrates the limitations of internal staffing models that consider only movement quantities or head-count levels. Despite constant quantities of employee movements across the four options, substantial differences in work-force value emerged. These concepts can be extended to encompass other decisions affecting internal and external employee flows, such as "make-or-buy" decisions between internal and external selection, reductions in work-force size, and systems involving more than two jobs.

Dealing With Uncertainty

Model 6 represents the most integrative utility framework, encompassing both internal and external recruitment, selection and separation/retention, as well as financial investment factors. Obviously, utility values based on such a model require estimates, and such estimates may be uncertain or variable. As with the earlier utility models, break-even analysis can address such uncertainty systematically and explicitly.

For example, Table 9 showed that using an assessment center for internal promotions reduces average programmer value by $625 per person-year, these productivity losses at the programmer level wipe out the $5.61 million advantage of better internal selection (that is, $302.51 million in Option 3 minus $296.90 million in Option 2. However, the $625 estimate of lost programmer value may be uncertain or controversial. How much of a productivity reduction could occur without eliminating the value of using the assessment center?

The results of options 3 and 4 in Table 9 suggest that when the difference in average value between the pre-promotion work force and the retained work force after promotion (programmer promotion effect) changes from zero to − $625, the total work-force value changes by − $23.83 million. This means that every dollar change in the programmer promotion effect changes total work-force value by $38,128 (that is, − $23.83 million/ − $625). Therefore, the programmer promotion effect that would exactly offset the $5.61 million advantage of improved programmer selection equals − $5.61 million ÷ $38,128. This produces a programmer promotion effect of − $147 per person-year. If promoting the most highly qualified programmers reduces the programmer work-force value by $147 per person-year or more, the total work-force value would be less than the $296.90 million work-force value obtained through random promotions and retentions. The key issue is not addressing the precise value of the programmer promotion effect, but rather whether it exceeds the critical value (− $147) that would negate the advantage of using the assessment center. The utility model aids this analysis by focusing on how different promotion systems affect the programmer work force.

Summary and Implications

Utility analysis models offer a way to summarize and integrate a large number of productivity-related consequences that might otherwise be ignored or incorrectly evaluated. As the examples have demonstrated, such summaries and integration are not limited to evaluating programs currently in place. Rather, utility models offer a framework for planning HR programs and activities. This explicit and systematic focus on productivity-related consequences will likely affect how managers throughout the organization perceive HR decisions and whether the resulting programs are implemented.

However, productivity-related consequences are only one consideration in HR decisions. Several constituencies must be considered, including not only managers concerned with productivity but also employees, regulatory agencies, and communities. Furthermore, organizations are never completely rational. Politics, personalities, tradition, and power often determine the outcomes of decisions and whether programs succeed or fail.[44]

Still, utility analysis models summarize productivity-related outcomes and can provide a more systematic way to consider the tradeoffs between productivity and other less tangible factors. Although a decision balancing a potential million-dollar return against possible negative effects on employee morale, legal vulnerability, or union animosity will always pose problems, the task may be easier when productivity consequences are better specified. At least decision makers will be operating from a common data set that can more appropriately address important organizational concerns.

Systematic Decisions Despite Limited Information

Every management function operates with uncertainty, yet dollar costs and returns are routinely considered in such decisions. Believing that "people problems" are simply too uncertain to measure provides a convenient excuse to avoid rigorous analysis, but the examples presented here illustrate that this attitude can also lead to unsystematic and incorrect decisions. Moreover, such a belief may create the impression that HRM produces only "soft" benefits to the organization.

Utility analysis encourages decision makers to identify sources of risk or uncertainty and examine their effects on decisions, rather than attempt to measure every variable precisely. Techniques such as break-even analysis and computer-assisted "what if . . ." analysis apply equally to decisions about human resources and to decisions about financial, marketing, or operational resources. Such techniques often clarify the nature of uncertainty and can actually enhance decisions by demonstrating that only very unlikely events could make HR programs unprofitable.

HR Decisions From Management's Perspective

Although the contributions and importance of HR decisions are often acknowledged abstractly (as in the common statement that "our people are our most important asset"), day-to-day decisions by line and top managers often belie this sentiment. HR programs are frequently the first targeted for budget cuts; managers often consider only the costs of HR programs or employee behaviors; and the substantial leverage of HR decisions that affect large numbers of employees and time periods is often ignored.

If one overwhelming message emerges from the illustrations presented here, it is that HR decisions can make a difference to organizational productivity, and that these decisions can be analyzed systematically and explicitly. Organizational decisions often are ultimately made by supervisors, line managers, and top management. If HR professionals are to influence these managers, they must demonstrate that HR issues can be analyzed within a management framework, and that such analysis provides essential and important information. Utility analysis models provide a starting point.

Ignoring HR implications or adopting convenient but faulty decision systems is a dangerous gamble that can cost millions. This conclusion seems logical when HR decisions are viewed within the framework of quantity, quality, and cost that applies to any management decision. In many cases, simply placing HR issues in this framework clarifies their importance and directs managers toward better decisions.[45] Actual decisions will involve different assumptions from those used here for illustration, but the principles illustrated by these examples provide a useful and general decision system. A long-term integrated research program is currently underway to enhance the utility models, develop improved decision support tools using computers, and explore how such models affect actual managerial decisions.[46]

Through using cost-benefit and utility concepts to analyze and present decisions, HRM decision makers should communicate better with supervisors, line managers, and top managers; make more effective HRM decisions; and contribute more to organizational productivity and competitiveness. Failing to employ these concepts may mean that supervisors, line managers, and top managers will continue to ignore HRM's contribution.

◆

Notes

1. Milkovich and Boudreau.
2. Gow.
3. Cascio; Flamholtz.
4. Fitz-Enz.
5. Mahler; Sheibar.
6. Rynes and Boudreau.
7. Compare Bierman, Bonnini and Hausman, Chapters 4–10.
8. Florin-Thuma and Boudreau; Landy, Farr, and Jacobs.
9. Mathieu and Leonard; Schmidt, Hunter, and Pearlman.
10. Boudreau and Milkovich, Chapter 8.
11. For other methods of addressing uncertainty, see Rich and Boudreau.
12. Boudreau and Berger (1985b); Milkovich and Boudreau, Chapters 10–13.
13. For more detailed summaries of these early models, see Boudreau (in press); Cascio; Hunter and Schmidt; Milkovich and Boudreau.
14. The validity coefficient ranges from −1.0 to +1.0, with zero indicating no linear relationship and higher values indicating a strongly positive linear relationship.
15. The success ratio was originally proposed by Taylor and Russell.
16. For examples of computer analysis methods, see Boudreau (1985 and 1987a).
17. These descriptions are adapted from Schmidt, Hunter, McKenzie, and Muldrow; and Boudreau (1987b).
18. This method uses the Brogden-Cronbach-Gleser utility model. See Brogden (1946a, 1946b, 1949); Brogden and Taylor; Cronbach and Gleser.

19. Standardized test scores can be estimated using Naylor-Shine tables.
20. Other researchers (e.g. Schmidt and Hunter) have estimated the standard deviation of applicant value as 20 percent of average productivity, or 40 percent of average salary among job incumbents. Still others have adopted detailed and complex methods based on behavioral anchors (e.g. Cascio and Ramos).
21. Schmidt, Hunter, McKenzie, and Muldrow.
22. Naylor-Shine tables, using a 50 percent selection ratio.
23. Schmidt, Hunter, McKenzie, and Muldrow.
24. Sackett et al.; Schmidt, Hunter, Pearlman, and Hirsh; Boudreau and Rynes.
25. Boudreau (1983a); Cronshaw and Alexander.
26. See Boudreau (1983a) for details regarding the application of financial parameters to utility analysis.
27. Compare to Rich and Boudreau.
28. See Boudreau (1983a).
29. Boudreau (1983b).
30. Boudreau and Rynes.
31. For estimates of recruitment costs, see American Management Association, Table 55.
32. Boudreau and Rynes.
33. Boudreau and Berger (1985b).
34. A similar application is described in detail in Boudreau and Berger (1985b).
35. These separation and retention costs were estimated through a review of costing literature. See Boudreau and Berger (1985b).

36. Boudreau (1985).
37. Boudreau and Berger (1985a).
38. Milkovich and Anderson.
39. See, for example, Anderson, Milkovich, and Tsui; Rosenbaum; Stewman and Konda.
40. See, for example, Doeringer and Piore; Thurow.
41. Boudreau (1987b).
42. Cascio and Silbey.
43. Boudreau (1987a).
44. Milkovich and Boudreau, Chapter 8.
45. Florin-Thuma and Boudreau.
46. Boudreau, Dyer, and Rynes.

◆

References

American Management Association, 1986. "Hiring Strategies and Costs: The AMA Report." New York: American Management Association.

Anderson, J.C., G.T. Milkovich, and A. Tsui 1981. "A Model of Intraorganizational Mobility." *Academy of Management Review* 6: 529–538.

Bierman, H. Jr., C.P. Bonnini, and W.H. Hausman 1981. *Quantitative Analysis for Business Decisions*. Homewood, IL: Irwin.

Boudreau, J.W. 1983a. "Economic Considerations in Estimating the Utility of Human Resource Productivity Improvement Programs." *Personnel Psychology* 36: 551–557.

Boudreau, J.W. 1983b. "Effects of Employee Flows on Utility Analysis of Human Resource Productivity Improvement Programs." *Journal of Applied Psychology* 68: 396–407.

Boudreau, J.W. 1984. "Decision Theory Contributions to HRM Research and Practice." *Industrial Relations* 23: 198–217.

Boudreau, J.W. 1985. "EXTMOV: A Spreadsheet Program for Quantifying External Employee Movement Decisions." Ithaca, N.Y.: Boudreau.

Boudreau, J.W. In press. "Utility Analysis in Human Resource Management Decisions." In *Handbook of Industrial-Organizational Psychology*, edited by M.J. Dunnette. 2nd ed.

Boudreau, J.W. 1987a. "MOVUTIL: A Spreadsheet Program for Analyzing the Utility of Internal and External Employee Movement." Ithaca, NY: Boudreau.

Boudreau, J.W. (1987b). "Utility Analysis Applied to Internal and External Employee Movement: An Integrated Theoretical Framework." Working paper, Center for Advanced Human Resource Studies, School of Industrial and Labor Relations, Cornell University.

Boudreau, J.W. and C.J. Berger. 1985a. "Decision-Theoretic Utility Analysis Applied to External Employee Movement." *Journal of Applied Psychology* Monograph 70: 581–612.

Boudreau, J.W. and C.J. Berger. 1985b. "Toward a Model of Employee Movement Utility." In *Research in Personnel and Human Resource Management*. Edited by K.M. Rowland and G.R. Ferris. Greenwich, CT: JAI Press.

Boudreau, J.W., L.D. Dyer, and S.L. Rynes. 1986. "Development of Utility Analysis Models for Manpower and Personnel Decision Making, and Investigation of Their Effects on Decision Processes and Outcomes." U.S. Army Research Institute, Contract SFRC #MDA903-87-K-0001.

Boudreau, J.W. and G.T. Milkovich. 1988. *Human Resource Decisions: Personal Computer (PC) Exercises in Personnel/Human Resource Management*. Plano, TX: Business Publications, Inc.

Boudreau, J.W. and S.L. Rynes. 1985. "The Roles of Recruitment in Staffing Utility Analysis." *Journal of Applied Psychology* 70: 354–366.

Brogden, H.E. 1946a. "On the Interpretation of the Correlation Coefficient as a Measure of Predictive Efficiency." *Journal of Educational Psychology* 37: 65–76.

_____. 1946b. "An Approach to the Problem of Differential Prediction." *Psychometrika* 14: 169–182.

_____. 1949. "When Testing Pays Off." *Personnel Psychology* 2: 171–183.

Brogden, H.E. and E.K. Taylor. 1950. "The Dollar Criterion—Applying the Cost-accounting Concept to Criterion Construction." *Personnel Psychology* 3: 133–154.

Cascio, W.F. 1987. *Costing Human Resources: The Financial Impact of Behavior in Organizations*. 2nd ed. Boston, MA: Kent Publishing Company.

Cascio, W.F. and R. Ramos. 1986. "Development and Application of a New Method for Assessing Job Performance in Behavioral/Economic Terms." *Journal of Applied Psychology* 71: 20–28.

Cascio, W.F. and V. Silbey. 1979. "Utility of the Assessment Center as a Selection Device." *Journal of Applied Psychology* 64: 107–118.

Cronbach, L.J. and G.C. Gleser. 1965. *Psychological Tests and Personnel Decisions*. 2nd ed. Urbana, IL: University of Illinois Press.

Cronshaw, S.F. and R.A. Alexander. 1985. "One Answer to the Demand for Accountability: Selection Utility as an Investment Decision." *Organizational Behavior and Human Decision Processes* 35: 102–118.

Doeringer, P. and M. Piore. 1971. *Internal Labor Markets and Manpower Analysis*. Lexington, MA: Heath-Lexington.

Fitz-Enz, J. 1984. *How to Measure Human Resources Management*. New York: McGraw-Hill.

Flamholtz, E. 1985. *Human Resource Accounting*. 2nd ed. San Francisco: Jossey-Bass.

Florin-Thuma, B.C. and J.W. Boudreau. In press. "Effects of Performance Feedback Utility on Managerial Decision Processes." *Personnel Psychology*.

Gow, J.F. 1985. "Human Resource Managers Must Remember the Bottom Line." *Personnel Journal* (April): 30–32.

Hunter, J.E. and F.L. Schmidt. 1982. "Fitting People to Jobs: The Impact of Personnel Selection on National Productivity." In *Human Performance and Productivity*. Edited by M.D. Dunnette and E.A. Fleischman. Hillsdale, NJ: Erlbaum.

Landy, F.J., J.L. Farr, and R.R. Jacobs. 1982. "Utility Concepts in Performance Measurement." *Organizational Behavior and Human Performance* 30: 15–40.

Mahler, W.R. 1979. "Auditing PAIR." In *ASPA Handbook of Personnel and Industrial Relations*. Edited by D. Yoder and H. Heneman, Jr. Washington, DC: BNA Books.

Mathieu, J.E. and R.L. Leonard Jr. 1987. "Applying Utility Concepts to a Training Program in Supervisory Skills: A Time-Based Approach." *Academy of Management Journal* 30: 316–335.

Milkovich, G.T. and J.C. Anderson. 1982. "Career Planning and Development Systems." In *Personnel Management*. Edited by K.M. Rowland and G.R. Ferris. Boston: Allyn and Bacon.

Milkovich, G.T. and J.W. Boudreau. 1988. *Personnel/Human Resource Management: A Diagnostic Approach*. Plano, TX: Business Publications, Inc.

Naylor, J.C. and L.C. Shine. 1965. "A Table for Determining the Increase in Mean Criterion Score Obtained by Using a Selection Device." *Journal of Industrial Psychology* 3: 33–42.

Rich, J.R. and J.W. Boudreau. 1987. "The Effects of Variability and Risk on Selection Utility Analysis: A Monte Carlo Analysis and Comparison." *Personnel Psychology* 40: 55–84.

Rosenbaum, J.E. 1984. *Career Mobility in a Corporate Hierarchy*. New York: Academic Press.

Rynes, S.L. and J.W. Boudreau. 1986. "College Recruiting in Large Organizations: Practice, Evaluation and Research Implications." *Personnel Psychology* 39: 729–757.

Sackett, P.R., N. Schmitt, M.L. Tenopyr, N. Kehoe, and S. Zedeck. 1985. "Commentary on Forty Questions about Validity Generalization and Meta-Analysis." *Personnel Psychology* 38: 697–798.

Schmidt, F.L. and J.E. Hunter. 1983. "Individual Differences in Productivity: An Empirical Test of Estimates Derived from Studies of Selection Procedure Utility." *Journal of Applied Psychology* 68: 407–414.

Schmidt, F.L., J.E. Hunter, R.C. McKenzie, and T.W. Muldrow. 1979. "Impact of Valid Selection Procedures on Work-Force Productivity." *Journal of Applied Psychology* 64: 609–626.

Schmidt, F.L., J.E. Hunter, and K. Pearlman. 1982. "Assessing the Economic Impact of Personnel Programs on Work-Force Productivity." *Personnel Psychology* 35: 333–347.

Schmidt, F.L., J.E. Hunter, K. Pearlman, and H.R. Hirsh. 1985. "Forty Questions about Validity Generalization and Meta-Analysis." *Personnel Psychology* 38: 697–798.

Sheibar, P. 1974. "Personnel Practices Review: A Personnel Audit Activity." *Personnel Journal* (March-April) 211–217.

Stewman, S. and S.L. Konda. 1983. "Careers and Organizational Labor Markets: Demographic Models of Organizational Behavior." *American Journal of Sociology* 40: 298–321.

Taylor, H.C. and J.T. Russell. 1939. "The Relationship of Validity Coefficients to the Practical Effectiveness of Tests in Selection: Discussion and Tables." *Journal of Applied Psychology* 23: 565–578.

Thurow, L. 1980. *Generating Inequality: Mechanisms of Distribution in the U.S. Economy.* New York: Basic Books.

———— ♦ ————

1.5

Evaluating Human Resource Effectiveness

Anne S. Tsui

Luis R. Gomez-Mejia

This chapter addresses two related questions: First, how does a firm determine if it is effectively utilizing its pool of human resources? Secondly, how does it assess the extent to which its HRM function is contributing to this goal? The first question focuses on the effectiveness of the firm's overall human resources, which is affected by the efforts of both line managers and those in the HR function. The second question examines the effectiveness of the HR function, which hinges on the efforts of the HR function's staff members themselves. The distinction between these two questions is important, although often obscured in the HR evaluation literature and in practice. As the following discussion makes clear, HR evaluations can strengthen not just the HR function, but the operations of the firm as a whole.

Purposes of HR Evaluation

For more than 40 years, many researchers and practitioners alike have advocated periodic evaluations of HRM generally, or the personnel function more specifically, through a systematic, formal process similar to a financial audit[1] which examines human resources with the same rigor accorded to other factors of production.[2] Potential benefits from such an evaluation include marketing the HR function, providing accountability, promoting change, and assessing financial impact.

Marketing the HR function

The HR function historically has been characterized as reactive;[3] an appendage to mainstream functions of finance, production, or marketing;[4] a dumping ground for obsolete executives;[5] and more interested in its own technologies than in serving the needs of its clients.[6] An HR evaluation can serve as a powerful tool to enhance the image of the HR function since it demonstrates to top management "what we have done for you lately." Information derived from an HR evaluation can help identify both tangible results such as compliance with government regulations and intangible benefits such as improvements in employee morale as well as provide top management with figures and information that affect the bottom line. This, in turn, can aid in marketing the HR function.[7]

Providing Accountability

Some analysts argue that the power and influence of personnel experts have increased over the past 15 years, but they attribute this development to changes in the regulatory system. Such a basis for power does not necessarily promote goodwill and acceptance by line management. Consequently, the argument continues that the HR function must develop power based on its ability to offer effective help in solving business-oriented problems.[8]

An HR evaluation can help ensure that the HR function is meeting both immediate and long-range goals.[9] It also can provide information to plan, implement, and monitor HRM activities by comparing actual versus expected performance levels.[10] An evaluation therefore serves as an important accountability tool to determine if the HR function is effectively utilizing its resources.[11]

Promoting Change

Information provided by an HR evaluation may promote recognition of needed changes, especially if various stakeholders see this information as new, objective, and unexpected.[12] As one analyst put it, "the power of objective data is great in getting attention, concern, and ultimately action."[13] By identifying strengths and weaknesses, an HR evaluation can energize corrective actions before problems get out of hand. It can also be used to plan long-term strategies[14] and to provide management with a system for allocating resources to those programs that significantly improve productivity and profits.[15]

Assessing Financial Impact

Some HR evaluations facilitate assessment of the relative financial advantages or disadvantages of various HR programs.[16] Hence, an HR evaluation can become an important tool both to market the HR function and to make rational decisions when choosing among alternative courses of action (such as choosing whether to develop an in-house day-care center or an employee assistance program).

This type of evaluation also has an important indirect benefit. By forcing HR managers to analyze the return on the corporation's personnel dollars, it teaches them to act "like entrepreneurs whose business happens to be people."[17] For example, one company calculates revenue and pretax earnings per employee, and tracks employee cost as a proportion of value added across divisions and over time.[18] The objective is to improve the financial return on human investments.

Approaches to HR Evaluation

Two major approaches to HR evaluation are the audit approach and the analytic approach, each of which offers several evaluation alternatives. Some methods focus on the HR function (for example, user reaction surveys), others focus on overall HR effectiveness (for example, cost-benefit analysis), and some, such as experimental design, can serve both purposes.

Audit Approach

Perhaps the best known approach, the audit focuses on a systematic review of the outcomes of HR subfunctions, such as staffing, training, and compensation. Two major types of audits, personnel indices and user-reaction measures, may be conducted, either individually or in combination.

Personnel Indices/Key Indicators

Personnel indices are potentially useful descriptive measures to help track and evaluate the impact of personnel programs.[9] The left-hand column of Table 1 shows a representative sample of 60 such indices broken down by the various HRM subfunctions. Many of these indices may prove useful for evaluating the effectiveness of

Table 1

Functional Audit Approaches to Evaluating HRM Effectiveness

Personnel Indices/ Key Indicators	Service-Oriented User-Reaction Measures
Staffing	
Average days taken to fill open requisitions	Anticipation of personnel needs
Ratio of applicants to requisitions per job family	Timeliness of referring qualified workers to line supervisors
Ratio of offers made to number of applicants	Treatment of applicants
Ratio of acceptances to offers made	Fairness in selection process
Ratio of minority/women applicants to representation in local labor market	Skill in handling terminations with respect to treatment of employees
Average days between application and formal response	Usefulness of selection tools
Per-capita recruitment costs	Assistance provided to line managers in staffing decisions
Average years of experience/ education of hires per job family	Adaptability to changing labor market conditions
Average test scores (where available) for hires	
Equal Employment Opportunity	
Ratio of EEO grievances to employee population	Communication of current EEO and affirmative action legal requirements/company policies
Ratio of EEO suits to employee population	Resolution of EEO grievances
Minority representation by EEO categories	Day-to-day assistance provided by personnel department in implementing affirmative action plan
Rejection rates of minorities by job categories	Aggressive recruitment to identify qualified women and minority applicants
Minority turnover rate	Lack of discrimination in hiring and promoting

Table 1 continued

Personnel Indices/ Key Indicators	Service-Oriented User-Reaction Measures
Wage and Salary Administration	
Ratio of payroll problems to number of employees	Fairness of existing job evaluation system in assigning grades and salaries
Ratio of "equal pay" complaints to number of employees	Consistency in applying compensation policies
Per-capita (average) merit increases	Competitiveness in local labor market
Ratio of recommendations for reclassification to number of employees	Resolutions of payroll problems
Ratio of exit interviewees citing pay as a reason for termination to number of employees	Relationship between pay and performance
Average merit increase per performance level	Employee satisfaction with pay
Ratio of protected classes' wages to nonprotected classes' wages	
Percentage of overtime hours to straight time	
Ratio of average salary offers to average salary in community	
Ratio of average salary to mid-point by grade level	
Benefits	
Average unemployment compensation payment (UCP)	Promptness in handling claims
"Experience rating" in UCP	Fairness and consistency in the application of benefit policies
Average Workers' Compensation payment (WCP)	Communication of benefits to employees
"Experience rating" in WCP	Assistance provided to line managers in reducing potential for unnecessary claims
Benefit cost per payroll $	
Percentage of sick leave to total pay	
Average annual premium for unemployment and Workers' Compensation insurance	

Table 1 continued

Personnel Indices/ Key Indicators	Service-Oriented User-Reaction Measures
Cost of employee benefits as a percentage of hourly base rates	
Average length of time taken to process claims	

Training	
Percentage of employees participating in training programs per job family	Extent to which training programs meet the needs of employees and the company
Percentage of employees completing training programs per job family	Assistance provided to line managers in identifying training needs and developing training programs
Percentage of employees receiving tuition refunds	Communication to employees about available training opportunities
Training hours per employee	Quality of induction/orientation programs
Training dollars per employee	

Employee Appraisal and Development	
Distribution of performance appraisal ratings	Assistance in identifying management potential
Psychometric properties of appraisal forms	Preparation given to employees for future advancement
	Organizational development activities provided by personnel department
	Support provided to line managers in setting up personal and organizational development programs

Careers	
Ratio of promotions to number of employees	Extent to which promotions are made from within
Percentage promoted by protected classes	Assistance/counseling provided to employees in career planning
Ratio of open requisitions filled internally to those filled externally	Relationship of promotions to proven merit

Table 1 continued

Personnel Indices/ Key Indicators	Service-Oriented User-Reaction Measures
Percentage of employees transferred between divisions and/ or geographically	Assistance/counseling provided to employees in transfer and relocation
Average years/months between promotions	

Work Environment/Safety	
Frequency/severity ratio of accidents	Assistance to line managers in organizing safety programs
Safety related expenses per $1000 of payroll	Assistance to line managers in identifying potential safety hazards
Plant security losses per square footage, e.g., fires, burglaries	Assistance to line managers in providing a good working environment (lighting, cleanliness, heating, etc.)
Ratio of OSHA citations to number of employees	

Labor Relations	
Ratio of concerted activities to number of employees	Assistance provided to line managers in handling grievances
Ratio of grievances by pay plan to number of employees	Assistance provided to line managers in handling routine employment actions (e.g., layoffs)
Frequency and duration of work stoppages	Efforts to promote a spirit of cooperation in plant
Percentage of grievances settled	Efforts to minimize interpersonal conflict
Average length of time to settle grievances	Efforts to monitor the employee relations climate in plant
	Corrective actions taken/ recommended before the outbreak of labor unrest.

Overall Effectiveness	
Ratio of personnel staff to employee population	Accuracy and clarity of information provided to managers and employees
Turnover rate	Lack of duplication or conflict in the types of services provided

Table 1 continued

Personnel Indices/ Key Indicators	Service-Oriented User-Reaction Measures
Absenteeism rate	Timeliness and adequacy of response to inquiries for assistance
Ratio of per-capita revenue to per-capita cost	Availability of staff for support
Net income per employee	Competence and expertise of staff
	Quality of consulting provided
	Creativity and resourcefulness in dealing with unusual situations
	Level of understanding exhibited by personnel department
	Working relationship between organizations and personnel department
	Overall personnel department support, considering all things

overall HR effectiveness and the HR function; others may be more appropriate for only one purpose.

Although these indicators are quantitative, none provides sufficient information when used alone. In combination, however, they may provide clues to the effectiveness of HR policies, programs, or activities. For example, almost 30 years ago, a group of General Electric plants combined several indicators (such as absenteeism, separations, and grievances) into an Employee Relations Index that served as a useful predictor of such measures as profitability, performance records, and supervisory ratings.[20]

Service-Oriented, User-Reaction Measures

A second alternative in the audit approach is to survey the HR function's customers, or clients, on the extent of their satisfaction with services received. Clients may include line executives and managers, employees, applicants, or even union officers. This method recognizes that the primary mission of the HR function is to provide users with services, rather than specific, tangible products. Hence, a "reputational" approach to HR evaluation seems logical.[21]

Clearly, this method focuses on the effectiveness of the HR function, not overall HR effectiveness throughout the organization.

Some analysts have attributed the perceived ineffectiveness of the HR function in many organizations to a production mentality.[22] That view leads HR managers to see their function as a manufacturing operation turning out uniform products for a homogeneous market rather than as a service organization providing unique offerings matched to diverse client needs. To these analysts, traditional personnel indices, such as those shown in the left-hand column of Table 1, reflect short-term countable criteria common to a production orientation. Overreliance on quantitative measures of effectiveness may give a false sense of objectivity and fail to assess whether services meet with the clients' satisfaction. This suggests using periodic studies of client perceptions of services rendered as the most appropriate way to measure effectiveness.

The right-hand column of Table 1 contains a representative sample of 55 service-oriented, "user-reaction" measures, each of which may be assessed through attitude surveys, discussions with employees, termination interviews, group meetings, and the like.

Analytic Approach

The analytic approach attempts to apply the scientific method or mathematical models to HR evaluation. Like the audit approach, this type of examination encompasses two general alternatives.

Experimental Design

Experimental procedures can be used to assess the effects of treatments on outcomes. As applied to HR effectiveness, the objective is to determine whether or not the introduction of particular personnel programs or practices (such as job enrichment, management training, or a new performance appraisal system) has the desired effect on relevant outcomes (for example, absenteeism and job satisfaction). The effectiveness of both overall HRM, through program administration, and the HR function, by selecting and designing the best program or policy, can be assessed this way.

Table 2 lists several experimental designs that may be used for HR evaluation. These vary in degree of scientific rigor and data requirements.[23] The simplest procedure involves the measurement of outcomes after a program has been introduced. A more elaborate

Table 2

Analytical Approaches to Evaluating Human Resource Management Effectiveness

Experimental Designs	*Cost/Benefit Analysis*
☐ Post hoc program effectiveness measures	
☐ Before-after program effectiveness measures	1. Human Resource Accounting ☐ Capitalization of salary ☐ Net present value of expected wage payments
☐ Before-after program effectiveness measures with control groups	☐ Returns on human assets and returns on human investment
☐ Reversal technique (measure of criterion variables is taken under baseline conditions, intervention is applied, criterion variable is measured second time, reversal is attempted, criterion variable is measured a third time)	2. Dollar Criterion ☐ Turnover costs (separation, replacement, and training) ☐ Absenteeism and sick leave (direct costs, opportunity costs, "spill over" costs). ☐ Economic impact of employee attitudes
☐ Comparison of effectiveness scores for separate "pilot projects" undertaken in different parts of the organization and/or at different points in time	☐ Financial costs of employee grievances ☐ Financial savings of a nonunion environment ☐ Financial returns of training programs
	3. Utility Analysis ☐ Pay off matrix for various personnel programs ☐ Taylor-Russell tables ☐ Naylor-Shine utility index ☐ Brogden-Cronbach-Gleser Model

design involves the measurement of outcomes both before and after program is introduced to determine whether or not the expected changes have occurred. To assure that other factors do not influence the results, a control group may be added. Another way to control for external factors is the reversal technique,[24] which involves introducing, withdrawing, and then reintroducing a program and measuring outcomes at each point. Comparing the results of pilot projects in different parts of an organization or at separate points in time is another possibility.[25]

Cost-Benefit Analysis

Several statistical procedures have been developed to estimate the financial costs associated with such problems as turnover, absenteeism, and grievances and the benefits accruing from various personnel programs designed to ameliorate these problems. Three types of study characterize this category: HR accounting or valuation, the dollar criterion, and utility analysis. Table 2 lists several representative measures for each type.

HR accounting attempts to measure the value of people as organizational resources.[26] A number of methods have been described,[27] all of which focus on overall HR effectiveness. The objective of the *dollar criterion approach* is to estimate the financial impact of such behaviors as absenteeism, turnover, and job performance.[28] Both the HR accounting and the dollar criterion methods attempt only to estimate the value of human resources to the firm and do not directly measure the effectiveness with which these resources are utilized.

Utility analysis, on the other hand, attempts to evaluate the dollar value of outcomes against the costs of producing them.[29] The best-known HRM utility models concern personnel selection,[30] but more recent models have addressed other types of personnel programs[31] as well as separation and replacement decisions.[32] With its current application to selection, training, and separation decisions, utility analysis tends to focus more on the effectiveness of the HR function than on overall HRM. (For more information on this method, see Chapter 1.4 of this volume.)

Current HR Evaluation Practices

HR Evaluation Approaches in Industry

As noted earlier, a vast literature dating back to the 1930s has exalted the benefits of HR evaluation and prescribed a variety of evaluation methods. But what is actually being done in this regard in the 1980s? To find out, the authors surveyed 900 HR executives chosen randomly from the American Society for Personnel Administration membership roster. Of the 70 firms responding to the survey, all reported some type of HR evaluation.

Demographic Characteristics of Respondents

Based on a comparison between survey respondents and non-respondents, it appears that large and high-performing firms are more likely to engage in HR evaluation.[33] A majority of the responding firms (over 70 percent) reported having higher profits than other companies in the same industry and having experienced improved performance levels over the past five years. The HR functions in these companies also tend to have greater than average resources, with personnel staff/employee ratios reported by the 70 respondents of 1 to 125; this compares with a national average of 1 to 167.[34]

Firms conducting HR evaluations are also more likely to follow aggressive product/market strategies. Fifty percent of the 70 firms were classified as "prospectors" in terms of their business strategies.[35] These companies attempt to be the "first movers" in new product lines and market areas, even if some of their efforts fail.

Aggressiveness and risk taking also characterize how these firms manage their financial and people resources. HR issues and business planning activities are highly integrated, and HR executives play an important role in business decisions. A majority (73 percent) serve on their firm's executive management committee or its equivalent, and nearly all (97 percent) have direct access to top management on an ongoing basis.

Responsibility for Evaluation

While responsibility for evaluating HR effectiveness is differentiated, it also is shared in many companies. In 61 percent of the survey companies, corporate or executive management is responsible for evaluating the HR function; in 40 percent, corporate HR administration is responsible; in 19 percent the HR research department does the job; and 3 percent use outside consultants.

On the other hand, line managers and supervisors have the responsibility of evaluating overall HR effectiveness in 56 percent of the companies; divisional executives perform these evaluations in 51 percent; and corporate management and corporate HR administration each is responsible in 42 percent of the companies. As with effectiveness evaluations of HR function, outside consultants are used infrequently.

Evaluation Process

Evaluations of both overall human resources and the HR function tend to be informal; over half of the companies (57 percent) reported this approach. Eighty-four percent of the respondents conduct evaluations at least annually. A smaller subset do evaluations when problems arise (20 percent), or when requested by management (11 percent). Responses to both structured and unstructured survey questions suggest that employee performance appraisal is the primary means for assessing overall HR effectiveness. In contrast, only three HR executives reported that their companies use financial performance as a criterion to evaluate overall HR effectiveness.

Utilization of Evaluation Findings

Seventy-three percent of the respondents indicated that they use information from evaluations of the HR function to improve the performance of specific functions such as staffing, compensation, or employee relations. Other frequently mentioned uses of the information include setting performance goals or objectives (67 percent), developing specific HR programs (61 percent), and evaluating the effectiveness of a particular HR department (61 percent). Slightly more than half of the responding companies use HR function evaluations to judge the performance of HR executives (59 percent) and HR managers (53 percent). Slightly less than half (47 percent) use the evaluations to allocate resources within the HR function.

The evaluation information on overall HRM is used for setting performance goals and objectives by 84 percent of the responding companies. Sixty-four percent use this information to evaluate managers, while 59 percent use it to evaluate divisional executives. About half the companies also use it to evaluate the performance of HR executives (50 percent) or HR managers (45 percent).

Effectiveness Criteria

An earlier literature review identified 56 indices or criteria that measure the effectiveness of the HR function, 35 criteria that measure overall HR effectiveness, and 20 criteria that measure the services provided by the HR function. The survey asked HR executives to indicate which of these criteria they use to judge the effectiveness of either the HR function or overall HR effectiveness. Table 3 summarizes the responses to the 20 service criteria, while Table 4 compares the effectiveness indicators of the HR function versus overall HRM.

As shown in Table 3, a large majority of the companies (76 percent) use cooperation of HR staff members as a criterion to judge the effectiveness of the HR function, while only one third of the companies use response time—the average amount of time taken to respond to inquiries from clients—in this fashion. Line executives' satisfaction with the HR function or department is used by nearly all the responding companies (90 percent). A majority also use satisfaction of line managers (84 percent) and employees (70 percent) to measure the effectiveness of the HR function.

Table 4 shows that most of the criteria shown are used to measure the effectiveness of both the HR function and overall HRM. However, some criteria are seen as more appropriate for one use than the other. For example, benefit costs as a percent of average salary are used to measure the effectiveness of the HR function in 70 percent of the companies, but only 44 percent use this to measure overall HR effectiveness. Average time to fill positions is also used more frequently for measuring the effectiveness of the HR function (64 percent) than for measuring overall HR effectiveness (32 percent). Other criteria used more often to evaluate the HR function than overall human resources include equal employment opportunity goals, training and development indices, and the number of union drives.

On the other hand, more companies use revenue per employee to measure overall HR effectiveness (47 percent) than the effectiveness of HR function (24 percent). Productivity and work quality indices are also used more often for assessing overall HR effectiveness than for assessing the HR function.

Summary of HR Evaluation Practices

The following conclusions can be drawn from the results of the HR evaluation practices survey:

Systematic, periodic evaluation of HR effectiveness does not occur frequently in American business organizations. Many firms do not evaluate HR effectiveness at all, and only 9 of the 70 firms reporting HR evaluations use the procedures described most fre-

Table 3

Use of HR Evaluation Criteria By Survey Respondents

	Companies Using Criterion	
Effectiveness Criteria	N	Percentage[a]
Personnel/HR Services		
Cooperation of HR staff	51	76%
Quality of HR staff	49	73
Quality of service	47	70
Quality of HR programs	46	69
Availability of HR staff	46	69
Innovativeness of HR staff	45	67
Integration of HR strategy with business management plan	44	66
Objectivity of HR staff	43	64
Proactivity of HR staff	42	63
Quality of advice	42	63
Openness of HR staff	37	55
Trustworthiness of HR staff	35	52
Number of employees who consult with HR staff	33	49
Number of managers who consult with HR staff	32	48
Handling of poor performers	31	46
Number of new ER or HR programs	23	34
Average response time to inquiries	22	33
Overall Effectiveness Criteria		
Executives' satisfaction	60	90
Line managers' satisfaction	56	84
Employees' satisfaction	47	70

[a]Percentage is based on a total of 67 companies. Three respondents did not complete this section of the survey.

quently in the literature. Most survey firms use indirect or informal methods for evaluations.

Larger and better-performing firms are more likely to engage in systematic HR evaluation. The HR function in these companies tends to have more resources, and this may reflect the added emphasis on HR evaluation. However, the causal relationship between a firm's financial performance and its practice of HR evaluation requires additional research. While the attention to evalua-

Table 4

Differential Use of Effectiveness Criteria By Survey Respondents

Effectiveness Criteria	Percent of Companies Using Criterion To Measure Effectiveness of:	
	Overall HR	HR function
Staffing Criteria		
New position hires[a]	73%	76%
Replacement hires	66	75
Average time to fill jobs	32	64
Acceptance ratio	20	27
Number of applicant complaints[a]	19	19
Recruitment data[b]	—	75
Performance Criteria		
Performance appraisal[a]	92	85
Involuntary terminations	56	64
Productivity indices	56	36
Work quality indices	34	18
Performance of new hires[a]	49	49
EEO Criteria		
EEO grievances	64	72
EEO suits	59	72
Minority turnover rate[a]	41	42
Number of minority job offers	36	55
Minority promotion rate	37	51
Offer rejected by minorities	15	27
Number of minority applicants[b]	—	55
Number of minority hires[b]	49	—
Training and Development Criteria		
Number of employees trained	61	72
Participant ratings[a]	49	52
Training cost per employee	37	51
Training hours per employee	34	43
Outcome measures (e.g., reduction in errors made)	36	43

	Percent of Companies Using Criterion To Measure Effectiveness of:	
Effectiveness Criteria		
Employee morale/attitudes criteria		
Grievance/complaint rate[a]	61%	60%
Average employee tenure	51	63
Voluntary terminations	56	63
Absenteeism rate	56	46
Job satisfaction	66	57
Number of accidents[a]	41	42
Number of union drives	27	36
Financial Criteria		
Benefit cost as a percent of average salary	44	70
Average salary per employee[a]	46	46
Cost per employee hired	27	45
Revenue ($) per employee	47	24
Pretax income per employee	17	7
Benefit cost per dollar of income[b]	29	—
HR budget per employee[b]	—	40

Table 4 continued

[a]The difference in percentages is not statistically significant. All other differences computed reach statistical significance at $P<.05$ or better.
[b]Indicates that this criterion was not included in this part of the survey, so no statistical test was computed.

tion may have contributed to more effective organizational performance, successful companies may also have greater resources to devote to this activity.

Firms conducting HR evaluations are more aggressive and risk taking in both their product/market strategies and in resource management. The integration between business planning and HRM in effect legitimizes the importance of the HR function. In these firms, HR executives play an active role in managing the business, and consequently are held accountable for their firm's overall success.

Operating executives, managers, and supervisors in firms conducting HR evaluations are responsible for the effectiveness of each employee. Corporate executives, both line and HR, are responsible for the effectiveness of the HR function. Information obtained through evaluations of employee effectiveness in turn becomes the tool used to assess managerial performance, as well as to set specific performance goals or objectives. This suggests that employee effectiveness is a primary responsibility of each supervisor or manager in these companies. The evaluation information on the HR function, on the other hand, is used for improving specific HR functions and developing HR programs.

No single criterion is used in all organizations to determine HR effectiveness. This suggests that effectiveness is a multi-criteria concept and that different companies find different criteria meaningful. However, employee effectiveness as measured by individual performance appraisals appears to be a widespread criterion for evaluating overall HR effectiveness. Client satisfaction, on the other hand, appears to be the most common criterion for evaluating the effectiveness of the HR function.

Client satisfaction receives a great deal of emphasis in evaluating the HR function, which reinforces its service-oriented role. This orientation also shows up in the importance given service criteria, such as cooperation, quality, and availability of HR staff members, as well as the quality of programs and services. These findings are based on HR executives' own perceptions; clients may place even greater emphasis on these service criteria.

Attitudes Toward HR Evaluations

The survey results clearly indicate skepticism about the value of HR evaluations. The approaches recommended in the HR evaluation literature have had little impact on actual practice, and the low response rate to the survey may well reflect a low practice rate.

Survey Responses

To verify this, a follow-up letter was sent asking nonresponding HR executives to indicate whether their firms engaged in periodic, formal evaluation of the HR function. The responses confirmed the original suspicion. Out of the 290 responses received, 90 (31 percent) reported that their firms do perform HR evaluation, mainly on an informal basis and rarely using the analytical approaches recommended by researchers. When asked about future plans, only 8 companies indicated having plans to implement HR evaluations and 17 felt such an evaluation would help the HR staff convince management of their contributions. The following comments reveal a general theme of skepticism about HR evaluation:

- Measuring key indices may be useful, but personnel people tend to get caught up in the measuring process and lose sight of overall goals. Credibility will come when we operate as business managers with an expertise in HRM rather than as HR managers. Personnel audits may actually reinforce the wrong image of what the department is doing.

- We honestly doubt that periodic evaluations or formal audits can enhance the prestige of the department. Businessmen look at the bottom line. Has HR really contributed by assisting in hiring top-notch employees? Has HR created innovative compensation and career ladder systems? A formal audit measures such things as how many interviews have taken place, [what] proportion of personnel files [were] processed on time, and how quickly grievances were processed. Who cares?

- Periodic evaluations have not accomplished much for us. We are now questioning whether the effort is worth the energy.

- Collection of such (evaluation) data is viewed by management as time consuming and not necessarily productive when intuitive judgement will suffice.

- Cost of collecting and analyzing the evaluation data tends to outweigh the benefits. We have better things to do with scarce staff time.

The Gap Between Prescription and Practice

The comments noted above suggest that doubts about the value of HR evaluation may have retarded its development in practice. The crucial question then becomes: Why has practice lagged behind prescription?

The survey responses suggest five possible reasons for this gap. These are: (1) fear of evaluation, (2) unclear purposes of evaluation, (3) measurement problems, (4) unclear focus of evaluation, and (5) lack of a meaningful framework to guide evaluation.

Fear of Evaluation

The reluctance to conduct evaluations of HR effectiveness is captured in the following responses of two HR executives: "We don't audit the function because we feel that senior executives would use it [the evaluation information] as a club. We get little management support—would make the situation worse if we audited," and "The evaluation information can be interpreted incorrectly by top management and lead to negative results for our department rather than demonstrating areas for further opportunities. I am not convinced that such an evaluation would accomplish anything other than demoralize the personnel managers."

These statements convey a lack of confidence by the HR executives in the effectiveness or contribution of the HR function. The resulting reluctance to perform evaluations is hardly new: Fifteen years ago, one researcher noted this fear of negative consequences if an evaluation fails to show worthwhile contributions by the HR function.[36]

Other decision-making research suggests that individuals tend to avoid taking risks when asked to choose between probable gains and losses or certain gains, even when the expected value of the probable gains is greater than the value of the gains that are certain.[37] In evaluations, keeping the status quo may be perceived as a certain gain that is preferable to the uncertainty of possible positive or negative outcomes. This preference is enhanced when the evaluation is linked to formal performance appraisals of the HR managers or executives.[38] Thus, fear is a plausible reason for the rarity of HR evaluations in practice.

Unclear Purposes

Unclear purposes of an HR evaluation contribute to this fear. Evaluation is central for organizational control,[39] since it provides information necessary for deciding how to allocate rewards and resources. However, evaluation also provides information for improving performance and setting new goals or objectives. The conflict inherent in the dual purposes of individual performance evaluations[40] also applies to evaluations of HR effectiveness. If management uses the information as a criterion for allocating financial resources, HR managers will take a different approach to the evaluation than if it is used to improve performance or develop programs.

Most authors find that identifying objectives at the outset is crucial to the success of the evaluation task;[41] otherwise, managers will fear and avoid the evaluation unless it is mandated by management. As one HR executive remarked, "We are not so sure what the real consequences of the evaluation would be. Trying to be too honest about strengths and weaknesses may lead to an inordinate attention being paid by senior executives to weaknesses while brushing aside the strengths."

Measurement Problems

Measurement problems may have delayed implementation of HR evaluations in many organizations. As discussed earlier, several procedures have been proposed for measuring virtually all aspects of HR effectiveness. A key unresolved issue concerns the validity of the data generated by such measurements. As noted by a survey respondent: "Evaluating the effectiveness of the HRM function is easy. Evaluating the validity of the evaluation is the tricky part."

The presence of invalid data has been recognized as a major problem in the design and administration of organizational control systems.[42] Invalidity may result from either intentional distortion or simply from the psychological reaction of employees to the measurement process. Ways in which the measurement process can influence work behavior include catalytic and motivational effects.[43] Measurement has a catalytic effect by influencing perception and limiting the search to only those dimensions which are measured, thus constraining alternatives in decision making. The motivational effect occurs when measurement is tied to reward systems. Individuals are motivated to perform well in those areas that are measured and rewarded, but not in those areas that are ignored. For example, if minority promotion rate is measured and rewarded, the HR function may pay more attention to the number of minorities promoted than the quality of the candidates or their success in the new positions.

To avoid these effects, it may be necessary to measure as many aspects of HRM as possible, an expensive proposition which may produce information overload. The difficulty of determining what to measure and how to obtain valid data may hinder the implementation of HR evaluation.

Two related aspects of this problem concern the definition of standards and interpretation of data. What level of turnover is optimal? How many grievances should an organization have? Because such questions are difficult to answer, some authors advise against prescribing any universal yardstick and instead suggest matching evaluation results to the unique expectations of management in each company.[44] Even this interpretation of data poses difficulties, since it is often not clear just what the data mean, and they may mean different things to different people within the same organization.[45]

In addition, it is often unclear to what extent performance on a specific measure can be attributed to the efforts of the HR function, to line managers' efforts, or to some other cause. Should the HR function be held accountable for controlling turnover? Is this a valid measure of the effectiveness of the HR function either alone or in conjunction with line managers? To what extent can employee performance be controlled by management? Is this a valid measure of overall HR effectiveness?

Many of the HR executives surveyed mentioned this difficulty of separating out the causal effects of personnel programs, personal factors, and environmental influences as their main concern with formal evaluations. This problem was succinctly captured in the following statement from one respondent:

> Most measures involved in the typical personnel audit (e.g., turnover, grievances, and absenteeism) vary more as a function of managerial behavior than as a result of any activities conducted by the HRM function. Our influence on these variables is very indirect. Unless we have direct authority over all managers, evaluating HR effectiveness (e.g., turnover trends) as an indicator of the HRM function's effectiveness would be meaningless. We can't be held responsible for things beyond our control. Therefore, why should we conduct evaluations that may fly in our face?

Unclear Focus

The problem of unclear focus is evident in the HR evaluation literature. Researchers have not clearly distinguished between evaluating the effectiveness of overall HRM and the effectiveness of the HR function or between evaluating the effectiveness of HR policy makers at the corporate level from evaluating the effectiveness of HR policy implementors (for example, HR function at the operating level). Greater clarity regarding level and focus in HR evaluation is indispensable for planning, conducting, and interpreting the results of HR evaluation.[46]

Lack of a Framework

The ambiguity in focus may be traced to the lack of a meaningful framework for evaluating HR effectiveness. A framework serves as a useful guide for identifying the evaluation objectives, for selecting an appropriate focus, and for defining meaningful criteria. It removes the ambiguity associated with the evaluation activity and helps to make causal inferences from the data.

Lack of a meaningful framework to guide the HR evaluation may pose the major obstacle to its becoming more widely used. To date, scholars have not adequately addressed such conceptual issues as the meaning of HR effectiveness, the responsibility for HR outcomes, and the relationship between HR evaluation and issues of organizational strategy, structure, and management values. An HR evaluation is a systemic task and requires a systems perspective to integrate its different elements. With such a perspective, it is possible that HR evaluation will become an activity to be endorsed, not feared.

A Proposed Integrative Framework for Evaluating HR Effectiveness

In an effort to help narrow the gap between prescription and practice in the evaluation of HR effectiveness, we offer here a conceptual framework based on a systems perspective. The first step in developing a model to evaluate HR effectiveness is to define exactly what is meant by "effectiveness."

As has been noted, effectiveness is an unclear concept with different meanings to different people. Many researchers consider the concept to be inherently subjective and political.[47] The meaning of even objective indicators has to be interpreted, and ultimately someone must establish standards. As one analyst comments, "[I]n the end, organizational effectiveness is what the relevant parties decide it should be. There is no higher authority to which we can appeal."[48]

To clarify the subjective nature of this concept, an effectiveness model must first identify those decision makers who play a significant role in determining HR effectiveness. Typically, these primary decision makers are HR and line managers; the HR effectiveness model must recognize the extent to which decisions and actions of the two types of managers affect the utilization of an organization's human resources. HR managers contribute to this effort in a variety of ways, although primarily by running an effective HR function. An HR manager, for example, may design benefit programs that enhance the retention of valued employees and control costs, and thus directly affect the firm's bottom line.

A framework capturing both the HR and line manager dimensions is presented in Figure 1. It shows how the decisions and activities of HR and line managers relate to the effectiveness of the HR function, overall HR effectiveness, and ultimately, organizational effectiveness.

Interaction Between Framework Elements

A systems perspective suggests that appropriately designed HR programs and activities must match the requirements and constraints of the firm's internal and external environments. Managerial decisions are affected by a variety of internal factors, including a firm's business strategy, technology, work-force characteristics, and culture or management philosophy, as well as external environmental conditions found in the economy, the labor market, and government legislation. HR managers, in particular, have a major responsibility to identify relevant organizational factors and to understand their implications for HR policies, systems, or programs. These managers play a critical role in scanning the external environment and in formulating strategies to cope with environmental constraints or to capitalize on environmental opportunities.[49] (For more on these points, see Chapters 1.1, 1.2, and 1.3 of this volume.)

The policies and programs designed by HR managers should enable line managers to meet operational requirements and business objectives. When HR policies fail to do this, line managers tend to ignore the prescribed policies in order to accomplish their own business objectives. Thus, effective HR managers must have an accurate understanding of the firm's business objectives and the roles of various line managers. They also must influence line management's perception and understanding of constraints on the firm that may require HR programming unrelated to immediate business objectives. In other words, they must be both "responsive" and "proactive" in their decisions and actions.

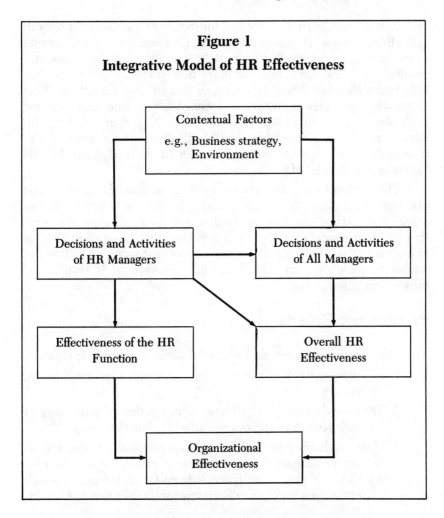

Figure 1

Integrative Model of HR Effectiveness

In the final analysis, the effectiveness of an HR function results directly from the decisions and actions of its HR managers. Overall HR effectiveness, on the other hand, is a direct result of the decisions and actions of line managers or of line managers and HR managers acting in concert. Organizational effectiveness, ultimately, results from the effectiveness of both the HR function and overall HRM.

This integrative approach departs from the traditional view of the HR function's role in organizational effectiveness since it treats

HR managers as both directly and indirectly responsible for overall HR effectiveness. It recognizes that HR managers design formal policies and programs that affect line managers' decisions and actions, and that they also formally or informally influence line managers through their advising or consulting activities. This approach holds HR managers as accountable as line managers for such outcomes as turnover, grievances, or employee morale. The survey results are consistent with this view, since most of the companies used these types of outcomes to measure both the HR function and overall HR effectiveness.

The subjective nature of the effectiveness concept suggests that HR outcomes (such as turnover and grievance activity) by themselves are neither effective nor ineffective. Instead, someone must determine the most appropriate criteria for measuring effectiveness of both the HR function and overall human resources, as well as the extent to which a particular level of achievement is considered effective or ineffective.

Effectiveness Criteria

HR effectiveness can be measured along three dimensions:
1. nature—whether the criteria measure a process or an outcome;
2. focus—whether the criteria examine the effectiveness of overall human resources or only HR function; and
3. form—whether the criteria are quantitative or qualitative measures. These three dimensions are presented in Figure 2 in the form of an Effectiveness Criteria Matrix, which also provides examples of criteria for each of the eight cells.

Process vs. Outcome

Effectiveness criteria reflect either processes or outcomes. Process criteria relate to the effectiveness of the activities or means employed to affect certain outcomes. Outcome criteria relate to the effectiveness of a desired end state or result. For example, the average time taken to fill a vacant position by the HR department is considered a process criterion, while line managers' satisfaction with the staffing process is an outcome criterion. Number of grievances is a process criterion, while employee loyalty to the company is an outcome criterion.

Figure 2

Effectiveness Criteria Matrix

	Overall HR Effectiveness		HR Function Effectiveness	
	Quantitative	Qualitative	Quantitative	Qualitative
Process	Cell 1 –Absentee- ism rate –Minority turnover –Grievances –Job acceptance rate	Cell 2 –Lack of conflict –Innova- tiveness –Union relations –Flexibility	Cell 5 –Average time to fill jobs –Cost per employee hired –No. of minority applicants –Training hours per employee	Cell 6 –Time to answer inquiries –Quality of HR services –Coopera- tiveness of HR staff –Quality of HR programs
Outcomes	Cell 3 –Revenue per employee –New inven- tions –Productivity –Loss of key employees	Cell 4 –Employee morale –Stakeholder approval –Company reputation for HR	Cell 7 –Value added on HR investment –HR budget per employee –No. of new ER programs –Personnel ratio	Cell 8 –Executive satisfaction –Line manager satisfaction –Employees' opinion of HR

Understanding why a particular effectiveness criterion is considered process or outcome can help clarify the relationship between the efforts of HR managers and line managers, and between the means and ends of managerial activities. Management values and/or corporate philosophy usually influence whether a specific criterion is considered a process or an outcome. For example, one company may consider employee morale to be a means to organizational success, while another company may consider it an end in itself.

Overall Human Resources vs. HR Function

Management philosophy also can influence which criteria will be used to measure overall HR effectiveness and which will measure only the HR function. Some organizations consider turnover and grievances to be criteria for measuring overall HR effectiveness; others use them to measure the effectiveness of the HR function; and the authors of this chapter advocate using these criteria for evaluating both. Meaningful HR evaluation must begin with determining, in advance, which criteria should be used to measure overall human resources, which should be used only to measure the HR function, and which should apply to both types of evaluations.

For measuring overall HR effectiveness, process criteria include such measures as absenteeism, scrap rate, and accidents. Outcome criteria can be defined in both financial terms, such as revenue per employee and return on investment, and nonfinancial terms, such as employee morale and psychological commitment.

For measuring the effectiveness of the HR function, process criteria include performance measures of specific HR subfunctions, such as staffing, training, compensation, and labor relations. In general, personnel or HR audits focus on these process criteria,[50] as do most of the indices found in Table 1. Examples of financial measures that are outcome criteria for the HR function include benefit costs as a percent of payroll or costs per hire. Nonfinancial outcome criteria can focus on client reactions, such as line managers' opinions of services or advice received from HR managers. Line managers' or client reactions are widely used criteria among the firms surveyed for this chapter.

Quantitative vs. Qualitative Criteria

Effectiveness criteria also may be measured either quantitatively or qualitatively. For example, employee turnover or grievances are quantitative measures; job satisfaction or reactions to training programs are qualitative criteria even though they may be measured on quantifiable scales. Cost per hire is a quantitative outcome criterion for measuring the HR function, while line managers' opinions of the HR function are a qualitative outcome criterion. Of the key indicators listed in Table 1, those in the left-hand column are predominantly quantitative, while those in the right-hand column tend to be qualitative.

The HR evaluation literature shows a bias favoring quantitative criteria.[51] Current practices among the survey firms do not suggest a dominance of quantitative criteria, and actual practices reported in the literature rely more on qualitative criteria, such as line manager or client reactions.[52]

However, neither quantitative nor qualitative criteria alone suffice for the total evaluation task. Rather, a combination approach utilizing both types of criteria is required.

Level of Analysis

The question of the level of analysis has received little attention in the management literature. Most authors focus on the HR function in their evaluation models,[53] and emphasize the operational effectiveness of the function in implementing personnel policies and in assisting line management in its HR activities. Other researchers focus on the effectiveness of HR policies[54] or programs[55] or on the entire HR function.[56] In the cases discussed in the literature, evaluations emphasize the appropriateness or effectiveness of policies or programs given organizational needs and user expectations.

Usually, no explicit distinction has been made between HR function evaluation at the corporate level and at the operating level. Yet, just as managers at different organizational levels confront different issues,[57] HR decisions and activities also differ at the strategic, or corporate, level; the management level; and the operating level of the firm.[58] Evaluation objectives and criteria therefore must also vary according to the organizational level at which the evaluation task is focused. Figure 3 summarizes the evaluation objectives and effectiveness criteria appropriate to each of the three organizational levels.

Strategic Level

At the highest level, key HR decisions involve the design of policies that meet the strategic challenges of the organization. Strategic challenges include business objectives, corporate values or culture, technology, and structure, as well as requirements or constraints of the external environment. (See Chapter 1.1 of this volume.)

The objective of the HR evaluation at this level is to assess the degree of strategic fit: that is, the appropriateness of HR policies for a particular set of strategic challenges. Outcome criteria seem most

Figure 3

Human Resource Evaluation at Different Organizational Levels

	Strategic	Management	Operating
HR Evaluation Objective:	Strategic Fit	Management Control	Service Delivery
	. . .through examining the appropriateness of HR policies	. . .through analyzing the cost–effectiveness of HR programs	. . .through assessing the quality of HR services
Effectiveness Criteria: Overall HR	Outcome Criteria –Qualitative and Quantitative (cells 3 and 4)	Outcome and Process Criteria –Quantitative (cells 1 and 3)	Process criteria –Qualitative and Quantitative (cells 1 and 2)
HR Function	Outcome criteria –Qualitative and Quantitative (cells 7 and 8)	Outcome and Process –Quantitative (cells 5 and 7)	Outcome and Process –Qualitative (cells 6 and 8)

Note: cell numbers refer to those shown in Figure 2.

meaningful for measuring the effectiveness of both overall human resources and the HR function at this level. For example, revenue per employee and employee morale may be used to measure overall HR effectiveness, while personnel ratios or client satisfaction may be meaningful for the effectiveness of the HR function.

Management Level

At the business or management level, key HR decisions involve the design of systems or programs consistent with policy guidelines which will facilitate the cost-effective implementation of business goals. The objective at this level is management control, and this is accomplished through analyzing the cost-effectiveness of HR programs. Both process and outcome criteria may be useful for measuring effectiveness of overall human resources and the HR function. However, quantitative criteria, such as the cost-effectiveness of HR programs to reduce turnover, improve morale, and promote innovativeness or productivity, may prove more useful for measuring overall HR effectiveness.

Operating Level

At the operating level, managers implement HR policies and programs and undertake actions or decisions which affect the attraction, motivation, and retention of employees. This level encompasses the hands-on HR practices of line managers and the day-to-day services provided by the HR function that directly affect HR outcomes.

The objective of an operational HR evaluation is to assess the effect of line managers' decisions and actions and the quality of services provided by the HR department. Process criteria are most appropriate for measuring overall HR effectiveness, while both process and outcome criteria seem appropriate for measuring the effectiveness of the HR function. In effect, the operating unit is held accountable for such overall HR effectiveness measures as absenteeism, grievances, or innovativeness, while the effectiveness of the HR function is measured by such criteria as the perceived quality of services, the cooperativeness of the HR staff, or overall satisfaction of such clients as executives, managers, or employees.

Client Satisfaction as an HR Effectiveness Criterion

Client or line managers' satisfaction increasingly is being advocated as a meaningful criterion of HR effectiveness.[59] As described in one article, "HR provides a service to *internal* customers—namely, line managers and workers on the firing line."[60] For this criterion, the focus is clearly on the HR function at the operating level, the organization's "firing line."

Using client satisfaction to measure the effectiveness of the HR function is not a new idea. It appears implicitly or explicitly as a criterion in almost all evaluation models, and it is used by over 80 percent of the firms surveyed for this chapter. The popularity of this criterion stems in part from the nature of the tasks performed by the HR function. The demand for personnel services is a derived demand; consequently, the HR function has value only to the extent to which it helps the rest of the organization achieve objectives.

Identifying Clients

The first step to achieving client satisfaction is to identify the customer for HR department services. This can be done in a number of ways. One analyst emphasizes the importance of understanding line management's expectations;[61] another suggests that an HR department "must research its markets and find out what its customers, primary producing departments, need, want, or will buy";[62] and another proposes the critical question of "Who is the customer?"[63] Others take a broader approach and recognize the presence of multiple interest groups or constituencies.[64] One analysis links recognition of various stakeholders' interests in HR policy design and practices not only to the internal well-being of the organization, but also to the success and ultimate survival of the enterprise.[65]

Assessing Clients' Needs

Various groups of managers or constituencies have different expectations and preferences for the activities performed by the HR function.[66] They also have different opinions regarding the department's effectiveness in meeting these expectations or preferences.[67]

Client satisfaction as a measure of HR effectiveness recognizes the subjective and political nature of the effectiveness construct. An organization that relies on a measure of client satisfaction to assess HR effectiveness should identify the critical constituencies, analyze their needs or expectations, determine the criteria that these stakeholders use in judging effectiveness, and, if necessary, influence constituency demands or expectations. For example, the personnel department may need to help line departments in setting objectives,[68] and to do this the HR function must understand the business objectives as well as the operational requirements or constraints of its clients, constituencies, or stakeholders, including line managers, top executives, and employees.

Prioritizing Constituencies

A major challenge in using the client satisfaction criterion to evaluate HR effectiveness is to determine the relative importance of different clients, given the difficulty of simultaneously meeting all clients' expectations. A recent study on the effectiveness of the HR function found top management received the most attention and nonmanagement employees the least attention from HR departments.[69] A related study suggests that nonmanagement employees and lower- to middle-level managers are more likely than upper-level executives to see a relationship between the effectiveness of the HR function and either an organization's overall HR effectiveness or its overall operating efficiency.[70]

These studies indicate that client satisfaction has important implications for managing the relationship of the HR department with important stakeholders or constituencies. At both the functional and organizational levels, client satisfaction begins with identifying the clients' expectations and defining desirable HR outcomes.[71] At the organizational level, client satisfaction determines how much approval or support will be given to HR policies and, to some extent, how outsiders view the company's HR effectiveness. At the function level, effectiveness relates more to reputation among internal clients such as executives, managers, and employees. A favorable reputation is essentially power "based on the ability to offer effective help in solving real problems."[72] In turn, this reputed power helps the HR function to influence the decisions and actions of its clients. In other words, using client satisfaction as a measure of effectiveness suggests a process that not only ensures that the HR function is delivering services relevant to client needs but also enhances the power or influence of the HR function.

Guidelines for Practitioners

The framework proposed here attempts to resolve some of the problems that have hindered HR evaluation and to provide guidelines for the evaluation task.

The following suggestions should help HR managers apply this integrative framework to the practice of HR evaluations in their organizations.

Assume Responsibility for HR Effectiveness

HR executives must assume responsibility for the effectiveness of both overall HRM and the HR function. They are just as responsible as line managers for such HR outcomes as turnover, morale, grievances, and productivity. This joint responsibility suggests that HR and line managers must work as partners to bring about desired HR outcomes. It also means that HR managers must be more active in influencing other managers' actions and decisions so as to enhance their own effectiveness.

Set Clear Objectives

The HR evaluation must have clear objectives. Is the objective to enhance administrative efficiency or to develop new HR initiatives? Is the objective to control costs or to improve programs? Clear objectives are necessary for the selection of an appropriate evaluation strategy.

Differentiate the Levels of Evaluation

An HR function has three levels of responsibilities, and these are usually differentiated at the three organizational levels. The first is policy development, which occurs at the strategic or corporate level. The second is cost control, which occurs at the management or business level. The third is service delivery, which is critical at the operating level. Evaluation objectives and effectiveness criteria should differ for each of the three types of responsibilities across the three organizational levels.

Adjust Evaluation Focus and Criteria to the Level of Analysis

Evaluation at the corporate level should focus on overall HR effectiveness and use outcome criteria, such as revenue per employee, benefit costs as percent of payroll, legal compliance, or product innovation. Evaluation at the management level should focus on quantitative effectiveness criteria for both overall HR and the HR function. Utility analysis of alternative HR systems or programs and cost indices applied to such HR subfunctions as staffing, training, compensation, and safety can be used. At the operating level, evaluation should focus on the impact of managerial decisions and the quality of services provided by the HR function. Process and qualitative criteria, such as absenteeism rate or cohesiveness (for overall HR) and client satisfaction (for one HR function) are appropriate effectiveness criteria.

Determine the Importance of Stakeholders or Clients

The HR function must determine the relative importance of various stakeholders and allocate attention and resources accordingly. For example, line managers and nonmanagement employees may be more important clients than line executives. Even though nonmanagement employees are the least powerful in the organizational hierarchy, it may be necessary to place more emphasis on this client to counteract the tendency to cater to the more powerful line executives.

Understand Stakeholder or Client Needs

Client satisfaction results from solving clients' problems and meeting their needs. This means that HR policies or decisions must reflect the requirements of line executives' business objectives, the operational requirements of line managers, and the personal expectations of nonmanagement employees. An HR function may enhance its effectiveness by spending more time understanding clients before developing HR technologies.

Involve the Clients

Input from stakeholders or clients may facilitate the process of defining desirable HR outcomes and designing HR policies or activities. HR committees at both the strategic and operating levels that have representation by important stakeholders or clients (such as line managers and nonmanagement employees in the operating units) are a useful mechanism to achieve this purpose. These committees can also serve as the assessors of the effectiveness of both overall HR and the HR function.

Utilize HR Evaluation Committees

A specialized HR evaluation committee comprised of stakeholders in HR effectiveness can also be formulated. Such a committee would define the focus, objectives, and criteria for measuring effectiveness. It would also serve as the judge for assessing effectiveness, informed by the data or information gathered through the evaluation process.

Use Evaluation Information Judiciously

Evaluation information should be used to achieve evaluation objectives, and not to allocate resources unless the objective is cost control. When the objective is assessing strategic fit or the quality of services delivered, the information should be used to improve HR systems and services and not to make budgetary decisions.

Emphasize the Operating HR Department

More emphasis should be placed on evaluating the effectiveness of the HR function at the operating level. The operational HR function has the greatest impact on employees' attitudes and behaviors. It also affects overall HR effectiveness by providing useful and relevant services to managers and employees. This requires an understanding of the needs and expectations of clients, which will occur only if the operating HR department has greater autonomy and more highly skilled staff than is currently the case.

This chapter has a reason for its focus on broad issues of HR evaluation rather than on tools, techniques, or procedures. As one HR executive responding to the survey expressed it, "Don't get hung up on procedural formula. Find out how HR can meet overall corporate objectives. If your value is obvious to management it saves a lot of questions. Go on the offense!" Evaluating HR effectiveness can be an effective way to "go on the offense" by enhancing the contribution of the HR function and the effective utilization of all employees.

◆

Notes

1. See, for example, Biles and Schuler; Dimick and Murray; Fitz-Enz (1980); French; Mahler; Merrihue and Katzell; Odiorne. Among the dozens of textbooks available in the 1980s, almost all contain some discussion of the topic and many devote an entire chapter to it (e.g., Holley and Jennings; Milkovich and Glueck; Peterson and Tracy; Werther and Davis).
2. Gomez-Mejia.
3. Jain and Murray.
4. Fitz-Enz (1980).
5. Peterson and Malone.
6. Bowen and Greiner.
7. Fitz-Enz (1980).
8. Jain and Murray.
9. Gray; Odiorne.
10. Lapointe; Mahler.
11. Harvey.
12. Biles; Hercus and Oades.
13. Mahler, p. 294.
14. Biles.

15. Cheek.
16. See, for example, Boudreau and Berger, and Cascio.
17. Fitz-Enz (1980), p. 41.
18. Dahl.
19. Ash; Biles and Schuler; Dunnette, Milkovich and Motowidlo; Fitz-Enz (1980); French; Lapointe; Mahler.
20. Merrihue and Katzell; see also Gomez-Mejia.
21. Tsui (1984).
22. Bowen and Greiner.
23. See Simon and Burstein for a highly readable description of these methods.
24. Luthans and Maris.
25. Gomez-Mejia, Page, and Tornow.
26. Flamholtz (1974).
27. Brummet, Pyle, and Flamholtz; Flamholtz (1974); Lev and Schwartz; Likert and Bowers.
28. Brogden and Taylor; Cascio.
29. Cronbach and Gleser.
30. Schmidt et al. (1979).
31. Schmidt, Hunter, and Pearlman.
32. Boudreau and Berger; see also Chapter 1.4 of this volume.
33. Over 50 percent of the respondents have more than 2000 employees compared to 27 percent of the nonrespondents.
34. As reported by the American Society for Personnel Administration and the Bureau of National Affairs Inc.
35. See Miles and Snow for a complete strategy typology.
36. Gordon.
37. Tversky and Kahnerman.
38. Peterson and Malone.
39. Flamholtz, Das, and Tsui.
40. Meyer, Kay, and French.
41. Biles; Gordon; Peterson and Malone.

42. Lawler.
43. Flamholtz (1979).
44. See, for example, Mahler.
45. Gordon; Peterson and Malone.
46. Dyer.
47. Cameron; Campbell; Kanter.
48. Campbell, p. 52.
49. See Chapter 1.3 of this volume for a detailed discussion of environmental scanning.
50. See, for example, Biles and Schuler; Fitz-Enz (1984); Mahler.
51. See, for example, Fitz-Enz (1980 and 1984).
52. Bolar; McAfee; Stone.
53. See, for example, Gray; McAfee; McLaughlin; Peterson and Malone; Rabe; Tsui (1984).
54. See, for example, Bolar.
55. See, for example, Gordon; Luthans and Maris; Schmidt, Hunter and Pearlman.
56. See, for example, Biles and Schuler; Gomez-Mejia; Keene; Lapointe; Mahler; Sheibar; Staltonstall.
57. Lorange; Schendel and Hofer.
58. Biles and Schuler; Devanna, Fombrun, and Tichy.
59. See, for example, Beer et al.; Tsui (1984).
60. Bowen and Greiner, p. 36.
61. Mahler.
62. Odiorne, p. 9-5.
63. Bowen and Griener.
64. Tsui (1984).
65. Beer et al.
66. Tsui (1987b); Tsui and Milkovich.
67. Tsui (1987a).
68. Odiorne.
69. Tsui (1987b).
70. Tsui (1987a).
71. Beer et al.; Bowen and Greiner; Mahler; Odiorne.
72. Jain and Murray, p. 107.

Editor's Note: In addition to the References shown below, there are other significant sources of information and ideas on evaluating HR effectiveness.

Articles

Balkin, D.B. and L.R. Gomez-Mejia. 1987. "A Contingency Theory of Compensation." *Strategic Management Journal* 8(1): 159–182.

Capelli, P. and R.B. McKersie. 1983. "Labor and Crisis in Collective Bargaining." Paper presented at an MIT/Union Leadership Conference, Boston.

Payne, B. 1951. "Evaluating the Personnel Department." *Personnel Journal* 29: 343–345.

Tichy, N.M., C.J. Fombrun, and M.A. Devanna. 1982. "Strategic Human Resource Management." *Sloan Management Review* 23: 42–61.

◆

References

ASPA/BNA Survey No. 47. 1984. "Personnel Activities, Budgets and Staff 1983–1984." *Bulletin to Management*, June 21. Washington, DC: The Bureau of National Affairs, Inc.

Beer, M., B. Spector, P.R. Lawrence, D.Q. Mills, and R.E. Walton. 1985. *Human Resource Management: A General Manager's Perspective*. New York: Free Press.

Biles, G.E. 1986. "Auditing HRM Practices." *Personnel Administrator* December: 89–93.

Biles, G.E., and R.S. Schuler. 1986. *Audit Handbook of Human Resource Management Practices*. Alexandria, VA: American Society for Personnel Administration.

Bolar, M. 1970. "Measuring Effectiveness of Personnel Policy Implementation." *Personnel Psychology* 23: 463–480.

Boudreau, J.W., and C.J. Berger. 1985. "Decision-theoretic Utility Analysis Applied to Employee Separations and Acquisitions." *Journal of Applied Psychology* 70: 581–612.

Bowen, D.E., and L.E. Greiner. 1986. "Moving From Production to Service in Human Resources Management." *Organizational Dynamics* Summer: 35–53.

Brogden, H.E., and E. Taylor. 1950. "The Dollar Criterion—Applying the Cost Accounting Concept to Criterion Construction." *Personnel Psychology* 3: 133–154.

Brummet, R.L., W.C. Pyle, and E.G. Flamholtz. 1969. "Human Resource Accounting in Industry." *Personnel Administration* July-August: 34–46.

Cameron, K. 1978. "Measuring Organizational Effectiveness in Institutions of Higher Education." *Administrative Science Quarterly* 23: 604–632.

Campbell, J.P. 1977. "On the Nature of Organizational Effectiveness." In Goodman, P.S. & Pennings, H.M. (eds.) *New Perspectives on Organizational Effectiveness*. San Francisco: Jossey-Bass, 13–55.

Cascio, W.F. 1982. *Costing Human Resources: The Financial Impact of Behavior in Organizations*. Boston: Kent Publishing Company.

Cheek, L.M. 1973. "Cost Effectiveness Comes to the Personnel Function." *Harvard Business Review* May-June: 96–105.

Cronbach, L.J., and G.C. Gleser. 1965. *Psychological Tests and Personnel Decisions.* 2nd ed. Urbana, IL: University of Illinois Press.

Dahl, H.L., Jr. 1979. "Measuring the Human ROI." *Management Review* 68: 44–50.

Devanna, M.A., C.J. Fombrun, and N.M. Tichy. 1984. "A Framework for Strategic Human Resource Management." In Fombrun, C., N.M. Tichy, and M.A. Devanna (eds.) *Strategic Human Resource Management.* New York: John Wiley & Sons.

Dimick, E.E., and V.V. Murray. 1978. Correlates of Substantive Policy Decisions in Organizations: The Case of Human Resource Management." *Academy of Management Journal* 21: 611–623.

Dunnette, M.D., G.T. Milkovich, and S.J. Motowidlo. 1973. "Possible Approaches for Development of a Naval Personnel Status Index (NPSI)." Unpublished technical report, Personnel Decisions, Inc., Minneapolis.

Dyer, L. 1984. "Studying Human Resource Strategy: An Approach and an Agenda." *Industrial Relations* 23(2): 156–169.

Fitz-Enz, J. 1980. "Quantifying the Human Resources Function." *Personnel Journal* 57: 41–52.

———. 1984. *How to Measure Human Resources Management.* New York: McGraw-Hill.

Flamholtz, E. 1974. *Human Resource Accounting.* Encino, CA: Dickenson Publishing Company.

———. 1979. "Toward a Psycho-Technical Systems Paradigm of Organizational Measurement." *Decision Science* 10(1): 71–84.

Flamholtz, E.G., T.K. Daz, and A.S. Tsui. 1985. "Toward an Integrative Framework of Organizational Control." *Accounting, Organizations and Society* 10: 35–50.

French, S.H., Jr. 1954. "Measuring Progress Toward Industrial Relations Objectives." *Personnel* 5: 338–347.

Gomez-Mejia, L.R. 1985. "Dimensions and Correlates of the Personnel Audit as an Organizational Assessment Tool." *Personnel Psychology* 38: 293–308.

Gomez-Mejia, L.R., R.C. Page, and W.W. Tornow. 1982. "A Comparison of the Practical Utility of Traditional, Statistical, and Hybrid Job Evaluation Approaches." *Academy of Management Journal* 25: 790–809.

Gordon, M.E. 1972. "Three Ways to Effectively Evaluate Personnel Programs." *Personnel Journal* 51: 498–510.

Gray, R.D. 1965. "Evaluating the Personnel Department." *Personnel* 42: 43–52.

Harvey, J.L. 1986. "Nine Major Trends in HRM." *Personnel Administrator* November: 102–109.

Hercus, T., and D. Oades. 1982. "The Human Resource Audit: An Instrument for Change. *Human Resource Planning* 5(1): 43–49.

Holley, W.H., and K.M. Jennings. 1987. *Personnel/Human Resource Management*. Chicago: Dryden Press.

Jain, H., and V. Murray. 1984. "Why the Human Resources Management Function Fails." *California Management Review* Summer: 95–111.

Kanter, R.M. 1981. "The Definition and Measurement of System and Individual Effectiveness, Productivity and Performance in Organizations: Critical Issues, Dilemma and New Directions. *Annual Review of Sociology*: 321–349.

Keene, C.M. 1976. "Personnel Management Reviews in a Multi-Campus State University." *Public Personnel Management* 5: 120–131.

Lapointe, J.R. 1983. "Human Resource Performance Indexes." *Personnel Journal* July: 545–553.

Lawler, E.E., III. 1976. "Control Systems in Organizations." In Dunnette, M.D. (ed.) *Handbook of Industrial and Organizational Psychology*. Chicago: Rand McNally.

Lev, B., and A. Schwartz. 1971. "On the Use of the Economic Concept of Human Capital in Financial Statements." *Accounting Review* 46: 103–112.

Likert, R., and D.G. Bowers. 1973. "Improving the Accuracy of P/L Reports by Estimating the Change in Dollar Value of the Human Organization." *Michigan Business Review* 25(2): 15–24.

Lorange, P. 1980. *Corporate Planning: An Executive View*. Englewood Cliffs, NJ: Prentice-Hall.

Luthans, F., and T.L. Maris. 1979. "Evaluating Personnel Programs Through the Reversal Technique." *Personnel Journal* 58: 692–697.

Mahler, W.R. 1979. "Auditing PAIR." In Yoder, D., and H.G. Heneman, Jr. *ASPA Handbook of Personnel and Industrial Relations*. Washington, DC: BNA Books.

McAfee, R.B. 1980. "Evaluating the Personnel Department's Internal Functioning." *Personnel* 57: 56–62.

McLaughlin, D. 1971. "Roadblocks to Personnel Department Effectiveness." *Personnel Journal* 50: 46–79.

Merrihue, W.V., and R.A. Katzell. 1955. "ERI-Yardstick of Employee Relations." *Harvard Business Review*: 91–99.

Meyer, H., E. Kay, and J.R.P. French, Jr. 1965. "Split Roles in Performance Appraisal." *Harvard Business Review* 43: 123–129.

Miles, R.E., and C.C. Snow. 1978. *Organizational Strategy, Structure, and Process*. New York: McGraw-Hill.

Milkovich, G.T., and W. Glueck. 1985. *Personnel: A Diagnostic Approach*. Dallas: Business Publications, Inc.

Odiorne, G.S. 1986. "Evaluating the Human Resources Program." In Famularo, Joseph J. *Handbook of Human Resource Administration* (2nd ed.). New York: McGraw-Hill.

Peterson, D.J., and R.L. Malone. 1975. "The Personnel Effectiveness Grid: A New Tool for Estimating Personnel Department Effectiveness." *Human Resource Management* 14: 10–21.

Peterson, R.B., and L. Tracy. 1979. *Systematic Management of Human Resources.* Reading, MA: Addison-Wesley.

Rabe, W.F. 1967. "Yardsticks for Measuring Personnel Department Effectiveness." *Personnel* 44: 56–62.

Schendel, D.E., and C.W. Hofer. 1979. *Strategic Management.* Boston: Little Brown.

Schmidt, F.L., J.E. Hunter, R.C. McKenzie, and T.W. Muldrow. 1979. "Impact of Valid Selection Procedures on Work-Force Productivity." *Journal of Applied Psychology* 64(6): 609–626.

Schmidt, F.L., J.E. Hunter, and K. Pearlman. 1982. "Assessing the Economic Impact of Personnel Programs on Workforce Productivity." *Personnel Psychology* 35: 333–347.

Sheibar, P. 1974. "Personnel Practices Review: A Personnel Audit Activity." *Personnel Journal* 53: 211–217.

Simon, J.L., and J.L. Burstein. 1985. *Basic Research Methods in Social Science.* 3rd ed. New York: Random House.

Staltonstall, R. 1952. "Evaluating Personnel Administration." *Harvard Business Review* 30: 93–104.

Stone, J.L. 1974. "The Use of an Applicant Service Questionnaire." *Public Personnel Management* 3: 155–158.

Tsui, A.S. 1984. "Personnel Department Effectiveness: A Tripartite Approach." *Industrial Relations* 23: 184–197.

──────. 1987a. "Assessing the Effectiveness of an Organizational Subunit: A Reputational Approach." (Working paper, Fuqua School of Business, Duke University.)

──────. 1987b. "Defining the Activities and Effectiveness of the Human Resource Department: A Multiple Constituency Approach." *Human Resource Management* 26(1): 35–69.

Tsui, A.S., and G.T. Milkovich. 1987. "Personnel Department Activities: Constituency Perspectives and Preferences." *Personnel Psychology* (in press).

Tversky, A., and D. Kahnerman. 1981. "The Framing of Decisions and the Psychology of Choice." *Science* 211: 453–458.

Werther, W.B., Jr., and K. Davis. 1981. *Personnel Management and Human Resources.* New York: McGraw-Hill.

─────── ◆ ───────

1.6

International HRM

Peter J. Dowling

International business activity has become increasingly important in the last five years, as numerous commentators and writers have noted. For many U.S. corporations, the importance of international business activities has steadily increased relative to domestic operations, and as Table 1 shows, a substantial proportion of these companies' operating profits now comes from overseas operations. Of the 50 companies listed in Table 1, 20 report that at least 40 percent of their total revenue results from foreign operations, while 21 receive at least 40 percent of their total operating profits from foreign operations. In addition, as many domestic industries mature, overseas expansion may be the only viable option for future growth. For example, the U.S. domestic fast-food industry is a $48.5 billion market characterized by an annual growth rate of 1 percent.[1] As a result, established companies such as McDonald's and Kentucky Fried Chicken are now looking to overseas markets to sustain their growth.

Shift Toward a Global Economy

This international expansion has led some analysts to argue that the distinction between domestic and international markets has become dysfunctional for many companies because of fundamental changes in the world economy.[2] For example, one observer has pointed out that in the financial area, "even purely domestic businesses that face foreign competition in their home market will have to learn to hedge against the currency in which their main competitors produce."[3] A second example concerns the link between global business perspective and economic success:

Table 1

Foreign Revenues and Operating Profits of the 50 Largest U.S. Multinationals

1986 rank	Company	Total revenue (millions)	Foreign revenue as % of total	Total operating profit (millions)	Foreign operating profit as % of total
1	Exxon	$69,888	72.0%	$5,219[a]	74.9%
2	Mobil	46,025[b]	59.5	1,407[a]	132.1
3	IBM	51,250	50.5	4,789[a]	66.5
4	Ford Motor	62,716	31.8	3,285[a]	25.1
5	General Motors	102,814	19.3	2,945[a]	D-P
6	Texaco	31,613	49.0	1,187	98.6
7	Citicorp	23,496	46.6	1,058[a]	49.3
8	EI du Pont de Nemours	26,907	37.0	1,791[c]	36.0
9	Dow Chemical	11,113	53.5	1,285	53.2
10	Chevron	24,352	23.0	1,055[d]	76.6
11	Bank America	12,483	37.3	−518[a]	P-D
12	Philip Morris	20,681	22.1	3,624	9.5
13	Procter & Gamble	15,439	29.1	709[a]	20.2
14	RJR Nabisco	15,978	28.1	2,617	18.8
15	Chase Manhattan	9,460	46.0	585[a]	20.3
16	ITT[e]	17,437	24.0	1,128	42.9
17	Eastman Kodak	11,550	35.9	724	53.7
18	Coca-Cola	8,669	46.4	1,372	62.5
19	Xerox[e]	13,046[b]	30.6	473	33.4
20	Amoco	18,478[b]	21.3	747[a]	35.2
21	General Electric	36,725[b]	10.4	4,303	17.2
22	United Technologies	15,669	24.3	73[a]	95.9
23	JP Morgan	6,672	54.8	873[a]	48.7
24	Goodyear	9,103	37.9	128	100.0
25	Hewlett-Packard	7,102	46.3	998	46.2
26	American Express	14,652	22.1	1,613[f]	15.4
27	Minn. Mining & Mfg	8,602	37.4	1,410	36.4
28	Unisys	7,432	42.9	384	78.4
29	Tenneco	14,529	21.5	1,203	15.8
30	Digital Equipment	7,590	41.1	955	64.2
31	Johnson & Johnson	7,003	43.3	330[a]	90.0
32	American Intl Group	8,876	33.8	749	61.4

Table 1 continued

1986 rank	Company	Total revenue (millions)	Foreign revenue as % of total	Total operating profit (millions)	Foreign operating profit as % of total
33	Sears, Roebuck	44,281	6.6	1,351[a]	1.9
34	CPC International	4,549	63.1	445	59.6
35	Colgate-Palmolive	4,985	54.1	362	47.8
36	FW Woolworth	6,501	41.5	456	34.4
37	Manufacturers Hanover	7,794	33.5	411[a]	30.4
38	NCR	4,882	50.9	588	43.5
39	Allied-Signal	11,794	20.9	605	26.0
40	Kraft	8,742	28.2	834	22.7
41	Bankers Trust New York	4,923	49.7	428[a]	22.4
42	American Brands[e]	6,221	38.3	847	23.7
43	K Mart[e]	25,350	9.3	1,028[f]	NA
44	Motorola	7,508	30.0	463	35.4
45	Monsanto	6,879	32.6	671	24.6
46	Atlantic Richfield	14,487	15.4	615[a]	23.7
47	GTE	15,112	14.1	1,184[a]	8.5
48	Chrysler	22,586	9.3	2,325[f]	16.3
49	Pan Am Corp	3,039	67.5	−324	19.8
50	Merck	4,129	49.0	1,039[f]	36.9

[a]Net income.
[b]Includes other income.
[c]Operating income after taxes.
[d]Net income before corporate expenses.
[e]Includes proportionate interest in unconsolidated subsidiaries and affiliates.
[f]Pretax income.
D-P: Deficit over profit.
P-D: Profit over deficit.
NA: Not available.

Source: Excerpted by permission of *Forbes* magazine, July 27, 1987, © Forbes Inc., 1987, pp. 152–154.

The "secret" of successful businesses in the developed world—the Japanese, the German carmakers like Mercedes and BMW, Asea and Erickson in Sweden, IBM and Citibank in the United States, but equally of a host of medium-sized specialists in manufacturing and in all kinds of services—has been that they base their plans and their policies on exploiting the world economy's changes as opportunities.

From now on any country—but also any business, especially a large one—that wants to prosper will have to accept that it is the world economy that leads and that domestic economic policies will succeed only if they strengthen, or at least do not impair, the country's (*or company's*) international competitive position. This may be the most important—it is surely the most striking—feature of the changed world economy. (italics added)[4]

Impact on Business Structures

This shift from national economies to a world economy has also affected the way in which organizations structure their international operations. Companies have begun to move away from traditional organizational arrangements, such as a foreign subsidiary with limited foreign equity, toward more flexible arrangements, such as various forms of joint ventures and international partnerships. While a literature has emerged on joint ventures,[5] international partnerships have received less attention. Some of the recurring characteristics of these partnerships that have been identified include:

1. Little or no direct joint investment by the partners
2. Some form of joint management of certain functions
3. Exchange of personnel and intensified inter-firm communication
4. Long-term commitments[6]

Examples of international partnerships include the European Airbus consortium, AT&T and Olivetti USA, General Motors Corp. and Hitachi, Inc., and Boeing Aerospace and the Japan Aircraft Development Corp. These partnerships alleviate problems facing companies entering overseas markets, such as the "enormous burdens on firms which would go it alone, greatly enhanced risk of commercial failure and of legal attack, a compelling need to gain rapid visibility and acceptance of products on all major markets, and intensified pressure to share risk and to participate in technological and managerial developments worldwide."[7]

HR Implications

The HRM implications of these developments in international business activity are both diverse and largely unexplored. Recent popular books have suggested that many U.S. companies need to re-assess their approach to doing business overseas—particularly in the area of managing human resources.[8] Indeed, some evidence does suggest that business failures in the international arena may often be linked to poor management of human resources. One detailed case study of a large U.S. multinational company drew the following conclusion:

> [T]he primary causes of failure in multinational ventures stem from a lack of understanding of the essential differences in managing human resources, at all levels, in foreign environments. Certain management philosophies and techniques have proved successful in the domestic environment: their application in a foreign environment too often leads to frustration, failure and underachievement. These "human" considerations are as important as the financial and marketing criteria upon which so many decisions to undertake multinational ventures depend.[9]

However, further research is needed to confirm these observations. The purpose of the present chapter is not to examine the international aspects of the functional areas of HRM, as recent reviews are available in the areas of compensation and benefits,[10] staffing,[11] training and development,[12] and industrial relations,[13] but to examine the main issues in the emerging field of international HRM and to speculate on future directions.

International HRM Literature

Although the topic of international HRM has received increasingly greater attention, the literature is still rather sparse. This observation is not all that surprising, as research on international management in general (of which HRM is one part, along with such fields as comparative management and international marketing) is not well developed. In fact, one study found that the internationalization of U.S. corporate activity has grown at a faster pace than the publication of international articles in U.S. management journals.[14] To a large extent this reflects the many difficulties inherent in international management research.

Many researchers, for example, have regarded the field of international management as a marginal academic area. Studies of this field have been criticized as descriptive and lacking in analytical rigor, ad hoc and expedient in research design and planning, self-centered in the frequent failure to incorporate existing research, and lacking a sustained research effort to develop case material.[15]

Another difficulty associated with international research is its cost. International studies are invariably more expensive than domestic studies,[16] which poses a liability for international researchers in a reduced funding environment. International research also tends to take more time, involve more travel, and require cooperation among host country organizations, government officials, and researchers. This in turn makes developing a stream of research much more difficult.

Finally, major methodological problems confront researchers in the area of international management.[17] These problems greatly increase the complexity of doing international research and are frequently impossible to solve with the rigor usually required by journal editors and reviewers.[18] The major methodological problems in this area are defining culture, the emic-etic distinction, static group comparisons, and translation and stimulus equivalence.

All of the problems associated with international management research apply equally to the field of international HRM. As consumers and prospective funders of research, personnel practitioners should be aware of these issues. In addition they should be aware of the poorly defined parameters of international HRM as a research field, and in particular the differences between domestic and international HRM in this respect.

International vs. Domestic HRM

Since the growth of international business enterprises has occurred rapidly and only recently, the lack of research on either international HRM or the differences between international and domestic HRM[19] is not surprising. Changes in HRM practices (for example, coping with the HR problems of a rapidly expanding overseas business operation) typically precede academic interest in these issues.[20]

To date, the only analyses of similarities and differences between domestic and international HRM have been written not by academics but by professionals in the field. One analysis identifies five broad categories to distinguish international from domestic HRM, with international HRM characterized by (1) a greater number of functions, (2) a wider variety of functions, (3) greater involvement in employees' personal lives, (4) different emphasis, and (5) more external influences.[21] It also noted that international HR managers are often called upon to cope with extremely complex and unique issues, such as the location of foreign assignments and

the establishment of foreign service premiums, cost-of-living allowances, and tax equalization policies.

A second, particularly useful analysis found that international
HRM differs from domestic HRM in terms of perspective, scope of
activities, and risk exposure. It proposed the three-dimensional
model of international HRM shown in Figure 1.[22] Specific elements
of the model include three broad HR functions of procurement,
allocation, and utilization; three national or country categories—the
host country where a subsidiary is located, the home country where
an international company is headquartered, and other countries
which provide labor or finances; and three types of employees—
local/host-country nationals, expatriate/parent-country, and third-
country nationals. International HRM is defined as the interplay between HR functions, countries, and types of employees.

Depending on the host-country context, a number of domestic
HRM activities are potentially transferable to the international area.
Figure 2 points out, for example, that the basic functional areas of
HRM do not change substantially between domestic and international environments. But it also reflects the earlier points that
international HRM involves a more diverse set of activities, serves a
more diverse population, and operates in a more complex external
environment. Thus, while domestic HRM provides some basis for
the development of international HRM, managers need to be aware
of the differentiating factors summarized in Figure 2. Failure to
recognize these factors—whether due to ethnocentrism, poor information, or lack of international perspective—frequently causes considerable difficulties in international operations.[23]

An Integrated Model of International HRM

Summarizing, it is clear that the following characteristics differentiate international from domestic HRM:

- Greater number of functions and activities

- Broader perspective

- Changing emphasis as employee mix of parent- and host-
  country nationals varies

- Greater risk exposure

- More external influences

Figure 1
International HRM Model

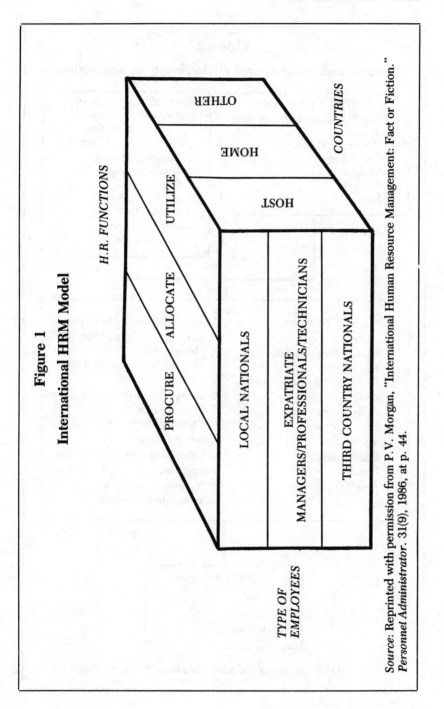

Source: Reprinted with permission from P. V. Morgan, "International Human Resource Management: Fact or Fiction." *Personnel Administrator.* 31(9), 1986, at p. 44.

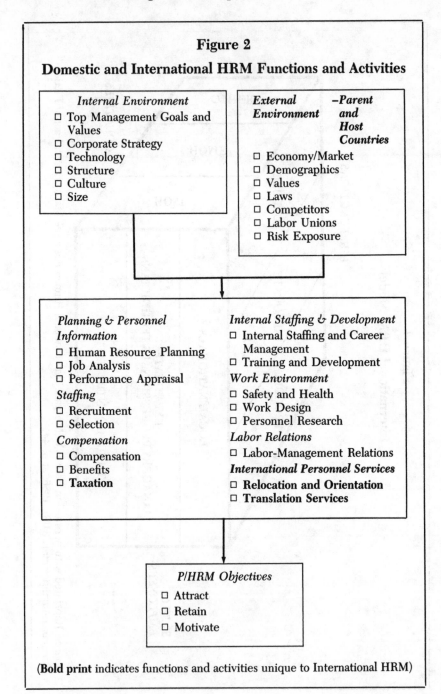

Figure 2

Domestic and International HRM Functions and Activities

Internal Environment
- ☐ Top Management Goals and Values
- ☐ Corporate Strategy
- ☐ Technology
- ☐ Structure
- ☐ Culture
- ☐ Size

External Environment — *Parent and Host Countries*
- ☐ Economy/Market
- ☐ Demographics
- ☐ Values
- ☐ Laws
- ☐ Competitors
- ☐ Labor Unions
- ☐ Risk Exposure

Planning & Personnel Information
- ☐ Human Resource Planning
- ☐ Job Analysis
- ☐ Performance Appraisal

Staffing
- ☐ Recruitment
- ☐ Selection

Compensation
- ☐ Compensation
- ☐ Benefits
- ☐ **Taxation**

Internal Staffing & Development
- ☐ Internal Staffing and Career Management
- ☐ Training and Development

Work Environment
- ☐ Safety and Health
- ☐ Work Design
- ☐ Personnel Research

Labor Relations
- ☐ Labor-Management Relations

International Personnel Services
- ☐ **Relocation and Orientation**
- ☐ **Translation Services**

P/HRM Objectives
- ☐ Attract
- ☐ Retain
- ☐ Motivate

(**Bold print** indicates functions and activities unique to International HRM)

The boldface type in Figure 2 indicates those functions and activities unique to international HRM. The following discussion examines each of the factors in detail to illustrate the main points of Figure 2.[24]

Greater Number of Functions and Activities

An international HR department must engage in a number of activities that are not at issue domestically. For example, at the corporate headquarters level, two major activities that differentiate international from domestic HRM are taxation and relocation/orientation; at the host-country level, the HR function provides three types of activities—administrative services, government relations activities, and translation services—not commonly found in domestic operations. Figure 3 shows the typical time allocations for international HRM functions at corporate headquarters and in a host country.

Taxation

Since expatriates typically have both domestic and host-country tax liabilities, tax equalization policies must be designed to eliminate any tax incentive or disincentive associated with a particular overseas assignment.[25] This task is complicated by the wide variation in tax laws across host countries and, in some cases, by a considerable time lag between completion of an expatriate assignment and settlement of domestic and international tax liabilities. To help resolve these difficulties, most large international firms retain the services of a major accounting firm for overseas taxation advice.

Relocation and Orientation

These activities also are performed domestically, but are less important since domestic relocation and orientation pose fewer complexities and potential problems.[26] In contrast, international relocation and orientation involve arranging predeparture training; supplying immigration and travel details; providing housing and schooling information; and finalizing compensation details concerning salary delivery, various overseas allowances, and taxation treatment. Many of these details may be a source of anxiety for the expatriate and require considerable time and attention to resolve.

Figure 3

Typical Time Allocations
For International HR Functions

CORPORATE HEADQUARTERS

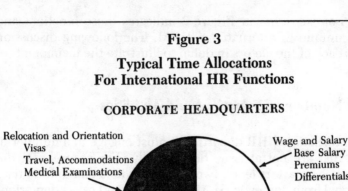

Relocation and Orientation
  Visas
  Travel, Accommodations
  Medical Examinations

Employment/
Human Resources
Planning

Occupational Safety

Labor Relations

Employee Benefits
  Health Care
  Retirement

Personnel
Systems and
Policies

Wage and Salary
  Base Salary
  Premiums
  Differentials

Equal Employment

Taxation

Training and
Development
  Supervisory Training
  Career Development

HOST COUNTRY

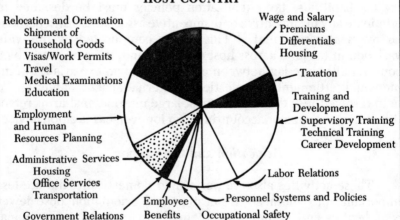

Relocation and Orientation
  Shipment of
  Household Goods
  Visas/Work Permits
  Travel
  Medical Examinations
  Education

Employment
and Human
Resources Planning

Administrative Services
  Housing
  Office Services
  Transportation

Government Relations

Employee
Benefits

Occupational Safety

Personnel Systems and Policies

Labor Relations

Wage and Salary
  Premiums
  Differentials
  Housing

Taxation

Training and
Development
  Supervisory Training
  Technical Training
  Career Development

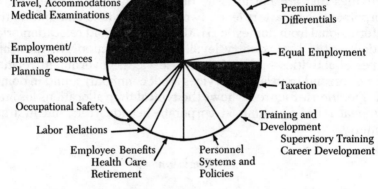

▨ ■ HR responsibilities more likely in the international than the domestic HR function.

Source: Reprinted with permission from F. Acuff, 1984. "International and Domestic Human Resources Functions." *Innovations in International Compensation.* Organization Resources Counselors. New York (Sept.), at p. 4.

Administrative Services

An international company also requires the services of international HR departments in its host countries to provide administrative services for expatriates. As one author has commented, "(A)nyone who has ever been responsible for an administrative service such as company-provided housing knows the importance of this function, where both employees and spouses often 'help' the human resource manager with interpretations of policy and procedure."[27] This can also be a relatively time-consuming activity.

Government Relations

While government relations may require less time than administrative services, it can play a very important role. This is particularly true in developing countries, where ambiguous eligibility and/or compliance criteria may mean that work permits and other important certificates are more easily obtained through personal relationships.

Translation Services

Translating internal and external personnel correspondence is an additional activity for an international HR department operating in a host country.[28] If an HR department is the major user of translation services, this role is often expanded to provide translation services to all departments and operations in the country.

Broader Perspective

Domestic HR managers generally administer programs for a relatively homogeneous group of employees who are covered by uniform compensation policies and taxed by a single government. Because international HR managers face the problem of designing and administering programs for more than one national group of employees (for example, parents, hosts, and third-country nationals who may work together), they must take a broader or more global view of issues. For example, an international perspective on benefits would endorse the view that all expatriate employees, regardless of nationality, should receive a foreign service or expatriate premium. Yet, some international companies which routinely pay such premiums to their parent-country nationals, even if the assignment is to a desirable location, do not pay a premium to foreign nationals assigned to the company's home country. Such a policy is dysfunctional because host- and third-country nationals tend to see such a policy as giving parent-country employees preferential treatment.[29] Complex equity issues arise when employees of various nationalities work together, and the resolution of these issues remains one of the major challenges in the international HRM field.[30]

The need for a broader perspective is implied, but not explicitly specified, in Exhibit 2 since it is a contextual factor that influences most aspects of international HRM. For example, the high cost of expatriate failure, the possibility of terrorist attacks on expatriates, the volatility of foreign exchange rates, and the need to change emphasis in personnel operations as a foreign subsidiary matures (that is, the shift from extensive use of parent-country nationals to hiring more host-country nationals for senior positions) would broaden the responsibilities of HR planning, recruitment, selection, compensation systems, benefits, and training and development.

Greater Involvement in Employees' Lives

A greater degree of involvement in employees' personal lives is necessary for the selection, training, and effective management of expatriate employees. The international HR department needs to ensure that the expatriate employee, and perhaps his or her family, understands all aspects of the compensation package provided for the assignment (for example, cost-of-living allowances, premiums, hypothetical taxes) and related matters, such as housing arrangements and health care. Many companies have a special administrative group to coordinate these programs and to provide services for expatriate employees, such as handling their banking, investments, and home rental while on assignment, and coordinating home visits and final repatriation.[31] For a domestic assignment, most of these issues either would not arise, or would be handled primarily by the employee rather than the HR department. This factor is recognized in the model in Figure 2 by the inclusion of international personnel services as a functional area.

Changing Emphasis as Employee Population Mix Varies

As foreign operations mature, the emphasis put on various HR functions changes. Over time, the need for expatriates usually declines as more trained host-country nationals become available. Resources previously allocated to such areas as expatriate taxation and relocation and orientation would be transferred to such activities as selection, training, and development of host-country nationals. The latter may involve, for example, a program to bring promising host-country nationals to corporate headquarters for developmental assignments. The need to change emphasis in personnel operations as a foreign subsidiary matures does not appear in Figure 2, but again it clearly broadens the responsibilities involved in HR planning, recruitment, selection, compensation systems, benefits, and training and development.

Risk Exposure

Risk exposure is captured by the external environment box of Figure 2. This factor highlights the finding that the human and financial consequences of failure in an international business are often more severe than in a domestic one. For example, expatriate failure (the premature return of an expatriate from an international assignment) is a persistent and costly problem for international companies.[32] Direct costs (salary, training costs, travel and relocation expenses) per failure to the parent company range between $55,000 and $80,000, depending on currency exchange rates and location of assignment.[33] Indirect costs, such as loss of market share and damage to overseas customer relationships, also may be considerable.[34]

A final aspect of risk exposure relevant to international HRM is terrorism. Major multinational companies now must consider this factor when planning international meetings and assignments,[35] and this has clearly affected the way in which employees assess potential international assignment locations.[36]

Greater Number of External Influences

Other aspects of the external environment, such as the type of government and the state of the economy in the various host countries, are obviously critical. In developed countries, labor is more expensive and better organized, and governments require compliance with guidelines on a wide range of issues, such as labor relations, taxation, and health and safety. These factors shape the activities of the international HR manager to a considerable extent. In less-developed countries, labor tends to be cheaper and less organized, and government regulation less pervasive, so these issues take less time. Instead, the HR manager may well become more involved in administering company-provided or -financed housing, education, and other services that are not readily available in the local economy.

Role of International HRM

With this understanding of the differences between international and domestic HRM, it is now possible to examine the role of international HRM in the context of the multinational enterprise. A particularly useful model for this purpose is the value chain model shown in Figure 4.[37] In this model, HRM is one of four support activities for a multinational firm's five primary activities. Since each of the primary and support activities involves human resources, the HRM function cuts across the entire value chain of a firm.

Multidomestic vs. Global Industries

This value chain model has recently been applied to the selection of appropriate strategies for multinational firms.[38] The industry (or industries if the organization is a conglomerate) in which the firm is involved forms the starting point for strategy formulation, since patterns of international competition vary widely from one industry to another. At one end of the continuum is the multidomestic industry, which is defined as an industry in which competition in each country is essentially independent of other countries. Traditional examples of multidomestic industries include retailing, distribution, and insurance. At the other end of the continuum is the global industry, which is defined as an industry in which a firm's competitive position in one country is significantly influenced by its position in other countries. Some examples of this type of industry include commercial aircraft, semiconductors, and copiers.

The key distinction between a multidomestic industry and a global industry is described as follows:

> The international industry is not merely a collection of domestic industries but a series of linked domestic industries in which the rivals compete against each other on a truly worldwide basis. . . . In a multidomestic industry, then, international strategy collapses to a series of domestic strategies. The issues that are uniquely international revolve around how to do business abroad, how to select good countries in which to compete (or assess country risk), and mecha-

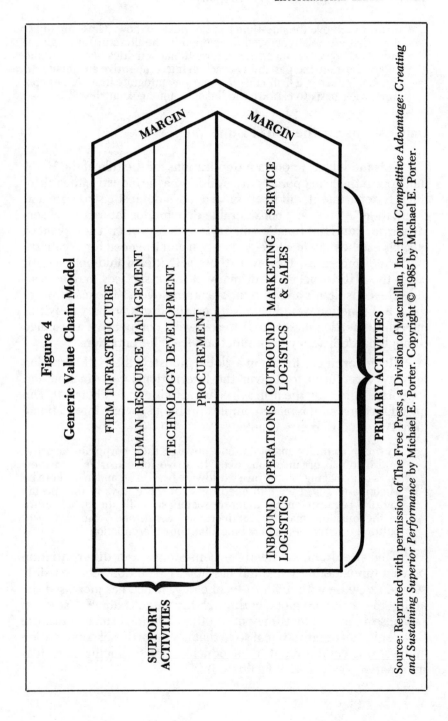

Figure 4
Generic Value Chain Model

nisms to achieve the one-time transfer of know-how. These are questions that are relatively well-developed in the literature. In a global industry, however, managing international activities like a portfolio will undermine the possibility of achieving competitive advantage. In a global industry, a firm must in some way integrate its activities on a worldwide basis to capture the linkages among countries.[39]

Implications for the HRM Function

This model has important implications for the role of the HRM function. If the firm operates in a multidomestic industry, the role of the HR department will likely have a more domestic structure and orientation. At times, a considerable demand for international services from the HRM function may arise, such as when a new plant or office is established in a foreign location and the need for expatriate employees increases. However, these activities would not be critical to the HRM role, indeed, many of these services may be provided by consultants and/or temporary employees. The main role of the HRM function would be to support the firm's primary activities in each domestic market so as to achieve a competitive advantage through cost/efficiency or product/service differentiation.[40]

However, if the firm is in a global industry, the HRM function must be structured to deliver the international coordination and support required by the firm's primary activities (see Figure 4). The need for coordination raises complex problems for any international firm. As one observer has noted:

> In order to build, maintain, and develop their corporate identity, multinational organizations need to strive for consistency in their ways of managing people on a worldwide basis. Yet, and in order to be effective locally, they also need to adapt those ways to the specific cultural requirements of different societies. While the global nature of the business may call for increased consistency, the variety of cultural environments may be calling for differentiation.[41]

This simultaneous need for consistency and differentiation poses a fundamental issue and has no easy solution. One possible solution may lie with modern technology, which has increased the ability to coordinate globally through the value chain.[42] A study of Japanese multinationals may offer other solutions since "Japanese firms enjoy an organizational style that is supportive of coordination and a strong commitment to introducing new technologies such as information systems that facilitate it."[43]

As for the HRM function, adopting a truly international concept of HRM should improve an organization's ability to work through the difficulties and complexities inherent in the process of implementing a global strategy. Such an international outlook would require headquarters to take the following steps:[44]

- Recognize that its own peculiar ways of managing human resources reflect some assumptions and values of its home culture

- Accept that these peculiar ways are not inherently better or worse than others but simply different, and are likely to exhibit strengths and weaknesses, particularly when used abroad

- Acknowledge that foreign subsidiaries may have other preferred ways of managing people that are not intrinsically better or worse, but could prove more effective when used locally

- Show a willingness not only to acknowledge cultural differences but also to take active steps toward discussing these differences and adapting HRM policy accordingly

- Build a genuine belief among all parties that more creative and effective ways of managing people could result from crosscultural learning

International HRM Practitioners: A 1986 Profile

The ideas presented in the previous section provide a starting point for examining how organizations overcome the problems of international HRM coordination. The following discussion examines data from a recent survey of international HRM practitioners to determine how well the issues noted earlier match the experience of actual practitioners.

Survey Methodology and Responding Companies

Data for this study were obtained through a survey sent to the 160 members of the International Chapter of the American Society for Personnel Administration (ASPA/I) in November 1986. The

Table 2
Profile of Companies Surveyed

Company Characteristic	Range		
	Minimum	Median	Maximum
Total World Sales (millions)	47	2,041	100,000
Percent Nondomestic Sales	3%	33.5%	70.0%
World Assets	7	2,190	100,000
Total Number of Employees (domestic and foreign)	1,100	16,500	405,435
Percent Foreign Employees	1%	27.5%	75.0%
Number of Countries in Which Company Operates	2	16	149
Years of Company's Involvement In Overseas Operations	1	25	86

Using the *Business Week* industry classifications, companies in this sample covered the following industries: service (5); conglomerate (4); special machinery (4); banks (3); electronics (3); aerospace (2); food processing (2); instruments (2); miscellaneous manufacturing (2); chemicals (1); containers (1); drugs (1); nonbank financial (1); office equipment (1); computers (1); publishing, radio, and television broadcasting (1); and tobacco (1).

questionnaire, developed by the author in consultation with a number of international HRM practitioners, sought information on respondents' companies in general, the structure of their international operations, and details of their international HRM activities.

Thirty-four questionnaires were returned, giving a response rate of 21.2 percent, one of the highest response rates to date on a survey distributed through ASPA/I.[45] These data provide a unique perspective because of the lack of information on what international HRM practitioners see as the major issues and problems in this emerging field.

Table 2 shows details of the variety represented among the respondents' companies, which range in size from very large to relatively small. The number of countries in which the responding companies operate (median 16) and the length of time in which

Table 3

**Structure of International Operations
and International HR Function**

Type of Structure	Companies Using	
International Operations	*Number*	*Percent*
National Subsidiaries with Local Coordination	4	11.8
International Divisions with Senior Management Reporting to Corporate President or CEO	5	14.7
World-Product or World-Matrix Organization	6	17.6
One or More Regional Headquarters To Coordinate National Operations	7	20.6
Mixed Forms	12	35.3
International HR Function		
Similar to International Operations	19	55.9
Different from International Operations	15	44.1

companies have been involved in international operations (median 25 years) have a wide spread, as does the range of industries represented in this sample.[46] World headquarters' location is the only characteristic of the sample that does not vary widely, with 31 of the 34 respondents reporting headquarters in North America.

Structure of HRM Function

The respondents report considerable diversity in the structure of their international operations. As Table 3 shows, the majority of companies use traditional structures, such as national subsidiaries, international divisions, regional headquarters, and world-product or world-matrix organization. However, a substantial minority use a mixed form of structure to manage their international operations. While most companies use the same form of organization for their HRM function as for their overall international operations, a number reported organizing their HR function differently. Those respondents using a different HR structure provide the following descriptions of how the HR function is organized:

HR function centralized at headquarters, with consulting arrangements provided from central headquarters; international organization is very small, so HR support provided from the U.S.; all offshore HR people report to U.S. headquarters (four companies).

HR policy developed through headquarters but implemented locally, according to each region's needs (three companies).

International personnel organization, with responsibilities for personnel activities outside the U.S. (three companies).

Separate corporate, group, and division international HR functions, that work closely together on a dotted-line basis, although each has core responsibilities unique to that level (three companies).

Differing HR arrangements, with local HR functions in those areas with larger operations, but all expatriates and third-country nationals on the head office payroll handled by corporate HR function (one company).

These alternative HRM structures reflect varying degrees of centralization and decentralization which presumably are influenced by a range of market and product factors. Inspection of the data indicates that companies with more than 50 years of overseas experience reported structuring their HRM function in a way different from the structuring of their international organizations.[43] Although further research is clearly needed, this finding may indicate that the longer companies operate internationally, the more likely they are to adapt their HR function to local or regional demands.

International HRM Activities

The majority of respondents (55.6 percent) report some formalized HR planning in their organizations, with another one-third (32.4 percent) describing the HR planning process as well-developed. Nearly three-quarters (73.5 percent) of the respondents indicate that their companies have formalized policies for expatriate selection, training, and compensation, and another 8.8 percent were in the process of developing such policies.

In addition, 61.7 percent of the companies in this sample have brought host- and third-country nationals to U.S. headquarters. In this case, there was a significant correlation between the length of time a company has been involved in overseas operations and the transfer of host- and third-country nationals to the U.S.—those companies with relatively limited experience in overseas operations tended not to transfer foreign employees to their U.S. operations.[47] Respondents described the purposes for bringing third- and host-country nationals to headquarters as follows:

- Specific job placement (eight companies)

- Training, technology transfer, product tours, further education about total company activities, and management development (six companies)

- Varied roles/purposes (two companies)

- Developmental assignments to further the employee's advancement in the foreign subsidiary (two companies)

- Job placement at several levels, including senior officer positions; training assignments conducted continuously so that some host- and third-country nationals are always at U.S. headquarters (two companies)

- Temporary assignments (one company)

Major Problem Areas

When asked to identify the major international HRM problem areas in their companies, respondents pinpointed both the contextual factors (internal and external environments) and all seven functions of the model of domestic and international HRM presented in Figure 2. Listed below are a number of the problem areas and specific difficulties cited by respondents.

Compensation: obtaining reliable local national compensation data; computerizing data on expatriate and third-country nationals into a comprehensive HR payroll system to improve service; extending stock purchase arrangements to employees outside the U.S.; offshore/split compensation payments to local national executives; escalating expatriation costs; cost and productivity of expatriates vs. local nationals; local currency devaluations (twelve companies).

Career development and training: development of managers into international managers; the need to increase cross-training exposure of U.S. management to foreign operations and culture, while similarly exposing foreign management staff to U.S. operations and culture; training for productivity improvement (eleven companies).

Internal and external business environment: policy development for off-shore operations during significant growth period; downsizing/restructuring; dealing with a maturing work force; slowdown in business resulting in loss of contracts and excess expatriate staff (eight companies).

Benefits: taxation, benefits/pensions for third-country nationals; local legislative changes in employment and benefit laws (seven companies).

HR planning and personnel: consistency of management practice within and between countries; appropriate level of HRM consistency between various international operations; lack of on-site HR personnel, inadequate skills of local HR staff; obtaining data resources in foreign locations without having to use consultants (seven companies).

Relocation and orientation: repatriation problems (six companies).

Staffing: staffing control, transfers, immigration rules (five companies).

Current Issues in International HRM

As with the discussion of current problem areas, when respondents were asked to identify the most important current issues in international HRM, their answers corresponded closely to this chapter's earlier discussion of differences between international and domestic HRM. The following list shows specific responses grouped by general topic.

Compensation/benefits/staffing: taxes, benefits, equitable compensation, maintaining a truly multinational work force in view of continually escalating costs (twelve companies).

Global orientation among top management: the necessity of learning to think globally, formalized training and development of a cadre of international executives within multinational firms, quality and consistency of management (seven companies).

Expatriate employees: expatriate selection criteria, duration of expatriate assignments, headquarter-expatriate communication, the changing role of the U.S. expatriate in the world; repatriates (six companies).

Labor relations and government relations: labor unions, government relations, administrative problems of identifying and dealing with legal issues that are different in each country, sending expatriates to China (six companies).

Cultural differences: living and working in a multicultural environment; facilitating the cultural interface of different and sometimes conflicting management styles and local business practices; performing crossnational "sensitization"; helping managers to deal with enormous complexity, volatility, and rapid changes; dealing with the issue of corruption; coping with prevailing belief among local nationals that they can run things in their own country, although they may not really be qualified/capable (six companies).

Coordination: more integration of international planning with business strategies, downsizing/restructuring, meshing strategic business unit and national or entity interests, matrix organization/decentralization and impact on worldwide HR policy and practice, consistency of use and enforcement of policy (five companies).

Career development: career planning and management development, career paths for local nationals, expatriate reassignment/replacement planning (five companies).

Status of international HRM function: Credibility with senior management, removing the common perception that international HRM is just an extension of the domestic HR function (three companies).

Conclusion

The survey data and its relationship to the issues discussed earlier in this chapter are important for a number of reasons. First, as perhaps the first survey of international HRM practitioners to be published, the information can serve as a benchmark for other researchers to use.[49] This survey also tends to confirm a number of trends found in the literature. For example, the mixed form of organizational structure used by a number of companies to manage their international operations indicates a move away from traditional patterns of organization.[50] Similarly, the finding that a number of companies structure their HRM function in a way different from their overall international operations may reflect both perceived and actual differences in the contribution of the HRM function to the company's value chain.

In addition, the problems and issues identified by respondents confirm that the international HRM field is in an early stage of development and could benefit from the model of international HRM presented in Figure 2. Most of the factors reported by respondents reflect problems in both defining the role of international HRM and adapting well-established HRM activities such as compensation and staffing to an international context. A number of respondents also seem to believe that senior management does not have a clear understanding of the similarities and differences between international and domestic HRM.

Finally, while not reported earlier, the survey also provided data on how HR academics can assist the development of the international HRM field: by conducting research, by developing courses, and by interfacing with practitioners in the field. This is, of course, the role that HR academics have had and will continue to have in domestic HRM—so while the context differs, the role for academics remains the same.

Progress in the field of international HRM will come about as issues are identified and strategies are implemented, and as the outcomes of these processes are documented and researched. As one author has observed:

> The challenge faced by the infant field of international human resource management is to solve a multi-dimensional puzzle located at the crossroad of national and organizational cultures. Research is needed on the various strategies that international firms are using as their own attempts at solving the puzzle.[51]

Despite the methodological problems inherent in international research, academics need to address the issues identified throughout this chapter. Practitioners can facilitate this process by offering researchers access to their organizations and assistance with research costs. One imaginative proposal that has been suggested would create a research cooperative funded by several international companies to define a common research agenda and offer a vehicle for sharing the costs of research.[48] Such a proposal warrants serious consideration.

◆

Notes

1. *Business Week* (1986a).   3. Ibid., p. 787.
2. Drucker.   4. Ibid., p. 791.

5. See Harrigan.
6. Robinson.
7. Ibid., p. 5.
8. See Copeland and Griggs.
9. Desatnick and Bennett, p. x. For an example of the difficulties that can arise in joint production ventures, see "AMC's Troubles in China: Jeep Venture Languishing Amid Conflict," *The New York Times*, April 11, 1986. Low worker productivity and "differing attitudes toward discipline" are cited as prime reasons why production levels at the Beijing plant are far below planned levels.
10. Ellison and Nicholas; Rayman and Twinn; Reynolds.
11. Dowling; Lorange; Root.
12. Dowling; Tung.
13. Blanpain; Poole.
14. Adler. In this study, Adler reviewed over 11,000 articles published in 24 management journals between 1971 and 1980, and found that 80 percent were studies of the United States conducted by American researchers.
15. Schollhammer.
16. Adler.
17. For a detailed analysis of the literature on methodological issues in international management, see the Fall 1982 Special Issue on Cross-Cultural Management of the *Journal of International Business Studies*, 14(2). See also Dowling and Nagel.
18. Adler.
19. This section of the chapter is based in part on a working paper by the author titled "International and Domestic Personnel/Human Resource Management: Similarities and Differences" (Working Paper No. 24, November 1986, Graduate School of Management, University of Melbourne, Australia).
20. Leap and Oliva.
21. Acuff.
22. Morgan.
23. See Desatnick and Bennett.
24. When reading the work of Acuff and Morgan, it is evident that Acuff tends to use the terms "function" and "activity" interchangeably, while Morgan is consistent in his use of these terms (e.g., he clearly describes translation services as an activity). Acuff highlights taxation and relocation and orientation under the heading of "more functions," but both are activities rather than functions. In our HRM model (Figure 2), taxation is listed as an activity under the compensation function, while relocation and orientation and translation services are listed as activities under the function of international personnel services. This function would also coordinate relocation and orientation activities with host-country HR departments.
25. Gajek and Sabo; Pinney.
26. Acuff.
27. Ibid., p. 4.
28. Morgan.
29. Robinson.
30. For a summary of the equity issues involved in international compensation, see Milkovich and Newman, Chapter 15.
31. For a discussion of the importance of these services, see Pulatie.
32. Tung.
33. Mendenhall and Oddou.
34. Zeira and Banai.
35. *Business Week* (1986b).
36. For a review of terrorism as it affects multinational companies, see Chapter 4 of Gladwin and Walter.
37. Porter (1985).
38. Porter (1986).
39. Ibid., p. 12.
40. For a detailed description of this HRM role, see Schuler and MacMillan.
41. Laurent, p. 97.

42. Porter (1986).
43. Ibid., p. 37.
44. Laurent. He notes that few organizations have taken these steps and that the difficulty has "more to do with states of mind and mindsets than with behaviors. As such, these processes can only be facilitated and this may represent a primary mission for executives in charge of international human resource management" (p. 100).
45. Personal communication from Patrick V. Morgan, vice president of ASPA/I, December 1986.
46. Correlation between length of time in which companies had been involved in overseas operations and degree of decentralization/centralization: r = .31, p<.05.
47. Correlation between length of time in which companies had been involved in overseas operations and transfer of foreign nationals to U.S. headquarters: r = −.54, p<.001.
48. Harvey.
49. Although several surveys have been conducted by consulting companies, these data are available on a restricted basis to clients or through private newsletters and, as such, do not constitute part of the public-domain literature on international HRM.
50. Robinson.
51. Laurent.

Editor's Note: In addition to the References shown below, there are other significant sources of information and ideas on International HRM.

Books

Child, J.D. 1981. "Culture, Contingency and Capitalism in the Cross-National Study of Organizations." In *Research in Organizational Behavior*, eds. L.L. Cummings & B.M. Staw, Vol. 111. Greenwich, CT: JAI Publishers.

Pucik, V. 1984. "The International Management of Human Resources." In *Strategic Human Resource Management*, eds. C.J. Fombrun, N.M. Tichy and M.A. Devanna. New York: John Wiley & Sons.

Torbiorn, I. 1982. *Living Abroad: Personal Adjustment and Personnel Policy in the Overseas Setting*. New York: John Wiley & Sons.

Gilroy, E.B., D.M. Noer, and J.E. Spoor. 1978. "Personnel Administration in the Multinational/Transnational Corporation." In *PAIR Policy and Program Management*, ed. D. Yoder and H.G. Heneman, *ASPA/BNA Handbook of Personnel and Industrial Relations*, vol. 7. Washington, DC: BNA Books.

Articles

Harvey, M.G. 1983. "The Executive Family: An Overlooked Variable in International Assignments." *Columbia Journal of World Business* 20(1):84–92.

Hixon, A.L. 1986. "Why Corporations Make Haphazard Overseas Staffing Decisions." *Personnel Administrator* 31(3):91–94.

Hofstede, G. 1983. "The Cultural Relativity of Organizational Practices and Theories." *Journal of International Business Studies* 14(2):75–89.

Kendall, D.W. 1981. "Repatriation: An Ending and a Beginning." *Business Horizons* 24(6):21–25.

Ondrack, D.A. 1985. "International Transfers of Managers in North American and European MNEs." *Journal of International Business Studies* 16(3), 1–19.

Ruff, H.J. and G.I. Jackson. 1974. "Methodological Problems in International Comparisons of the Cost of Living." *Journal of International Business Studies* 5(2):57–67.

Torbiorn, I. 1985. "The Structure of Managerial Roles in Cross-Cultural Settings." *International Studies of Management & Organization* 15(1):52–74.

Consulting Firms
Organization Resource Counselors, 1211 Sixth Ave., New York, NY 10036.

Moran, Stahl & Boyer, Inc., International Division, 900 28th St., Suite 200, Boulder, CO 80803.

◆

References

Acuff, F. 1984. "International and Domestic Human Resources Functions." *Innovations in International Compensation*, Organization Resource Counselors September: 3–5.

Adler, N.J. 1983. "Cross-Cultural Management Research: The Ostrich and the Trend." *Academy of Management Review* 8: 226–232.

Blanpain, R. 1985. *The OECD Guidelines for Multinational Enterprises and Labour Relations 1982–1984: Experience and Review.* Deventer, The Netherlands: Kluwer.

Business Week. 1986a "How U.S. Executives Dodge Terrorism Abroad," May 12: 41.

———. 1986b. "McWorld? McDonald's Is Raising Golden Arches From Berlin to Bangkok. But Can the Company Export Its Unique Management Style?" October 13: 60–66.

Copeland, L. and L. Griggs. 1985. *Going International: How to Make Friends and Deal Effectively in the Global Marketplace.* New York: Random House.

Desatnick, R.L. and M.L. Bennett. 1978. *Human Resource Management in the Multinational Company.* New York: Nichols.

Dowling, P.J. 1986. "Human Resource Issues in International Business." *Syracuse Journal of International Law and Commerce* 13(2): 255–271.

Dowling, P.J. and T.W. Nagel. 1986. "Nationality and Work Attitudes: A Study of Australian and American Business Majors." *Journal of Management* 12: 121–128.

Drucker, P.F. 1986. "The Changed World Economy." *Foreign Affairs* 64(4): 768–791.

Ellison, L.M. and D.A. Nicholas. 1986. "Employee Benefits and Special Policies." In *Handbook of Human Resources Administration*, ed. J.J. Famularo, 2d ed. New York: McGraw-Hill.

Gajek, M. and M.M. Sabo. 1986. "The Bottom Line: What HR Managers Need to Know About the New Expatriate Regulations." *Personnel Administration* 31(2): 87–92.

Gladwin T.A. and I. Walter. 1980. *Multinationals Under Fire: Lessons in the Management of Conflict*. New York: John Wiley & Sons.

Harrigan, K.R. 1986. *Managing for Joint Venture Success*. Lexington, MA: Lexington Books.

Harvey, M.G. 1983. "The Multinational Corporation's Expatriate Problem: An Application of Murphy's Law." *Business Horizons* 26(1): 71–78.

Laurent, A. 1986. "The Cross-Cultural Puzzle of International Human Resource Management." *Human Resource Management* 25: 91–102.

Leap, T. and T.A. Oliva. 1983. "General Systems Precursor Theory as a Supplement to Wren's Framework for Studying Management History: The Case of Human Resource/Personnel Management." *Human Relations* 36: 627–640.

Lorange, P. 1986. "Human Resource Management in Multinational Cooperative Ventures." *Human Resource Management* 25: 133–148.

Mendenhall, M. and G. Oddou. 1985. "The Dimensions of Expatriate Acculturation: A Review." *Academy of Management Review* 10: 39–47.

Milkovich, G.T. and J.M. Newman. 1984. *Compensation*. Plano, Texas: Business Publications.

Morgan, P.V. 1986. "International Human Resource Management: Fact or Fiction." *Personnel Administrator* 31(9): 43–47.

Pinney, D.L. 1982. "Structuring an Expatriate Tax Reimbursement Program." *Personnel Administrator* 27(7): 19–25.

Poole M. 1986. *Industrial Relations: Origins and Patterns of National Diversity*. London: Routledge & Kegan Paul.

Porter, M.E. 1985. *Competitive Advantage: Creating and Sustaining Superior Performance*. New York: The Free Press.

_____. 1986. "Changing Patterns of International Competition." *California Management Review* 28(2): 9–40.

Pulatie, D. 1985. "How Do You Ensure Success of Managers Going Abroad?" *Training and Development Journal* 39(12): 22–23.

Rayman, J. and B. Twinn. 1983. *Expatriate Compensation and Benefits: An Employer's Handbook*. London: Kogan Page.

Reynolds, C. 1986. "Compensation of Overseas Personnel." In *Handbook of Human Resources Administration*, ed. J.J. Famularo, 2d ed. New York: McGraw-Hill.

Robinson, R.D. 1978. *International Business Management: A Guide to Decision Making*, 2d ed. Hinsdale, IL: Dryden Press.

―――. 1986. "International Strategic Partnerships." Paper presented at the Annual Conference of the Academy of International Business, London.

Root, F.R. 1986. "Staffing the Overseas Unit." In *Handbook of Human Resources Administration*, ed. J.J. Famularo, 2d ed. New York: McGraw-Hill.

Schollhammer, H. 1975. "Current Research on International and Comparative Management Issues." *Management International Review* 15(2–3): 29–40.

Schuler, R.S. and I.C. MacMillan. 1984. "Gaining Competitive Advantage through Human Resource Management Practices." *Human Resource Management* 23(3): 241–255.

Tung, R.L. 1981. "Selection and Training of Personnel for Overseas Assignments." *Columbia Journal of World Business* 16(1): 68–78.

―――. 1984. "Strategic Management of Human Resources in the Multinational Enterprise." *Human Resource Management* 23: 129–143.

Zeira, Y. and M. Banai. 1984. "Present and Desired Methods of Selecting Expatriate Managers for International Assignments." *Personnel Review* 13(3): 29–35.

―――――― ◆ ――――――

Author Index

Authors appearing in this Index appear in the Notes and References at the end of each chapter. The individual authors of the chapters appear here also. Anyone referenced in the body of the text will appear in the Subject Index.

Subject Index

A

Age Discrimination in Employment
  Act   1–13
Allen-Bradley   1–17
American Hospital Supply
  Corp.   1–57
American Society for Personnel
  Administration   1–197,
  1–245
Arthur Andersen and Co.   1–67
Assessment centers
  utility model   1–175—1–179
Atlantic Richfield Co.   1–108
AT&T   1–74, 1–231
Audits of HR programs   1–128,
  1–189—1–195
Auto Workers, United   1–17, 1–37
Availability analysis in HR
  planning   1–62—1–64, 1–71

B

Bank of America   1–17
Behavioral dynamics   1–54
Benefits, employee
  international HRM and   1–250
Boeing Aerospace   1–231
Boise-Cascade Corp.   1–108
Break-even analysis in utility
  analysis   1–139—1–166
Bureau of Labor Statistics   1–16
Business environment. See also
  Environmental scanning
  HR planning and   1–59—1–66,
  1–72—1–78
  HR strategy and   1–12, 1–15, 1–19,
  1–22—1–27, 1–35—1–40,
  1–72—1–78
  International HRM and   1–259

Business planning, strategic
  HR planning and   1–47—1–87,
  1–101

C

Canada   1–76
Career development   1–249
Caterpillar Tractor Co.   1–75
Champion International Corp.   1–108
Chaparral Steel   1–2, 1–10, 1–18,
  1–27, 1–28
Chase Manhattan Bank   1–108
Citicorp   1–60
Civil Rights Act, Title VII   1–13
Club of 1,000   1–92
Commitment, employee, as HRM
  goal   1–8, 1–16, 1–22, 1–25,
  1–28
Compensation, employee. See also
  Benefits; Pay plans
  international HRM and   1–249
Competence, employee, as HRM
  goal   1–8, 1–22, 1–25—
  1–26, 1–28
Competence profile   1–66
Competitive advantage   1–67, 1–73
Competitive analysis in HR
  planning   1–65—1–67
Composition, organizational, as HRM
  goal   1–8, 1–22, 1–25, 1–28
Computers, use of in utility
  analysis   1–161, 1–171,
  1–178
Contribution, employee, as HRM
  goal   1–8, 1–22, 1–25, 1–28
Control Data   1–7
Corning Glass Works   1–17
Correlation coefficient   1–143. See
  also Validity coefficient